ALL AT SEA

The Policy Challenges of Rescue, Interception, and Long-Term Response to Maritime Migration

Kathleen Newland with Elizabeth Collett,
Kate Hooper, and Sarah Flamm

Migration Policy Institute

*Foreword by Peter Sutherland, United Nations
Special Representative of the Secretary-General*

September 2016

Migration Policy Institute
Washington, DC

Library of Congress Cataloging-in-Publication Data

All at sea: the policy challenges of rescue, interception, and long-term response to maritime migration / by Kathleen Newland, Elizabeth Collett, Kate Hooper, and Sarah Flamm.
pages cm
Includes bibliographical references.
ISBN 978-0-9831591-6-2

1. Emigration and immigration--Government policy. 2. Emigration and immigration-
-Government policy--Case studies. 3. Ports of entry--Security measures. 4. Ports of entry-
-Security measures--Case studies. I. Title.
JV6271.N48 2015
325'.1--dc23

                            2015020086

Cover Photo: A. D'Amato, UNHCR (via Flickr.com)
Cover Design: Marissa Esthimer, MPI
Typesetting: Liz Heimann, MPI

Suggested citation: Newland, Kathleen with Elizabeth Collett, Kate Hooper, and Sarah Flamm. 2016. *All at Sea: The Policy Challenges of Rescue, Interception, and Long-Term Response to Maritime Migration.* Washington, DC: Migration Policy Institute.

Printed in the United States of America.

TABLE OF CONTENTS

FOREWORD

By Peter Sutherland

Desperate migrants and refugees risking their lives at sea frame one of the defining issues of this young century. With conditions in their home countries intolerable, and no country to welcome them, they shock our collective conscience and reveal the inadequacy of both national policies and international cooperation. Unauthorized maritime migration, too often accompanied by appalling suffering and shocking death rates, has put to the test friendly relations among neighbors, long-established maritime traditions, the cohesion of the European Union, and the humanitarian commitments of the international community. The policy responses to these challenges are by no means adequate, but the issues cannot be ignored.

Kathleen Newland and her co-authors from the Migration Policy Institute have put the challenges and the dilemmas of maritime migration starkly in perspective in this compelling volume. Although the issue did not get the attention it deserves until people started pouring across the Mediterranean, this book also covers the boat people of the Caribbean, the Bay of Bengal, and the Andaman Sea, as well as the maritime approaches to Australia. It puts the policy conundrums in vivid language: squeezing the balloon, the blind men and the elephant, and wicked problems. But it also offers practical policy recommendations as well as analysis, while asserting unequivocally that there will be no single, simple solution to these flows.

The failure to cooperate and share the responsibilities of protection at sea will lead—is leading—to greater disorder in international migration corridors and to less protection for refugees. Countries of first asylum and frontline coastal states are experiencing growing pressure from refugee and unauthorized migrant arrivals. If these states are overwhelmed and left to face these challenges unaided, they may resort to pushbacks to even less-capable countries, or tolerate irregular departures to other countries. They may suffer from growing lawlessness associated with the presence of criminal elements attracted by smuggling opportunities.

The costs of not cooperating are high, and they escalate if cooperation does not even begin until a crisis is very nearly out of control. This is the challenge confronting policymakers in the face of unauthorized maritime migration—and this book will help to prepare them for timely action.

Peter Sutherland
United Nations Special Representative of the Secretary-General
for International Migration

PREFACE

In 2013, the Australian Department of Immigration and Border Protection invited me to take part in a series of high-level strategic discussions in Canberra, addressing some of the most perplexing, and often contentious, issues in migration policy. These confidential discussions brought policymakers from several departments of the Australian government together with academic experts from a small number of countries and practitioners from international organizations and nongovernmental organizations. One meeting was devoted to irregular maritime migration, and that led the Department's Irregular Migration Research Programme to commission the Migration Policy Institute (MPI) to do a study of unauthorized movements by sea in several parts of the world. At first, we imagined that this would be a simple matter of updating a publication that MPI had issued in 2006, but it quickly became apparent that a new and more ambitious work would be required. Movements by sea had become more complex, widespread, and dangerous, presenting what often seemed to be intractable problems for policymakers. At the time the work began, in early 2014, the Mediterranean crisis had yet to assume the dimensions that would rock Europe, the Caribbean was relatively quiet, movements across the Bay of Bengal and the Red Sea/Gulf of Aden got little attention outside (or even inside) their regions, and Australia was just embarking on it its radical new operation to stop boat arrivals.

From that point forward, unauthorized maritime migration exploded onto national and international policy agendas, seizing the attention of governments, the media, and publics worldwide. Crisis followed upon crisis. With the manuscript in first draft in the spring of 2015, the team at MPI was updating every week and struggling to keep up with events and policy turns. After several months, we decided to put the book aside and wait until things settled down a little, or at least until we could gain some perspective on current events. We returned to the manuscript in 2016 and decided to draw a line under the narrative with the end of that summer. Maritime migration was far from disappearing from public view, but some common themes had emerged—enough, we hope, to support a useful analysis and practical recommendations.

One thing that readers of this book should not expect to find is a solution to the movement of people by sea to places that are not prepared to welcome them—or even to let them land. This issue is too difficult, dynamic, and complex for a once-and-for-all solution. The multiple

state- and nonstate actors; the mixed flows of refugees and nonrefugees; the overlapping and sometimes contradictory legal regimes; the
fluctuating state policies; the secondary movements of people from
countries of first asylum; the constantly shifting sources, routes, and
destinations; and the inter-relatedness with other equally complex
problems guarantee that combining control of sea routes and protecting the lives and rights of refugees and migrants will require a long,
hard, and persistent effort. Policy will have to be flexible, adaptive, and
oriented toward the long term. Bringing together the pieces of a puzzle
that constantly shifts shape and dimension is a particular policy challenge and one that governments, civil society, the private sector, and
international organizations must tackle together.

Kathleen Newland, Washington, DC, September 2016.

CHAPTER I

MARITIME MIGRATION
A Wicked Problem

By Kathleen Newland

Introduction

As the world's migrant and refugee populations climbed past post-World War II records in 2015,[1] the most dramatic images of migration were of those who travel by sea: a ship on fire within half a mile of land dooming 366 of its 521 passengers; boats built to hold 50 crammed to standing-room-only with five times that many; two sisters, champion swimmers, towing their foundering boat to safety; a little boy's body lying facedown in the sand.[2] Just a tiny proportion of the world's international migrants travel by sea without permission to enter their intended destination country, on vessels that are not authorized to enter that country's ports. This double irregularity constitutes the bulk of what is known as irregular

---

1　United Nations Department of Economic and Social Affairs (UN DESA), *International Migration Report 2015: Highlights* (New York: United Nations, 2016); United Nations High Commissioner for Refugees (UNHCR), *Global Trends: Forced Displacement in 2015* (Geneva: UNHCR, 2016), 5.

2　See, for example, Zed Nelson, "Lampedusa Boat Tragedy: A Survivor's Story," *The Guardian*, March 22, 2014; UNHCR Regional Office for South-East Asia, "Mixed Maritime Movements in South-East Asia—2015," accessed August 9, 2016; Heather Saul, "Yusra Mardini: Olympic Syrian Refugee Who Swam for Three Hours in Sea to Push Sinking Boat Carrying 20 to Safety," *The Independent*, August 5, 2016; Helena Smith, "Shocking Images of Drowned Syrian Boy Show Tragic Plight of Refugees," *The Guardian*, September 2, 2015.

maritime migration,[3] which receives an outsize share of attention from the media and politicians (and therefore the public) and absorbs significant shares of the financial and human resources devoted to making and implementing migration policy.

Unauthorized migration by sea is exceptionally dangerous. Some land routes—those that cross deserts or regions with high levels of violent crime—also present grave natural or manmade threats to migrants, but deaths rarely occur *en masse*. In contrast, it is not uncommon for one incident at sea to result in hundreds of fatalities, and deaths in the single and double digits have become so common that they are no longer newsworthy. In the Mediterranean alone, more than 3,700 migrants were lost at sea in 2015, and another 3,165 in the first eight months of 2016.[4] The global total of migrant deaths at sea is difficult to calculate; an unknown number of boats sink without leaving a trace of their passengers. By one estimate, for every corpse that washes up on the shores of developed countries, at least two others are never recovered.[5]

Most unauthorized maritime migration involves "mixed" flows—that is, groups of people traveling along the same routes and using the same forms of transportation, but with different motivations and needs. State authorities often find it difficult to distinguish between refugees, traveling to seek international protection, and migrants traveling in search of a better life, which they may define in terms of economic opportunity, access to education, reunification with relatives, or some other desired outcome. A state's obligation to refugees and other people

---

3 "Irregular maritime migration" usually refers to this double lack of permission to enter a country's territory; in this context, the Migration Policy Institute (MPI) prefers the more specific terms "unauthorized migrants" traveling on "unauthorized vessels." Some unauthorized migrants are detected as they go through the immigration and customs procedures at seaports after arriving on regularly scheduled commercial or private vessels (or, in rare cases, after being rescued from shipping containers). They may be refused permission to enter because of inadequate documentation, criminal records, public-health concerns, or other issues. Meanwhile, in most developed countries, the majority of unauthorized migrants have entered the country legally but subsequently overstay or abuse the terms of their visas. This study does not examine these phenomena, but focuses on unauthorized migrants traveling on unauthorized vessels.
4 Tara Brian and Frank Laczko, eds., *Fatal Journeys Volume 2: Identification and Tracing of Dead and Missing Migrants* (Geneva: International Organization for Migration, 2016), 5; International Organization for Migration (IOM), "Migration Flows – Europe: Recent Trends," updated August 28, 2016.
5 Leanne Weber and Sharon Pickering, *Globalization and Borders: Death at the Global Frontier* (Basingstoke, UK: Palgrave Macmillan, 2011).

legally eligible for protection is vastly different from its obligations to other migrants. The 148 states that are party to the 1951 United Nations Convention on the Status of Refugees or its 1967 Protocol are bound by the obligation of nonrefoulement, that is, a prohibition from expelling or returning a refugee back to a territory where his or her life or freedom would be threatened.[6] In fact, some experts argue that nonrefoulement has achieved the status of customary law and is binding even for states that are not party to the 1951 Convention or 1967 Protocol.[7] While international law—and most national laws—draw a bright line between refugees and other migrants, the difference in reality is not so clear-cut.

Unauthorized maritime migration troubles the public imagination and resonates in the broader policy debate on many levels. Boats heading to shore without notice conjure up echoes of "invasion" that threaten to undermine national sovereignty and challenge existing legal regimes. Then there are the heart-rending images of suffering and death when boats founder and their passengers drown—occasionally in full view of cameras that relay the pictures around the world.

Policies that aim to address unauthorized maritime migration are rife with unintended consequences. In many cases, deterrence measures raise concerns that refugees' claims for international protection are not being adequately considered. Policy measures may also trap migrants and refugees in a dangerous limbo between their origin and intended destination, in the hands of ruthless smugglers or in indefinite detention. For example, the Thai government crackdown on smuggling in the spring of 2015 led smugglers to abandon migrants at sea, leaving thousands adrift without adequate food or water (see Chapter 3). Intensified measures to deter or intercept unauthorized boats have taken most migrant journeys out of the hands of amateurs and placed them firmly in the hands of professionals, many of whom are part of organized-crime networks that make huge profits from people smuggling. Attempts by individual states to prevent unauthorized arrivals have sometimes soured their relations with neighboring countries and countries of origin or transit. Perhaps the most extreme unintended consequence is that more humane policies toward boat arrivals may encourage unauthorized journeys and result in even more deaths at sea.

---

6   United Nations General Assembly, "Convention Relating to the Status of Refugees," July 28, 1951.
7   See, for example, Guy S. Goodwin-Gill, *The Refugee in International Law*, 2nd edition (Oxford, UK: Oxford University Press, 1996).

Reflecting the fear and emotion that it inspires, maritime migration is often met with crisis-driven responses. The focus of policy over the past ten to 20 years has shifted, in different contexts, between rescue (followed by processing of asylum or immigration claims) and deterrence.

President Silvio Berlusconi of Italy, for instance, controversially negotiated the involuntary return of unauthorized maritime migrants with the Gaddafi regime in Libya in 2009,[8] a practice that continued until the European Court of Human Rights ruled that such returns, with no asylum screening, violated European law (see Chapter 2).[9] In October 2013, under a different government and following a very visible disaster in which 366 people drowned within half a mile of the Italian island of Lampedusa, Italian leaders instituted a massive search-and-rescue mission in the Mediterranean that brought future survivors to Italian territory.

Australia offers another example of policy volatility. In 2001 the Australian government put a strict denial-and-deterrence regime in place. When the opposition Labor Party came to power in 2008, it removed many elements of this regime, only to reinstate most of them between 2011 and 2013, while also developing new initiatives (such as supporting the resettlement of refugees in other countries of the Asia-Pacific region). After the 2013 general election, a new administration reinforced the strict deterrence regime with a zero-tolerance policy for unauthorized boat arrivals (see Chapter 5).

I. Territorial Asylum and Its Discontents

The seemingly intractable problem of unauthorized maritime migration points to a deep fault line in the international migration and asylum regime. The territorial basis of asylum means that refugees must enter the territory of a state other than their own in order to claim protection. International law grants everyone the right to leave his or her country, but does not establish a corresponding right to enter another country without the consent of that country's authorities. The measures that capable states have taken to prevent the entry of unauthorized migrants make it extremely difficult for refugees to

---

8   EurActiv, "Italy's Immigration Deal with Libya Sparks Uproar," EurActiv, June 11, 2009.

9   *Hirsi Jamaa and Others v. Italy*, Application no. 27765/09 (European Court of Human Rights, 2012).

access their territory—and these are the states that offer the best prospect not only of protection but also of a secure and even prosperous future. For many refugees in more easily accessible but relatively poor countries of first asylum, life is extremely precarious. Although they have been granted international protection, many choose to move on in hopes of a better life, only to find that all legal avenues of entry to another country are closed to them.

For most asylum seekers, the only way to enter any state other than their own is through unauthorized means, including unauthorized travel by boat; there are no established international mechanisms to apply for protection as a refugee while still within one's own country (although some states have at times made special, usually temporary, provisions for in-country processing of refugee claims). In fact, the 1951 Convention's definition of a refugee specifies a person who is *outside* his or her country.[10]

However, once a refugee has managed to reach the territory of another state, the state in question not only is obliged to avoid refoulement, but is also enjoined from penalizing refugees for entering illegally.[11] Not surprisingly, many highly motivated migrants who do not qualify for refugee protection apply for asylum nonetheless, in the hope of being allowed to stay in their intended country of destination. The difficulty of determining refugee status—and the volume of asylum claims— overburdens refugee-determination systems in even the world's richest countries.

After untold hardships that may include assault and extortion by smugglers, prolonged detention, and extremely long waiting periods for the processing of their claims, people with recognized refugee status often still struggle to survive. Many countries of first asylum are themselves desperately poor and unable to provide adequately for refugee arrivals; 86 percent of the refugees under the United Nations High Commissioner for Refugees (UNHCR) mandate worldwide are hosted by developing countries.[12] Even middle-income host countries, such as Turkey, stagger under the weight of huge numbers of long-term refugees. Relatively few countries of first asylum allow refugees to work legally. Unsurprisingly, many refugees opt to leave them in search of greater physical and economic security. But other than for the tiny proportion (less than 1 percent) of refugees who are selected for resettlement in a

---

10 United Nations General Assembly, "Convention Relating to the Status of Refugees," Article 1.
11 Ibid, Article 31.
12 UNHCR, *Global Trends*.

third country, the international mechanisms available to assist refugees' onward movement are extremely limited. Meanwhile, the lines between the refugee and the "economic migrant" have been blurred beyond easy distinction. Refugees move on from first-asylum countries for economic reasons, and many so-called economic migrants flee from mortal threats.

II. Who's Who

Of the various types of unauthorized movement, maritime migration is particularly difficult to address. This is in large part because of the sheer number of actors—of different types and from different states—who are involved in the process:

- *National authorities.* Prominent among the state actors responsible for preventing unauthorized maritime migration are immigration agencies (in many cases located within home affairs or justice ministries), border protection agencies (coast guards and land-based agencies), departments of foreign affairs, departments of defense, armed forces (in particular naval forces), and national search-and-rescue operations. Legislatures, executives, and courts establish the laws and policies that frame state actions.

- *Private-sector interests.* Commercial actors, in particular the shipping industry but also fishing vessels and even pleasure boats, are often on the frontlines of maritime rescue.

- *International organizations.* Several are central to maritime migration operations: the International Maritime Organization (IMO), is the custodian of the *Law of the Sea*; UNHCR is responsible for ensuring the protection of refugees and asylums seekers; the United Nations Office for Drugs and Crime (UNODC) coordinates state efforts to combat international organized crime, including human trafficking; and the International Organization for Migration (IOM) provides migration advice and services to states and, at the request of states, to migrants. UNHCR and other multilateral bodies, such as the United Nations Children's Fund (UNICEF) and the United Nations Office of Legal Affairs, also play a role in specific circumstances. The Special Representative of the Secretary-General for International Migration (SRSG) seeks to manage, among other issues, the politics of the international community in relation to maritime flows.

- *Regional bodies.* The European Union (EU) border-control agency, Frontex, and other regional actors take part—and sometimes take the lead—in confronting unauthorized traffic by sea.

- *Civil-society organizations.* Many nongovernmental organizations (NGOs) defend the dignity and human rights of migrants and insist on the proper functioning of asylum systems. Some provide legal assistance and humanitarian support to migrants in transit. A small number of NGOs take direct action to rescue migrants at sea.

- *Criminal syndicates.* All over the world, criminal networks have incorporated people smuggling and human trafficking into their business lines.

At the base of this jumble of actors are the networks of migrants, intending migrants, and their families and communities in both destination and origin countries. Members of these networks have a wide range of motives for planning, assisting, and undertaking journeys that are usually expensive and often extremely dangerous.

Each of the actors in international maritime migration responds to different laws, regulations, incentives, norms, and operational standards, making for an exceptionally complex and dynamic policy environment. The debate around unauthorized maritime migration resembles the story of the blind men and the elephant.[13] Some comprehend it through a humanitarian lens and see it primarily as a protection issue. Others consider it a national security threat, others a question of law and order, and still others an economic phenomenon. Overlaid on these views is a common political perception—in Western countries at least—of unauthorized maritime migration as a public relations disaster for governments when they appear to be unable to control their borders, thereby failing one of the fundamental tests of national sovereignty. The lens through which unauthorized maritime migration is viewed—humanitarian, national security, law enforcement, or politics—often determines the thrust of the policy response.

---

13 In the story, a group of blind men touch an elephant to learn what it is like. Depending on which part of the creature touched, each man came away with a dramatically different description of the elephant. One grasped the trunk and said an elephant is like a snake; one the ear (a fan), one the leg (a tree), and so on. An argument ensued, and while each man was in a sense correct in a limited sense, none could give an accurate description of the whole creature.

III. Who's Where

Unauthorized maritime migration is most prevalent in waters that connect poorer regions with richer ones, particularly at times when the poorer area is experiencing armed conflict or political turmoil accompanied by repression and violence. This book offers five case studies of regions in which the sea functions not as a moat but a highway: the Mediterranean, the Bay of Bengal region, the Gulf of Aden/Red Sea, the maritime approaches to Australia, and the Caribbean.

Among these five, one of the largest and least remarked flows is that between the Horn of Africa and Yemen. The routes, dimensions, and even the direction of migration across the Gulf of Aden and Red Sea fluctuate with the course of conflicts in the region and the policies of the primary destination, Saudi Arabia. From 2010 through 2013, these waters saw more migrant crossings annually than any other region, topping 100,000 in 2011 and 2012.[14] Most migrants travel from Ethiopia or Somalia to Yemen, with the aim of reaching the labor markets of Saudi Arabia or another Gulf state. As the conflict in Yemen escalated in 2014, however, people also began to cross in the other direction—both returning migrants and Yemeni refugees. This maritime region is one of the world's most dangerous, with migrants not only facing the perils of the sea journey but also armed conflict on both shores and vicious smuggling gangs. But the flows between the Horn of Africa and the Middle East are a long way from the major Western media markets and get only a fraction of the public attention given to the other four cases presented here.

Outside the five case study regions, many other notable maritime routes are used by unauthorized migrants. Maritime migration to the United Kingdom diminished markedly since the Channel Tunnel connected the island nation with the European continent by rail. Nonetheless, unauthorized migrants still travel by sea, either hiding themselves in trucks on cross-channel ferries or being concealed by smugglers in shipping containers. In the French port of Calais, 7,414 migrants were arrested in the first six months of 2014 as they attempted to arrange a channel crossing.[15] In August 2014, 35 migrants (including children) were found in a shipping container at Tilbury docks, Essex; one had died, and all survivors were suffering from dehydration and hypothermia. They had arrived on a container ferry from Zeebrugge, Belgium

---

14 UNHCR, "Record Number of African Refugees and Migrants Cross the Gulf of Aden in 2012" (press briefing, UNHCR, Geneva, January 15, 2013).

15 The Economist, "Migration into Europe: A Surge from the Sea," The Economist, August 16, 2014.

via a route that had been opened only two weeks before[16]—evidence of professional smugglers' tremendous adaptability and opportunism.

Island states large and small are, obviously, likely to see a higher proportion of unauthorized migrants arriving by sea than states with land borders.[17] Island territories that lie on or near major sea lanes or in close proximity to high-emigration areas are particularly vulnerable. Italy's Lampedusa, Spain's Canary Islands, Australia's Christmas Island, the uninhabited Mona Isles of the U.S. Commonwealth of Puerto Rico, and France's overseas department of Mayotte in the Mozambique Channel have all been entry points for unauthorized migrants to a greater or lesser extent at various times. They put a destination country's territory in much closer reach of would-be migrants. For destination countries, the cost of patrolling waters around distant possessions is high. Australia has gone so far as to "excise" its island territories, including Christmas Island, from its "migration zone," so that people who reach these territories without permission cannot claim asylum.[18] The United States is said to be considering the same for the uninhabited Mona Islands to discourage smugglers from depositing their passengers there, where they can claim asylum or (in the case of Cuban migrants) claim the benefits of a U.S. policy that grants automatic legal status to Cubans who reach U.S. land borders.[19]

IV. The Legal Framework of Maritime Rescue and Interception

Maritime migration differs crucially from movement by land or air in that people who move on the high seas are not constantly within the jurisdiction of a state. A migrant cannot board or land on a scheduled flight except at an airport located on the territory of a state, nor can

---

16 BBC News, "Tilbury Docks: Man Dies After 35 Found in Container," BBC News, August 16, 2014.

17 For most countries, the largest numbers of unauthorized migrants arrive by air with temporary visas and overstay or abuse the terms of their visas.

18 People who enter Australian territory via an excised zone cannot make a valid application for a visa without special permission from the Minister for Immigration and Border Protection.

19 Author communication with a U.S. Department of Homeland Security (DHS) official, Washington, DC, June 2014. Cuban migrants who reach U.S. territory are automatically paroled into the United States, whereas those intercepted at sea are returned to Cuba or to the U.S. Naval Station at Guantánamo for refugee processing.

they leave one state by land without entering the territory of another. People traveling in international waters, however, enter a realm in which the jurisdiction of states is less comprehensive and much easier to avoid. This reality, in contrast to the increasingly tight control that many states exercise over their airports and land borders, is one of the factors driving unauthorized maritime migration.

Aboard a ship, passengers and crew are under the jurisdiction of the shipmaster, who is, at least in theory, under the jurisdiction of the state whose flag the ship flies (the flag state). But some countries offer flags of convenience for a price (including land-locked Mongolia),[20] and some make no attempt or have no capacity to enforce their own laws or international treaties, including the *Law of the Sea*. It is often difficult to contact the authorities of such a state to confirm jurisdiction when such a vessel is challenged on the high seas for suspected smuggling or trafficking.

Some boats that carry unauthorized migrants are unflagged, unregistered, or operate under false pretenses with a flag they have no right to bear. These vessels are effectively stateless and answer to the law of no state even in theory. Many small craft, such as fishing vessels and private yachts, are unregistered but are still entitled to carry the flag of a state. This can make it very difficult to identify the state responsible for the vessel.

A body of treaty law negotiated among states brings the rule of law to the high seas, which are outside the law of any one state. The obligation to rescue people regardless of their nationality, legal status, or the circumstances in which they are found is codified in the widely ratified 1974 Convention for the Safety of Life at Sea (SOLAS), the 1979 Convention on Maritime Search and Rescue (SAR), and the Protocol of 1988 relating to SOLAS. (But the tradition of rescue at sea long predates the modern conventions that lay out the obligations of flag states and shipmasters to come to the aid of persons in distress.) SAR divides the world's seas into search-and-rescue regions and obligates state parties to cooperate in patrolling them and summoning rescue operations when needed. Search-and-rescue missions alert nearby ships to the presence of a vessel in distress, and those notified are obliged to do their best to rescue people in danger, including by taking them on board (embarking them) if it is necessary and can be done safely.

---

20 The International Transport Workers' Federation (ITF) identifies 35 states that register ships under flags of convenience. See ITF, "Flags of Convenience: Avoiding the Rules by Flying a Convenient Flag," accessed September 10, 2016.

The most comprehensive treaty on maritime law, the 1982 United Nations Convention on the Law of the Sea (UNCLOS), also specifies the obligation to rescue and assist people in peril on the sea. UNCLOS Article 98(1) reads: "Every state shall require the master of a ship flying its flag, in so far as he can do so without serious danger to the ship, the crew or the passengers: (a) to render assistance to any person found at sea in danger of being lost; (b) to proceed with all possible speed to the rescue of persons in distress, if informed of their need for assistance, in so far as such action may reasonably be expected of him."[21]

In addition to rules on rescue, UNCLOS provides for the possibility of interception and interdiction of ships that are believed to pose a threat to peace and security. Known as "the right of visit," Article 110 of the treaty creates an exception to the principles, also codified in the treaty, of noninterference with ships, freedom of navigation on the high seas, and the sole jurisdiction of the flag state. A suspect ship may be inspected by authorities from a state-operated vessel (such as a warship or a coast guard vessel) with the permission of the flag state, if that state can be determined. If the ship is found to pose no threat, compensation must be provided. UNCLOS does not specifically mention migrant smuggling as a ground for exercising the right of visit, but "smuggling and trafficking of persons at sea" is among the threats to maritime security specified by the United Nations Office of Legal Affairs.[22] In addition, the Migrant Smuggling Protocol to the United Nations Convention against Organized Crime gives states the right to board and search ships suspected of migrant smuggling with the permission of the flag state, and to "take appropriate measures" in such cases.[23]

The legal framework for maritime migration goes far beyond the *Law of the Sea*.[24] When passengers are rescued at sea, or the vessel on which they are traveling is intercepted, other bodies of law may come into play: refugee law prohibits the return of refugees to a state where they would face danger to life and liberty, human-rights law proscribes arbi-

---

21 United Nations General Assembly, "United Nation Convention on the Law of the Sea," Article 98 (1), December 10, 1982.

22 United Nations Secretary-General, *Oceans and the Law of the Sea* (New York: United Nations, 2008).

23 United Nations General Assembly, "Protocol against the Smuggling of Migrants by Land, Sea and Air, Supplementing the United Nations Convention against Transnational Organized Crime," Article 8.

24 See Efthymios Papastavridis, *The Interception of Vessels on the High Seas: Contemporary Challenges to the Legal Order of the Oceans* (Oxford, UK: Hart, 2013).

trary detention, and transnational criminal law enjoins the obligation to combat the smuggling and trafficking of persons. The intersection of these different bodies of law, the laws of individual states, and regional statutes creates an intricate legal structure with plentiful opportunities for differing interpretations.

The complexity of the legal framework embodied in international treaty law is multiplied by widely differing national and, in the case of the European Union, regional jurisprudence on unauthorized maritime migration. For example, the U.S. Supreme Court ruled in 1993 that neither the 1967 Protocol to the Refugee Convention nor the U.S. domestic legislation implementing the Protocol apply to actions taken by the U.S. Coast Guard on the high seas, and therefore that Haitians intercepted outside U.S. territorial waters could be returned directly to Haiti without first determining if they qualify for refugee status.[25] The European Court of Human Rights, on the other hand, ruled in 2012 that European flag states are responsible for the protection of migrants picked up by state vessels even if the interdiction takes place in international waters—thus confirming that Italy's pushbacks of migrants to Libya were a violation of the European Charter of Fundamental Rights.[26] As a result of this decision, Frontex adopted new rules for its sea operations that take into account the nonrefoulement obligations of EU Member States.[27]

In 2011, the High Court of Australia declared the Australian government's plan to transfer asylum seekers to Malaysia for processing invalid on the grounds that Malaysia is not legally bound to provide protection for asylum seekers, access to effective procedures, or refugee protection since the agreement between the two countries was not legally binding and Malaysia is not a signatory to the 1951 Refugee Convention or its 1967 Protocol.[28]

UNHCR takes the position, argued in *amicus curiae* briefs in several court cases, that the obligations incurred under the Refugee Convention apply wherever the authorities of a state have jurisdiction or exercise "effective control" of a person, whether that person is in the

---

25 *Sale v. Haitian Centers Council, Inc.* 509 U.S. Reports 155 (1993).

26 *Hirsi Jamaa and Others v. Italy.*

27 Yves Pascouau and Pascal Schumacher, "Frontex and the Respect of Fundamental Rights: From Better Protection to Full Responsibility" (policy brief, European Policy Centre, Brussels, June 2014).

28 *Plaintiff M70/2011 v. Minister for Immigration and Citizenship & Anor*, 244 CLR 144 (High Court of Australia, 2011).

territory of that state or not.[29] A number of states party to the Refugee Convention, such as the United States and Australia, do not take this view. The inconsistency in national jurisprudence makes it difficult to establish a consensus—whether in word or action—on the treatment of people intercepted at sea.

V. The Problem of Disembarkation

Some of the most vexatious questions surrounding maritime migration concern the disembarkation of people rescued or intercepted at sea. The maritime conventions require that states cooperate to disembark rescued people at a "place of safety" on dry land, but do not specify which port should take this responsibility. It could be the nearest port, the next port of call on the rescue ship's itinerary (which would minimize the cost of disrupting a voyage to conduct a rescue), a port governed by the rescued people's country of origin (unless they are claiming asylum), or a port in the territory of the flag state. Since international law gives no firm instruction on the port of disembarkation, shipmasters and states are left to exercise discretion. The Executive Committee of UNHCR has stated that rescued people should normally disembark at the next port of call—and indeed this is expected unless there is good reason to make an exception. But the committee has also recognized that the next port of call may not be the most appropriate.[30] Amendments to the SAR and SOLAS conventions, discussed below, have helped to clarify the issue of disembarkation procedurally, if not substantively.

Once migrants disembark and are admitted to the country where that port is located, they enter the territory of a state, which from that moment has certain obligations toward them. To some extent, these obligations depend on the international legal instruments to which the state is party, such as the United Nations Convention Relating to the Status of Refugees and the United Nations Convention against Torture. (However, as noted above, many legal experts consider nonrefoulement of refugees to be established customary international law.) These

---

29 See, for example, UNHCR, "Submission of the Office of the United Nations High Commissioner for Refugees – Seeking Leave to Intervene as Amicus Curiae" (UNHCR submissions in the High Court of Australia in the Case of *CPCF v. Minister for Immigration and Border Protection and the Commonwealth of Australia*, September 15, 2014).
30 See UNHCR, "Background Note on the Protection of Asylum-Seekers and Refugees Rescued at Sea," Section II (31) (background note, UNHCR, Geneva, March 18, 2002).

instruments may prohibit the state from returning a rescued person to his or her country of origin. In order to determine the correct course of action, the state must have some means, direct or indirect, of determining whether a person is a refugee (or has some other protected status) and is therefore eligible for protection. In many cases, states will go to considerable lengths to avoid taking on these obligations, particularly if illegal immigration is a controversial issue in domestic political debates (where refugee status determination is often framed as a costly and burdensome process). Several high-profile incidents of rescue at sea, the most notorious of which involved the *MV Tampa* in 2001, have demonstrated this reluctance.

In August 2001, the Norwegian container ship *MV Tampa*[31] rescued 433 asylum seekers from a boat that was sinking in international waters between Indonesia and Australia's Christmas Island in Indonesia's search-and-rescue zone. The container ship had been alerted to the incident by the Australian Maritime Safety Authority (AMSA). After the rescue, the shipmaster followed standard procedures in heading toward Indonesia (which was the next port of call), but turned back toward Christmas Island after the extreme agitation of some of the rescued passengers, who insisted on reaching Australian territory, made him fear for the safety of both the crew and the people they had rescued.

Although AMSA initially deferred to the shipmaster's judgment, the Australian government refused permission to disembark the passengers on Christmas Island and went so far as to threaten legal action against the shipmaster if he were to attempt to do so. An impasse ensued for three days as the *Tampa* waited just outside Australian territorial waters for a resolution. Indonesia (the next port of call and the point of embarkation), Australia (the nearest port), and Norway (the flag state) all refused to accept the passengers. With conditions on board deteriorating (the *Tampa* was designed and provisioned for a few dozen, not hundreds, of people), the shipmaster declared an emergency on board and moved into Australian waters. The *Tampa* was intercepted and boarded by Australian military forces and its passengers transferred to an Australian military vessel. After negotiations between the Australian government and the government of Nauru, the passengers were transferred to Nauru, where UNHCR agreed to oversee the process of refugee determination and resettlement procedures. Eventually most of the passengers rescued by the *Tampa* were resettled as refugees in New Zealand, Australia, and several other countries.

---

31 See Ernst Willheim, "MV Tampa: The Australian Response," *International Journal of Refugee Law* 15, no. 2, Oxford University Press (2003): 159-91.

In the aftermath of the *Tampa* incident, the IMO Member States adopted amendments to SOLAS and SAR. The purpose of the amendments, which were adopted in 2004 and came into force in 2006, is to match the shipmaster's obligation to render assistance with a corresponding obligation on the part of states to "coordinate and cooperate" to allow the shipmaster to hand over the responsibility of caring for people rescued at sea and allow these people to disembark in a safe place.[32] The state that is in charge of the search-and-rescue zone in which a vessel in distress is detected is expected to take responsibility for ensuring that such cooperation and coordination take place. Ideally, the people rescued will be brought to a safe point for disembarkation with the least possible disruption to the itinerary of the rescuing ship—of particular importance to commercial vessels. UNHCR and IMO have also jointly issued guidelines for the implementation of the amendments.[33] But while the procedures to be followed after a rescue-at-sea operation have been clarified, the actual site of disembarkation often remains contentious.

When states cannot agree on which port should be used—and occasionally when passengers refuse to disembark at an agreed port—the rescuing ship is forced to delay the progress of its journey, at considerable cost and inconvenience to its owners, master, and crew. The chance that disembarkation procedures will be contentious and drawn out, or that the crew of a rescuing vessel will be prosecuted for assisting illegal immigration (as happened in Italy in 2007 when the crew of a Tunisian fishing boat landed a group of rescued migrants on Lampedusa[34]), creates the incentive for commercial ships to shirk their duty of rescue and leave people in peril. In one instance in 2007, shipwrecked migrants were left clinging to a tuna pen in the Mediterranean for three days. Their vessel had foundered in the Libyan search-and-rescue area, and Malta—the flag state of the ship towing the tuna pen—refused to pick them up.[35] They were eventually rescued by an Italian naval vessel.

Migrants—including the survivors of the 2013 shipwreck off the Italian island of Lampedusa that resulted in the death of 366—often tell of being ignored by multiple merchant ships or fishing boats before being rescued. This is the most serious consequence of states' failure to

---

32 International Maritime Organization (IMO), *Rescue at Sea: A Guide to Principle and Practice as Applied to Migrants and Refugees* (London: IMO, 2004).
33 Ibid.
34 Peter Popham, "Tunisian Fishermen Face 15 Years' Jail Time in Italy for Saving Migrants from Rough Seas," *The Independent*, September 19, 2007.
35 Consiglio Italiano per i Refugiato (CIR), *Report Regarding Recent Search and Rescue Operations in the Mediterranean* (Rome: CIR, 2007).

cooperate on the issue of disembarkation. And if commercial vessels traveling through sea lanes known to be used by migrants turn off their communications equipment to avoid being caught up in migrant-rescue dramas, others will also be lost at sea—fishermen, yachtsmen, and merchant seamen. To a worrying extent, states' lack of cooperation on this issue threatens the rescue-at-sea regime for everyone.

The interception of migrants at sea is surrounded by similar problems. An important difference, however, is that the main purpose of interception is to prevent unauthorized migrants from disembarking at their intended destination. The intercepting authority, typically an agent of the intended destination state, takes control of a boat in order to prevent its onward movement, return it to the port of embarkation, or compel it to alter course. But if the boat is unseaworthy, what started as an interception may become a rescue, and the intercepting vessel may have to take the passengers and crew aboard.

UNHCR and many legal scholars take the view that by voluntarily taking control of a boat that is still seaworthy, the intercepting author- ity acquires the same obligations that it would have if it had landed the passengers on its territory (especially if the interception takes place within its territorial waters). But some states, including the United States and Australia, reject the interpretation that interception of a vessel at sea means they must provide asylum to any refugees found to be among the passengers on board. Rather, they construe their obligation narrowly, as a requirement not to take actions that result in refugees being returned to a territory where their lives or freedom would be in danger. Denying people the ability to reach their intended destination or moving them to a third state, even without their consent, does not amount to refoulement.[36]

VI. The Politics of Unauthorized Maritime Migration

The domestic politics surrounding unauthorized maritime migra- tion are toxic in several countries where unauthorized maritime migration—because of its visibility and drama—has at certain times become a proxy for a broader debate on migration in general and illegal

---

36 Many legal scholars agree, if reluctantly, that "the simple denial of entry of ships to territorial waters cannot be equated with breach of the principle of nonrefoulement." See Goodwin-Gill, *The Refugee in International Law*, 166.

immigration in particular. Wedge politics, enabled by the treatment of boat arrivals in elements of the popular media, fan public disquiet by invoking images of invasion and criminality. The fact that Australia was facing a general election at the time of the *Tampa* incident undoubtedly added to the heat of the domestic debate surrounding the event within the country and of the exchanges with the other countries involved. Similarly, President Clinton's 1992 refusal to lift the interception program in the Caribbean (by which Haitians were turned back wholesale, without review) was said to have derived from the political backlash he endured as governor of Arkansas during the "Mariel boatlift" of Cubans in 1981, when Cubans sent to Arkansas' Fort Chaffee for processing broke out of the base and rioted.[37] Right-wing politicians throughout Eastern and Central Europe benefitted from public resistance to the arrival in their countries of hundreds of thousands of migrants who had traveled through Greece and up through the Balkans in 2015 and 2016. By contrast, approval ratings for German Chancellor Angela Merkel plummeted in the year after she opened Germany's borders to refugees and migrants stranded in Austria (September 2015 to September 2016), and her party lost the state elections in her own constituency, coming in behind a far-right, anti-immigrant party.[38]

In some cases, domestic politics works in favor of boat arrivals—or at least some of them. For example, the legacy of the Cold War and the continuing power of the Cuban lobby in the United States sustain the extraordinary "wet foot/dry foot" policy that permits Cuban maritime migrants who successfully reach dry land in U.S. territory to remain and quickly adjust to permanent resident status (see Chapter 6). At the same time, Cubans intercepted at sea are returned to Cuba for in-country processing or, if they wish to claim asylum, taken to the U.S. naval station in Guantánamo Bay[39] for refugee status processing; if found to be refugees, the U.S. government seeks a third country to accept them for resettlement.

Unauthorized maritime migration is often portrayed as an artefact of the international asylum regime when, in fact, it is also one of the major threats to the regime. Both domestic politics and good relations among states demand that the institution of asylum serves the protection purpose for which it was intended and does not act as a back door

37 Justin Wm. Moyer, "The Forgotten Story of How Refugees Almost Ended Bill Clinton's Career," *Washington Post,* November 17, 2015.

38 Deutsche Welle, "Politicians Blame Merkel's Refugee Policy for Defeat in Regional Elections," Deutsche Welle, September 5, 2016.

39 The refugee-processing facility in Guantánamo is unrelated to the U.S. military prison holding terrorism suspects.

to illegal immigration. State efforts to prevent maritime arrivals—in response to public disquiet often stoked (or even invented) by political rhetoric—too often run roughshod over the procedures established to distinguish refugees from those migrants not in need of international protection. Such efforts may also undermine the availability of international protection for refugees.

There are good reasons to safeguard the integrity of the asylum system that has offered protection to millions of refugees since it was established on a global basis in 1951. First, the public in a receiving country is unlikely to give refugees the welcome they need in order to rebuild their lives if people who claim to be refugees are seen to be abusing the system in large numbers. Second, the organized-crime networks that prosper from human smuggling and trafficking undermine the rule of law in origin, destination, and transit countries. (Most states have committed themselves to combating organized crime by acceding to the Palermo Protocols to the United Nations Convention against Transnational Organized Crime.) Third, and most important, people may be lured to put their lives in danger by traveling illegally by boat if they believe that the asylum system is so lax as to allow almost anyone to migrate to any country of his or her choice.

While these are all important reasons to protect the integrity of the asylum system, the system is put at risk when public officials paint all maritime migrants as "queue jumpers," cheats, and criminals. Even those migrants who do not qualify for protection should be treated with dignity. Migrants may claim asylum in the genuine belief that they are refugees, or in the hope that the story they tell will persuade adjudicators that they are. For many migrants who have neither family ties in their desired destination nor sought-after skills to offer employers, asylum may appear to be the only way to access the "promised land." This does not mean that they should be allowed to remain, but it does mean that they should be treated humanely.

The international politics of unauthorized maritime migration are also fraught with tensions in many cases, pitting countries of intended destination against origin and transit states, littoral states against interior ones, and flag states against intercepting states. Even as the divergent short-term interests of states make it difficult for them to cooperate on maritime migration, these interests are threatened by the lack of international cooperation. At the international level, too, states have suffered reputational damage after taking actions that are seen as inhumane or contrary to the spirit, if not the actual letter, of inter

national refugee law or the law of the sea—or that shift the burden of
refugee protection onto poorer and less capable states.

VII. "Bad Actors" and the Manipulation of Rescue: Engineered Helplessness

The smugglers who organize unauthorized maritime migration do not
make the distinction between refugees and nonrefugees. It is reason-
able to believe that most people who bear the expense and run the risks
of unauthorized maritime migration are extremely anxious to leave
their home countries, even if they do not conform to the definition of a
refugee in international law. Smugglers prey upon the desperation of
would-be migrants and refugees, and often mislead potential clients
about the prospects of reaching their desired destination and being
allowed to stay there.

While some smugglers see themselves as agents performing a service
for their clients—and do their best to deliver that service—the entry of
criminal elements into the business puts many migrants in the hands
of ruthless operators. Stories of migrants forced to disembark in deep
waters offshore; jammed into unseaworthy boats; denied food, water,
and breathable air; and thrown overboard or murdered by smugglers seem to be growing in frequency. For example, UNHCR reported
that "On 15 July [2014], 29 people were found dead from apparent
asphyxiation in the hold of a fishing boat, and details are emerging of
a horrifying incident in which as many as 60 people were stabbed and
thrown overboard as they sought to escape from the hold. A total of 131
people are missing and presumed dead from the incident, including a
newborn baby."[40] In September 2014, an even more horrifying incident
was reported, in which smugglers deliberately sank a boat carrying
as many as 500 migrants (including about 100 children). According
to survivors interviewed by IOM officers, the migrants had refused
to cooperate with smugglers' instructions to board a smaller and less
seaworthy boat to continue their journey; only 11 people survived.[41]
With a similar disregard for human life, smugglers abandoned at sea
thousands of migrants and refugees from Bangladesh and Myanmar to
avoid a crackdown by the government of Thailand in 2015. And in the

---

40 UNHCR, "Urgent European Action Needed to Stop Rising Refugee and Migrant
Deaths at Sea" (press release, July 24, 2014).
41 Tara Brian and Frank Laczko, eds., *Fatal Journeys: Tracking Lives Lost during
Migration* (Geneva: IOM, 2014).

Gulf of Aden, smugglers are so determined to avoid an encounter with Yemeni law enforcement that if one seems inevitable, they will simply throw their human cargo overboard (see Chapter 4).

The tactics of smugglers evolve as coastal defenses against them are strengthened. In the past, the most common maritime people-smuggling operations mirrored other kinds of smuggling, attempting to reach the coast of the destination country without being apprehended. Today, common tactics include deliberately drawing attention to dangerously unseaworthy boats carrying migrants, providing boats with only enough fuel to reach international waters in locations where rescue efforts are known to be common, or disabling a migrant boat as soon as a coast guard or search-and-rescue vessel approaches. These tactics transform an interception into a rescue and make it impossible to return the vessel to the point from which it set out. Employees of the smugglers or the migrants themselves are instructed to hole the vessel or disable its engine, rendering themselves in distress and in need of rescue.

Smugglers tend to be not only ruthless but opportunistic. They are often extremely well informed about the practices of coast guards and other law enforcement bodies as well as the mechanisms that trigger protection responses from states. Further, smugglers have been known to coach migrants in the behaviors and stories that are likely to gain them entry—and perhaps permission to remain—in a country of destination.

Because of its low risk (for the owners and managers of smuggling outfits) and high profits, people smuggling is an attractive business for many actors, from poor fishermen to multibillion-dollar criminal cartels. Survivors of one deliberately wrecked ship reported that they had paid US $2,000 each for passage across the Mediterranean,[42] putting the gross from that voyage alone at US $1 million. While most people worldwide are smuggled through land borders and airports, those who travel by sea are put at greatest risk and are most dependent on a smuggler to arrange the voyage. The United Nations Office on Drugs and Crime reports that "though more migrant smuggling occurs by air, more deaths occur by sea."[43]

---

42 IOM, "IOM Says New Witnesses Provide Further Details of Mediterranean Shipwreck Tragedy" (press release, September 16, 2014).

43 United Nations Office on Drugs and Crime (UNODC), *Issue Paper: Smuggling of Migrants by Sea* (Vienna: UNODC, 2011), 12.

VIII. Policy Responses, Part I: Law Enforcement, Denial, Diversion, and Deterrence

Law enforcement efforts to arrest and prosecute people smugglers encounter a number of challenges. Smugglers who can be caught in the act are usually low-level operators and can easily be replaced, leaving unscathed the higher-level organizers of unauthorized sea voyages whose fingerprints on the crime can be difficult to detect. It may also be difficult to find witnesses who are willing to testify in court proceedings against smugglers. People smuggling is often just one of many business lines of loosely organized criminal organizations. When authorities crack down on people smuggling, the organizations responsible can simply lie low and concentrate on other activities until the pressure lifts or they figure out alternative routes or mechanisms. In addition, smuggling operations are often deeply interpenetrated with the local community (in a fishing village, for example), including local authorities.[44]

In the face of such complexity, law enforcement efforts often depend on intelligence gathering with respect to intended boat departures. The U.S. government has conducted surveillance flights along the coast of Haiti to monitor boat building, for example. The Australian Minister for Immigration and Border Protection has emphasized the importance of cooperating with other states in the region, stating that "more than 85 percent of Customs and Border Protection detections at the border come from intelligence."[45] Annual joint operations instigated by successive European Union presidencies have designated a two-week period for intensive interception of unauthorized migrants at and within EU borders; these operations are aimed "at weakening the capacity of organized-crime groups to facilitate illegal immigration to the EU and . . . to collect information, for intelligence and investigation purposes, regarding the main routes followed by migrants to enter the common area and the modus operandi used by crime networks to smuggle people toward the EU."[46]

---

44 Graeme Hugo, "The New International Migration in Asia: Challenges for Population Research," *Asian Population Studies* 1, no. 1 (2005): 93-120.

45 Address by Scott E. Morrison, Minister for Immigration and Border Protection, Australian Government, to the Lowy Institute for International Policy, "A New Force Protecting Australia's Borders," Sydney, Australia, May 9, 2014.

46 Council of the European Union, "Joint Operations 'Mos Maiorum,'" (Note from the Presidency to the Delegations, July 10, 2014).

Beyond straightforward law enforcement, attempts by states to reduce, or indeed stop, unauthorized maritime migration generally employ three mechanisms: (1) denial of access to the territory of the destination country, (2) diversion to other destinations or channels, and (3) deterrence. All three types of measures are designed to make the cost-benefit analysis for migrants so unfavorable that they abandon the attempt at a sea journey. Some policies overlap the three categories.

Denial of access to the coast of an intended destination requires significant investment in patrol capacity, as well as the ability to compel unauthorized vessels to alter their courses or abandon their journeys. Ships forced to return to their port of departure may simply wait for another moment to set sail. Law enforcement vessels sometimes tow unauthorized boats out of their territorial sea or contiguous zone into international waters or from the high seas into the territorial waters of the state from which they embarked. To make sure that unauthorized migrants can return to their departure point, authorities have repaired disabled vessels or offloaded passengers from unseaworthy boats into lifeboats and pushed them back toward the shore. Other times, intercepting authorities destroy boats that have been returned so that they cannot be used for another attempt. Unlike a border fence, a sea barrier is never fixed and requires continuous investment. U.S. Coast Guard patrols to deny migrants access to U.S. territory have been in place in the Caribbean since 1981, and have slowed but not stopped unauthorized maritime migration.

Diversion of maritime migrants takes two very different forms. The first seeks to direct migrants from unauthorized channels into legal ones by opening up opportunities to receive visas to people who otherwise would not be eligible. In October 2014, U.S. Citizenship and Immigration Services (USCIS) announced the creation of the Haitian Family Reunification Parole program, which would accelerate the arrival of Haitian family members of U.S. citizens and legal permanent residents. It focuses on would-be migrants with an approved family-based visa petition who might otherwise wait years for a slot to open. In announcing the program, which took effect in early 2015, the U.S. Deputy Homeland Security Secretary said, "The United States strongly discourages individuals in Haiti from undertaking life-threatening and illegal maritime journeys to the United States."[47] Opening the U.S. H-2 visa categories (low-skilled temporary labor) to Haitians after the 2010 earthquake may have also served to deter some unauthorized maritime

---

47 U.S. Citizenship and Immigration Services (USCIS), "DHS to Implement Haitian Family Reunification Parole Program" (news release, October 17, 2014).

migration, although this was probably not the primary intention. Meanwhile, EU Member States have discussed the creation of "humanitarian visas" for refugees in North Africa and the Middle East as an alternative to the need to undertake unauthorized migration to seek asylum in Europe.

A harsher diversionary tactic is to direct an unauthorized boat's passengers to destinations other than the one intended. The U.S. practice of diverting U.S.-bound unauthorized migrants in the Caribbean to Guantánamo and then to a third country if they are found to be refugees, without the possibility of being resettled in the United States, is one example. Australia, too, has followed this practice, and offers fewer options for resettlement. Asylum seekers are sent to processing centers in Papua New Guinea and Nauru,[48] and, since 2013, Australia has made it clear that people found to be refugees through procedures in these countries will not be resettled in its territory. Instead, they have the choice of settling in Papua New Guinea or Nauru, being resettled in Cambodia, or waiting for the possibility of resettlement in another country or voluntarily deciding to return home (see Chapter 6).

The third mechanism for slowing or stopping unauthorized maritime migration is deterrence. The softer end of the spectrum of deterrence relies on dissuasion. For example, information campaigns (as implemented by the United States, Australia, and European countries in various contexts) explain the dangers of illegal maritime voyages, the ruthlessness of smugglers, the difficulties of living without papers in the destination country, the likelihood of apprehension, and the challenges to finding a job. Assessments of information campaigns do not indicate that they have a significant impact on unauthorized travel, however.[49] Asked how effective such campaigns were, one Malian migrant who attempted to travel to Spain on a flimsy rubber dinghy told *The New York Times*, "It can't be worse than Mali. Europeans want to scare us away, but they don't have a clue what kind of problems we leave behind."[50]

---

48 Government of Australia and Government of Papua New Guinea, "Regional Resettlement Arrangement between Australia and Papua New Guinea," July 19, 2013.

49 See, for example, Maybritt Jill Alpes and Ninna Nyberg Sørensen, "Migrant Risk Warning Campaigns Are Based on Wrong Assumptions" (policy brief, Danish Institute for International Studies, Copenhagen, May 5, 2015).

50 Rafael Minder and Jim Yardley, "Desperation Fuels Trips of Migrants to Spain," *The New York Times*, October 4, 2013.

On the hard side of deterrence policy is detention. Conditions in detention centers for unauthorized migrants are often harsh, as reported by numerous, highly critical reports by human-rights organizations.[51] More important, however, confinement keeps migrants away from what is for many the primary goal of mobility: the chance to make a living.

Deflection, as described above is an effective form of deterrence. When migrants don't succeed in reaching their goal, word quickly gets back to intending migrants, their families, and communities that unauthorized travel by sea is not worth the risks and expense. By consistently substituting an undesirable location for the intended one, policymakers hope to discourage people from migrating without authorization. More importantly, by making it extremely difficult for smugglers to provide the service that they have promised, such policies disrupt their business models. Migrants will be unwilling to pay large sums to smugglers to reach a desired destination if they are likely to end up in another country where they have no ties or prospects.

Considerable evidence indicates that interception policies, too, work to deter unauthorized maritime arrivals, at least for as long as they are in place. In 2006, nearly 40,000 unauthorized boats arrived on Spanish territory, the majority in the Canary Islands. After Spain increased patrols off the coast of West Africa and stationed night-vision cameras along its own southern coasts, the number of boat arrivals dropped to 3,804 by 2012.[52] Australia saw an even more dramatic decline within a single year after implementing Operation Sovereign Borders in September 2013. The operation aimed to deny unauthorized maritime migrants access to Australian territory by intercepting their boats and, where safe to do so, removing them from Australian waters. From a high of 48 boat arrivals in July 2013, just five arrived in October of the same year; there have been no arrivals since. (Passengers on an unauthorized vessel that sank in July 2014 were rescued and brought temporarily to the Australian mainland before being transferred to Nauru.)[53]

---

51 See, for example, the collection of reports released by *The Guardian* detailing abuse, self-harm, and negligence in the Australian detention center on the island of Nauru. See Nick Evershed, Ri Liu, Paul Farrell, and Helen Davidson, "The Nauru Files: The Lives of Asylum Seekers in Detention Detailed in a Unique Database," *The Guardian,* August 10, 2016.

52 Minder and Yardley, "Desperation Fuels Trips of Migrants to Spain."

53 Speech by Lieutenant General Angus Campbell, Australian Army, to the Australian Strategic Policy Institute, "Operation Sovereign Borders: Initial Reflections and Future Outlook," Barton, Australia, May 15, 2014.

The strict enforcement of policies to return unauthorized migrants to their countries of origin also functions to deter new arrivals. But such policies are far from comprehensive in most destination countries. When authorities contemplate returning migrants, various consider-ations—primarily humanitarian, legal, and political—often come to the fore. For example, children's cases are meant to be decided on the basis of what is in the "best interests of the child," and this standard may preclude returning children to the country they just escaped. Similarly, according to the Refugee Convention, refugees are not meant to be penalized for using illegal means to enter another country's territory to seek asylum, nor are they to be sent back to a place where their lives or freedom would be in danger. But, as noted above, they are not infre-quently deflected back to transit countries or subjected to perfunctory determination procedures that leave them vulnerable to refoulement.

In some countries, the presence of a politically influential diaspora or another type of support group may discourage politicians from imple-menting strict return policies. The United States' "wet-foot/dry-foot" policy—which protects Cubans who manage to evade interception at sea and land on U.S soil from deportation and gives them a fast track to permanent residence—is one of the few nonreturn policies for nonrefu-gees that is written into legislation. The policy encourages continued departures from Cuba because success, even if the sea patrols make it unlikely, brings such a great reward. But the policy also appears to have deflected more risk-averse Cuban migrants toward land routes (most of them via Mexico) that they can access via air or a relatively short sea voyage. Haitian migrants, on the other hand, are almost uniformly returned directly to Haiti and are routinely detained if apprehended on U.S. soil.

France has shown some reluctance to deport francophone Africans back to countries of origin in turmoil, even if they do not meet strict refugee criteria, perhaps because of domestic constituencies that vocally oppose such practices on humanitarian grounds. Moreover, deporting an unwilling migrant who is determined not to be moved is an expensive and unpleasant procedure, which authorities often seek to avoid. The conviction, even if based on slim anecdotal evidence, that if migrants can just reach the intended destination, they will be allowed to stay, is a powerful stimulant of unauthorized journeys. And yet states find it difficult to counter this through strict return policies. The decision to force an involuntary departure is not an easy one.

IX. Policy Responses, Part II: Rescue, Protection, and Burden Sharing

While many governments have pursued the three Ds of denial, diversion, and deterrence (as described above), others have opted to focus on (1) rescue, (2) the protection of refugees and the humane treatment of other migrants, and (3) the establishment of frameworks for multinational burden sharing. Italy's widespread search-and-rescue operation in the Mediterranean, Mare Nostrum, is a prime example. It was instituted in October 2013, following a shipwreck off Lampedusa, and remained in operation for 14 months, despite the objection of some EU Member States that saw it as a magnet for unauthorized maritime migration. In fact, the surge in maritime migration across the Mediterranean had started at least three months before Mare Nostrum was put in place and continued after it ended.

At a cost of 9 million euros per month, Mare Nostrum could not be sustained by Italy alone. What replaced it was a much smaller operation mounted by Frontex. Confined to patrols within 30 miles of the European coast and with one-third the financial resources of Mare Nostrum and a fraction of its maritime assets, Operation Triton did not have an explicit search-and-rescue mandate. Its vessels would engage in rescue if they encountered people in distress, but its remit did not cover most of the migration routes across the Mediterranean. It took another terrible tragedy, in April 2015, to galvanize further EU response. At least 700 people are reckoned to have died in the worst single shipwreck in modern times, leaving only 29 survivors.[54] In the aftermath, the resources devoted to Operation Triton increased to almost the level devoted to Mare Nostrum, and national assets from EU Member State navies and coast guards (including those from Germany, Greece, Ireland, Italy, and the United Kingdom) were deployed in the Mediterranean for search-and-rescue operations. Migrant crossings surged in the spring of 2015; 5,000 to 6,000 people were rescued each weekend as the weather improved. Despite the calmer weather and the enhanced search-and-rescue capacity, the death toll continued to rise, reaching 3,763 by the end of the year.[55]

---

54 Alessandra Bonomolo and Stephanie Kirchgaessner, "UN Says 800 Migrants Dead in Boat Disaster as Italy Launches Rescue of Two More Vessels," *The Guardian*, April 20, 2015.

55 IOM, "Missing Migrants Project – Latest Global Figures," accessed September 10, 2016.

The mounting death toll in the Mediterranean between 2013 and 2015 prompted many—including the presidents of Malta and Italy, Pope Francis, and a quartet of the most senior international officials dealing with migration—to call for further action.[56] The Pope's appeal for moral action based on solidarity with migrants generated one of the more innovative responses. Private citizens based in Malta created and funded the Migrant Offshore Aid Station (MOAS), which operates a private rescue ship, the *Phoenix*, in the Mediterranean Sea and, for one season in 2016, in the Andaman Sea .[57] Even before its first official mission began, in August 2014, *Phoenix* rescued a fisherman and his 5-year-old son from a boat whose engine had stopped working. *Phoenix* and its crew of 16 operated the 40-meter ship over 60 days at sea in its first summer, at a cost (including the vessel and its equipment) of several million euros.[58] More than 3,000 people were saved in the summer of 2014. By its second anniversary, MOAS had been involved in the rescue of about 25,000 migrants in the Mediterranean, and had been joined by several other private rescue vessels. Doctors without Borders also joined MOAS to provide medical care on board and assistance to migrants following rescue.[59]

In the Red Sea and Gulf of Aden, the Yemeni Coast Guard cooperates with UNHCR to rescue migrants and apprehend smugglers. Its vessels bring migrants ashore, where they are provided with medical treatment, food, water, and temporary shelter. Somali refugees receive *prima facie* recognition[60] from the Yemeni authorities. UNHCR runs refugee status-determination procedures for arrivals of other nationalities who wish to apply for asylum—although many prefer to avoid registration and move on as soon as they can to look for work, primarily in Saudi Arabia. Saudi Arabia, meanwhile, is constructing a fence along the more traversed sections of the Yemeni border to deny unauthorized access to

---

56 For the latter, see UNHCR, "Joint Statement on Mediterranean Crossings" (press release, April 23, 2015).

57 BBC News, "Malta: Private Migrant Rescue Boat Saves Fishermen," BBC News, August 26, 2014.

58 *The Malta Independent*, "First MOAS Mission on Wednesday, Fisherman and Young Son Rescued," *The Malta Independent*, August 25, 2014.

59 Doctors Without Borders, "MSF and MOAS to Launch Lifesaving Operation for Migrants in Mediterranean" (press release, April 9, 2015).

60 Migrants are granted *prima facie* recognition as refugees when a receiving state acknowledges the severity of conditions in their country of origin (or, in the case of stateless persons, their country of habitual residence) and offers refugee status without the need to complete an individual refugee status-determination process.

Saudi territory and has expelled nearly 1 million unauthorized migrant workers since 2012, including about 150,000 from Ethiopia.[61]

The humanitarian actions of rescue and protection on national territory present a conundrum to countries such as Italy and Yemen, which are seen by most migrants as transit countries en route to more desirable destinations such as Germany, Sweden, and Saudi Arabia. This has created tension in some cases. For example, several top European destinations accused Italy of not being vigilant about registering and fingerprinting migrants rescued by Mare Nostrum as required by European regulations in order to avoid its responsibility (as the first point of entry into the European Union) to consider their asylum applications.

A third policy response puts rescue and protection in a broader framework of international cooperation, by seeking other countries to share the consequences of rescue and interception. Burden sharing is a form of international cooperation in which states voluntarily take on responsibility for refugees or migrants who, under international law, would fall under the responsibility of other states. Cooperation of this kind on maritime migration poses particular challenges. The responsibility to protect refugees is often interpreted differently across states. The burden (for it is often seen in those terms) falls much more heavily on some countries than on others by accident of geography. Other states may volunteer to share these burdens, but there is no legal obligation to do so—although the 1951 Refugee Convention (Article 35) does obligate states to cooperate with UNHCR. The same reluctance to accept or share responsibility also comes into play when refugees are rescued at sea, especially if the flag state of the rescuing ship is poor or overburdened. In the case of interception by a capable state, it may be more difficult to convince other states to share the responsibility of protection.

- The mechanisms of burden-sharing are many and varied, but tend fall into one of four categories:

- Permission to relocate migrants or refugees to a particular state's territory

- Provision of technical assistance in managing flows and establishing legal and institutional frameworks

- Financial assistance in the care of migrants in general and protection of refugees in particular

---

61 Benno Muchler, " Ethiopian Migrants Expelled by Saudis Remain in Limbo Back Home," *The New York Times,* January 7, 2014.

- Common frameworks for dealing with refugees and asylum seekers, often including an agreed upon division of labor among the participating states.

One example of burden sharing through physical relocation is a 2007 agreement between the U.S. and Australian governments to transfer refugees intercepted at sea by one country for settlement in the other.[62] Australia agreed to resettle 40 Cuban refugees as early as 1981. Later formalized under a U.S.-Australia Mutual Assistance Arrangement, the two governments agreed to resettle up to 200 refugees processed in the other country every year. Both governments feared that providing settlement in their own territory would draw more people to embark on a dangerous, unauthorized journey—and were under political pressure to halt inflows. Stopping short of refoulement, the governments believed they could disrupt this magnet effect by preventing the few who managed to pass the high hurdle of refugee recognition from reaching their desired destination. In April 2010, *The Australian* reported a suspected "swap" of three Cuban refugees held by the United States for 28 Tamil refugees rescued by the customs ship *Oceanic Viking*.[63]

Although the numbers exchanged under this arrangement are small, the idea that even *bona fide* refugees cannot choose their destination is important to the U.S., Australian, and EU governments, among others. The U.S. government will not permit refugees from Cuba and Haiti interdicted at sea to settle in the United States, even after U.S. authorities have determined their claims to be valid. Instead, the refugees are held in a facility at the U.S. naval base in Guantánamo, Cuba until a third country agrees to accept them.[64] Australia has made agreements with Cambodia, Nauru, and Papua New Guinea to resettle refugees in these countries. And the Dublin Regulation allows EU Member States to return asylum seekers to their first point of entry into the EU space.

Many countries that are on the front lines of unauthorized maritime migration flows, whether floods or trickles, lack the infrastructure and administrative capacity to adjudicate asylum claims and provide care to refugees and asylum seekers. Wealthier states often provide technical assistance to reinforce (or in some cases, create) this capacity, as European countries have in North African states such as Morocco. In other cases, UNHCR provides assistance or, in the absence of a national

---

62 Rob Taylor, "U.S. and Australia Strike Refugee Exchange Deal," Reuters, April 17, 2007.

63 Paul Maley and Paige Taylor, "Cuban Refugees from US Arriving Here in Exchange for Tamils," *The Australian*, April 6, 2010.

64 Cath Hart, "Refugee Swap Not Binding, Says US," *The Australian*, April 20, 2007.

framework, will process asylum claims directly. In Indonesia, for example, UNHCR processes asylum claims and provides protection, while IOM runs facilities to house migrants while they await status determination and either repatriation or resettlement. Australia funds much of the cost of these operations under a tripartite arrangement with Indonesia and IOM. As of May 2014, more than 10,000 refugees and asylum seekers were in Indonesia, with nearly 17 percent in 13 detention centers located across the country.[65]

The largest-scale incidence of burden sharing to date occurred in the aftermath of the Vietnam War, as large numbers of refugees left Vietnam by boat (see Chapter 3). Many were attacked by pirates en route; others were endangered by bad weather and unsafe, overcrowded vessels. Hundreds of thousands made their way to Southeast Asian countries that refused to consider them for permanent settlement. In 1979, the United Nations convened a groundbreaking conference of international stakeholders in Geneva.[66] As a result, worldwide resettlement commitments more than doubled the following year. Participating countries (with guidance from UNHCR) negotiated a number of agreements to address the particular circumstances of migrants at sea—many of whom reported being bypassed by ships that refused to respond to their distress. In particular, under the DISERO program that began in 1979 (DISERO being a derivation of "Disembarkation Resettlement Offers"), several countries agreed to accept any Vietnamese refugee rescued at sea by a ship of a country that was not itself participating in the resettlement of these refugees. Additionally, under a companion program begun in 1985, called Rescue at Sea Resettlement Offers (RASRO), 15 countries pledged to resettle a specified number of the refugees rescued at sea.[67] At the same time, an orderly departure program (ODP) was put in place to give people a safer, managed alternative to dangerous sea journeys. As the pace of resettlement exceeded the rate of boat arrivals, government officials were optimistic that the crisis had passed.

However, in the late 1980s, departures from Vietnam again surged, in part because of drought in North Vietnam and the hardships faced amid the country's ongoing political and economic transitions. Most of the

---

65 Vivian Tan, "Tricked by Smugglers, It's Sink or Swim for Afghan Youth" (UNHCR news release, May 16, 2014).

66 W. Courtland Robinson, "The Comprehensive Plan of Action for Indochinese Refugees, 1989–1997: Sharing the Burden and Passing the Buck," *Journal of Refugee Studies* 17, no. 3 (2004): 319-33.

67 USCIS, "This Month in Immigration History: July 1979," accessed September 21, 2016.

people making up these flows did not conform to the 1951 Convention definition of a refugee. In response, the Comprehensive Plan of Action (CPA) was established in 1989 to handle the outflows, particularly the hundreds of thousands of Vietnamese "boat people." One of the goals of the CPA was to resettle—in an orderly, organized manner—those refugees who could neither remain in other Southeast Asian countries nor return to Vietnam, in order to avoid another mass departure by boat.[68] Over time, more than 1 million refugees were resettled in Western Europe, North America, Australia, and New Zealand. Those who had landed in states in the region and were found not to be refugees were returned to Vietnam.[69] As a result of the CPA, the number of boat departures dropped considerably, and the plan is generally thought to have been a success. The Indochinese refugee experience remains the outstanding example of burden sharing connected with unauthorized maritime migration.

No recent experiences come close to the scale of the burden-sharing experience in Indochina. Echoes of the experience can be detected in the insistence by Indonesia and Malaysia in 2015 that, in return for agreeing to shelter the migrants and refugees from Myanmar and Bangladesh stranded at sea, the boat arrivals would have to be resettled elsewhere within a year of arrival. The European approach to unauthorized maritime migration from the 1990s to the present, as governed by the Dublin Regulation, seems almost the reverse of the post-Vietnam experience: rather than relieving the pressures of boat arrivals on frontline states (in this case Greece and Italy), the terms of the Dublin agreement allow EU Member States to return refugees who have moved within Europe to the EU Member State in which they first arrived, unless they have family ties in the state to which they moved. Meant to deter migrants from filing asylum applications in multiple states ("asylum shopping"), it has left the littoral states of the northern Mediterranean to cope with at least three overlapping waves of boat arrivals. First came migrants fleeing the Balkan wars of the early 1990s through Albania and Greece across the Adriatic Sea (as well as by land), followed by large numbers from sub-Saharan Africa transiting through Libya. The most recent wave was prompted by the transitions following

---

68 Robinson, "The Comprehensive Plan of Action."

69 Later programs (such as the Humanitarian Resettlement Program and the McCain Program) were put in place by agreements between the U.S. and Vietnamese governments that allowed people who had missed the September 30, 1994 application deadline for the Orderly Departure Program (ODP) to apply for resettlement in the United States. The Resettlement Opportunities for Vietnamese Returnees (ROVR) program provided a second chance at resettlement for people who had been returned under ODP.

the Arab Spring, war and repression in sub-Saharan Africa, and—dominating recent movements—the Syrian civil war.

The limits to burden sharing came into sharp focus with the dramatic increase in boat arrivals across the Mediterranean between 2013 and 2015. Although border management has been a cooperative venture in the European Union since the creation of Frontex in 2004, primary responsibility for border control and for processing boat arrivals still rests with individual states.[70] According to UNHCR, nearly 85 percent of the estimated 165,000 unauthorized maritime arrivals to Europe in 2014 arrived in Italy, whose Mare Nostrum operation had rescued about 150,000 people by the time it ended on October 31, 2014.[71] In 2015, the numbers of Mediterranean crossings soared, as the traffic shifted from the central route from Libya to Italy toward the much shorter crossing from Turkey to the Greek islands. More than 1 million migrants crossed the Mediterranean in 2015.[72]

After the huge shipwreck in April 2015 that killed approximately 800 migrants, and the enhanced rescue operations that followed, the European Commission proposed an obligatory distribution scheme for maritime arrivals, but EU Member States could not reach a consensus on its terms. Several Member States were simply unwilling to participate, leaving Greece, Italy, and the two most popular onward destinations, Germany and Sweden, with the great majority of the migrants.

An unshared burden can lead to further disorder in migration corridors. Countries of first asylum and frontline littoral states, overwhelmed by growing numbers of refugees and unauthorized maritime arrivals, may resort to pushbacks to even less capable countries or tolerate unauthorized departures to other countries. Transit countries

---

70 Frontex is the European Agency for the Management of Operational Cooperation at the External Borders of the Member States of the European Union, established by EU Council resolution on October 26, 2004. Currently, 26 states, not all of them EU Member States, are members of Frontex, which coordinates the external border controls of the states belonging to the Schengen area. The 26 states of the Schengen area have abolished all internal borders in favor of a single external border. Common rules and procedures are applied with regard to visas for short stays, asylum requests, and border controls. See EU-Lex, "The Schengen Area and Cooperation," updated August 3, 2009. The Schengen area has 44,000 kilometers (km) of external sea borders (compared to only 9,000 km of external land borders). See Frontex, "Roles and Responsibilities," accessed September 10, 2016.
71 UNHCR, *Central Mediterranean Sea Initiative: So Close, Yet So Far from Safety* (Geneva: UNHCR, 2014).
72 IOM, "Mixed Migration Flows in the Mediterranean and Beyond, Reporting Period 2015," accessed September 21, 2016.

may suffer from growing lawlessness, sparked by the criminal elements involved in human smuggling (but who do not confine themselves to that line of business). Although the costs of failure are high, effective burden sharing requires an act of will and a commitment of resources that many countries seem unable to muster—at least until a crisis is very nearly out of control.

X. Conclusions: A Wicked Problem

Unauthorized maritime migration surges and retreats in response to circumstances—conflict, repression, political turmoil, and economic decline—in countries of origin, as well as conditions and policy responses in the desired countries of destination. Paradoxically, some of the states that take the hardest lines on maritime migration, such as the United States and Australia, have the most open immigration policies overall. But they insist on choosing, rather than being chosen by, immigrants. These states set the rules of entry, and deal harshly with people who attempt to violate those rules—especially those who arrive by sea.

The second decade of the 21st century has seen surges in maritime migration in several regions: the Mediterranean, the Bay of Bengal, the Gulf of Aden/Red Sea, the southern Indian Ocean approaches to Australia, and the Caribbean. Such movements present daunting challenges to states seeking to reconcile the sovereign control of their borders with international obligations to protect refugees and to treat all people humanely and with dignity. Australian policy, for instance, has brought maritime arrivals under control, at least for the time being. But this control has come at a high cost in terms of financial expenditure, the erosion of protection mechanisms, and the reputation of the country.

Unauthorized maritime migration is everywhere characterized by complexity. The multiplicity of state- and nonstate actors, the mixed flows of refugees and nonrefugees, the overlapping and sometimes contradictory legal rulings, the fluctuating state policies, the secondary movements of people from countries of first asylum, and the constantly shifting parameters of sources, routes, and destinations—all these factors and more make maritime migration an extremely difficult issue to resolve. An apparent solution to the problem in one setting is likely to reflect not true resolution but deflection or diversion—a process of "squeezing the balloon" so that the problem emerges or intensifies elsewhere. The construction of a 7.5-mile border fence between Turkey and Greece in 2012, for example, all but stopped migration across the land border but resulted in a surge in maritime migration across the Aegean Sea between the Turkish coast and the nearby Greek islands. Greek police reported that maritime arrivals doubled in the first six months of 2014 to more than 25,000, even as unknown numbers went undetected.[73]

Marie McAuliffe and Victoria Mence have suggested that unauthorized maritime migration displays many of the characteristics of a "wicked problem," borrowing a term used by urban planners to describe a complex, hard-to-resolve social problem.[74] The originators of the term, Horst Rittel and Melvin Webber, identified two of the major challenges in confronting wicked problems as (1) defining the problem and (2) identifying solutions—or, in their words, "finding where in the complex causal networks trouble really lies" and then "identifying the actions that might effectively narrow the gap between what is and what ought to be."[75] Defining the problem is difficult because wicked problems are both causes and symptoms of other problems—and, like the blind men and the elephant—the explanation of the problem depends on the perspective of the observer. Unauthorized maritime migration is intimately connected to poverty, repression, and violence in migrants' countries of origin and to the growth of organized crime, the perception of disorder in destination countries, the erosion of international norms, and dozens of other equally wicked problems. And such problems, Rittel and Webber point out, are not likely to be definitively solved, "but only re-solved—again and again."[76] This implies that states will have to learn to live with imperfection, and engage in a continuous process of trial and error.

Policymakers need better tools to make that process more productive. These may include:

1. Better collection and sharing of data on maritime migration would solidify the evidence base for policymaking. The Regional Mixed Migration Secretariat (RMMS) for the Horn of Africa-Yemen region, established in 2011, is a useful model for

---

73 *The Economist*, "Migration into Europe."
74 Marie McAuliffe and Victoria Mence, "Global Irregular Maritime Migration: Current and Future Challenges" (occasional paper 07/2014, Irregular Migration Research Programme, Department of Immigration and Border Protection, Government of Australia, Canberra, April 2014).
75 Horst W. J. Rittel and Melvin M. Webber, "Dilemmas in a General Theory of Planning," *Policy Sciences* 4, no. 2 (1973): 155–69, 159.
76 Ibid., 160.

organizing data collection and research on regional migration, including migration by sea. States could also benefit from sharing intelligence findings on the involvement of organized crime in the smuggling or trafficking of migrants.

2. Better evidence and analysis of the causes of maritime migration and the motivations of migrants would help to define the nature of the problem. War, poverty, and repression are undoubtedly root causes, but the patterns of boat departures do not map on to them as closely as one might expect. For example, the average number of Sri Lankan boat arrivals in Australia held steady from 2008 to 2011, at fewer than 500 per year. In 2012, however, the number jumped to about 6,400. No other country experienced this kind of increase, suggesting that conditions in Sri Lanka were not the determining factor.[77] What caused the surge? The decision to migrate illegally is complex. In addition to their own personal situations, migrants take into account the nature of border protection regimes, the costs of clandestine travel, the danger of the voyage, the presence of a known community (perhaps including family or friends) at the intended destination, the availability of rescue, the chances of being allowed to stay, and the likelihood of being able to earn a living. Information about these and other factors is transmitted with great speed and variable accuracy. Understanding the sources of information on which migrants rely is an important part of understanding the dynamics of migration.

3. Monitoring the impact of policies can establish feedback loops that help policymakers understand whether their actions are having the intended results, or producing unintended and undesirable consequences. Better data can help establish correlations, but not necessarily causation. Interviewing migrants who are rescued or intercepted at sea as soon after they disembark as possible can offer valuable insights, provided it is done with appropriate sensitivity to their experiences and their potential need for protection.

4. These three tools are all helpful in the difficult task of defining the problem of maritime migration. Identifying the goals of policy in this area and the actions that might bring them

---

77 Dinuk Jayasuriya and Marie McAuliffe, "Placing Recent Sri Lankan Maritime Arrivals in a Broader Migration Context" (occasional paper 02/2013, Irregular Migration Research Programme, Department of Immigration and Border Protection, Government of Australia, Canberra, October 2013).

closer is even more challenging, not least because of the number of actors involved and their competing priorities. Identifying policy goals, even within a single government, requires cooperation across departments and agencies with varying objectives and operating procedures. Identifying common objectives among destination, transit, and origin countries is much more complex. Complex, crosscutting problems like unauthorized maritime migration lend themselves to a task force or standing committee, in which multiple perspectives can be represented at the national or regional level. The rare breakthrough in addressing maritime migration at the global level has tended to come out of a crisis-driven conference format, as with the Comprehensive Plan of Action or the amendments to the SARS and SOLAS conventions relating to disembarkation.

The issues surrounding maritime migration that are most in need of breakthroughs in international cooperation include:

1. A global recommitment to the universal norms of rescue at sea, with particular emphasis on further development of burden sharing on a regional or global basis so that frontline states do not bear a disproportionate share of responsibility for migrants and refugees who reach their shores.

2. Provision of international protection to refugees who travel by boat, and respect for the dignity, human rights, and basic needs of other maritime migrants.

3. The opening of channels for legal migration as an alternative to clandestine sea journeys.

4. Measures to oppose the involvement of organized criminal organizations in migrant smuggling.

These problems are not subject to technical solutions. The persistence and complexity of the problem motivated UNHCR to make "Protection at Sea" the theme of a global initiative in 2014-15. Its ambition to reduce loss of life and abuse of unauthorized migrants traveling by sea, and to make sure that states' responses to maritime migration are protection-sensitive continues. Rescue at sea was also one of the themes of the United Nations General Assembly High-Level Meeting on Large Movements of Refugees and Migrants held on September 19, 2016. The outcome document of the summit said: "We commend the efforts already made to rescue people in distress at sea. We commit to intensifying international cooperation on the strengthening of search and rescue mechanisms. We will also work to improve the availability of accurate data on the whereabouts of people and vessels that are stranded at sea."[78] Maritime migration also remains high on regional cooperation agendas, whether in Europe, the Americas, Australasia, or the Horn of Africa.

One-dimensional responses are unlikely to be effective in addressing the whole phenomenon of maritime migration and have been seen to produce unintended, and often unwelcome, consequences. Governments may choose to live with these. Alternatively, they may adopt a set of responses that is tactically flexible and capable of adapting to changing circumstances while remaining strategically anchored in rule of law, the imperative of safety, and respect for human dignity.

---

78 United Nations General Assembly, "Outcome Document for 19 September 2016 High-Level Meeting to Address Large Movements of Refugees and Migrants," Draft for Adoption, July 29, 2016.

Works Cited

Alpes, Maybritt Jill and Ninna Nyberg Sørensen. 2015. Migrant Risk Warning Campaigns Are Based on Wrong Assumptions. Policy brief, Danish Institute for International Studies, Copenhagen, May 2015. www.diis.dk/en/research/migration-risk-warning-campaigns-are-based-on-wrong-assumptions.

BBC News. 2014. Tilbury Docks: Man Dies After 35 Found in Container. BBC News, August 16, 2014. www.bbc.com/news/uk-england-28817688.

———. 2014. Malta: Private Migrant Rescue Boat Saves Fishermen. BBC News, August 26, 2014. www.bbc.com/news/blogs-news-from-elsewhere-28936649.

Bonomolo, Alessandra and Stephanie Kirchgaessner. 2015. UN Says 800 Migrants Dead in Boat Disaster as Italy Launches Rescue of Two More Vessels. *The Guardian*, April 20, 2015. www.theguardian.com/world/2015/apr/20/italy-pm-matteo-renzi-migrant-shipwreck-crisis.

Brian, Tara and Frank Laczko, eds. 2014. *Fatal Journeys: Tracking Lives Lost during Migration*. Geneva: International Organization for Migration (IOM). www.iom.int/files/live/sites/iom/files/pbn/docs/Fatal-Journeys-Tracking-Lives-Lost-during-Migration-2014.pdf.

———. 2016. *Fatal Journeys Volume 2: Identification and Tracing of Dead and Missing Migrants*. Geneva: IOM. http://publications.iom.int/system/files/fataljourneys_vol2.pdf.

Campbell, Angus. 2014. Speech by Lieutenant General, Australian Army, to the Australian Strategic Policy Institute. Operation Sovereign Borders: Initial Reflections and Future Outlook, Barton, Australia, May 15, 2014. www.aspi.org.au/_data/assets/pdf_file/0016/21634/SovereignBorders_Reflections.pdf.

Consiglio Italiano per i Refugiato (CIR). 2007. *Report Regarding Recent Search and Rescue Operations in the Mediterranean*. Rome: CIR. www.europarl.europa.eu/hearings/20070703/libe/cir_report_en.pdf.

Council of the European Union. 2014. Joint Operations "Mos Maiorum." Note from the Presidency to the Delegations, July 10, 2014. www.statewatch.org/news/2014/sep/eu-council-2014-07-10-11671-mos-maioum-jpo.pdf.

Deutsche Welle. 2016. Politicians Blame Merkel's Refugee Policy for Defeat in Regional Elections. Deutsche Welle, September 5, 2016. www.dw.com/en/politicians-blame-merkels-refugee-policy-for-defeat-in-regional-elections/a-19526368.

Doctors Without Borders. 2015. MSF and MOAS to Launch Lifesaving Operation for Migrants in Mediterranean. Press release, April 9, 2015. www.doctorswithoutborders.org/article/msf-and-moas-launch-lifesaving-operation-migrants-mediterranean.

Economist, The. 2014. Migration into Europe: A Surge from the Sea. *The Economist*, August 16, 2014. www.economist.com/news/europe/21612228-illegal-migration-causing-strains-across-continent-surge-sea.

EU-Lex. 2009. The Schengen Area and Cooperation. Updated August 3, 2009. http://
   eur-lex.europa.eu/legal-content/EN/TXT/?qid=1412793270717&uri=URIS
   ERV:l33020.

EurActiv. 2009. Italy's Immigration Deal with Libya Sparks Uproar. EurActiv, June 11,
   2009. www.euractiv.com/section/justice-home-affairs/news/italy-s-immi-
   gration-deal-with-libya-sparks-uproar/.

Evershed, Nick, Ri Liu, Paul Farrell, and Helen Davidson. 2016. The Nauru Files:
   The Lives of Asylum Seekers in Detention Detailed in a Unique Database.
   The Guardian, August 10, 2016. www.theguardian.com/australia-news/ng-
   interactive/2016/aug/10/the-nauru-files-the-lives-of-asylum-seekers-in-
   detention-detailed-in-a-unique-database-interactive.

Frontex. N.d. Roles and Responsibilities. Accessed September 10, 2016. http://fron-
   tex.europa.eu/operations/roles-and-responsibilities/.

Goodwin-Gill, Guy S. 1996. *The Refugee in International Law*, 2nd edition. Oxford, UK:
   Oxford University Press.

Government of Australia and Government of Papua New Guinea. 2013. Regional
   Resettlement Arrangement between Australia and Papua New Guinea, July
   19, 2013. http://dfat.gov.au/geo/papua-new-guinea/pages/regional-reset-
   tlement-arrangement-between-australia-and-papua-new-guinea.aspx.

Hart, Cath. 2007. Refugee Swap Not Binding, Says US. *The Australian,* April 20, 2007.
   www.theaustralian.com.au/news/nation/refugee-swap-not-binding-says-
   us/story-e6frg6nf-1111113376696.

Hirsi Jamaa and Others v. Italy. 2012. Application no. 27765/09, European Court of
   Human Rights. http://hudoc.echr.coe.int/eng?i=001-109231.

Hugo, Graeme. 2005. The New International Migration in Asia: Challenges for Population Research. *Asian Population Studies* 1 (1): 93-120.

International Maritime Organization (IMO). 2004. *Rescue at Sea: A Guide to Principle
   and Practice as Applied to Migrants and Refugees.* London: IMO. www.imo.
   org/en/OurWork/Facilitation/personsrescued/Documents/Rescueat-
   SeaGuideENGLISH.pdf.

International Organization for Migration (IOM). 2014. IOM Says New Witnesses
   Provide Further Details of Mediterranean Shipwreck Tragedy. Press release,
   September 16, 2014. www.iom.int/news/iom-says-new-witnesses-provide-
   further-details-mediterranean-shipwreck-tragedy.

———. 2016. Migration Flows – Europe: Recent Trends. Updated August 28, 2016.
   http://migration.iom.int/europe/.

———. N.d. Mixed Migration Flows in the Mediterranean and Beyond, Reporting
   Period 2015. Accessed September 21, 2016. http://doe.iom.int/docs/
   Flows%20Compilation%202015%20Overview.pdf.

———. N.d. Missing Migrants Project – Latest Global Figures. Accessed September
   10, 2016. http://missingmigrants.iom.int/latest-global-figures.

International Transport Workers' Federation (ITF). N.d. Flags of Convenience: Avoiding the Rules by Flying a Convenient Flag. Accessed September 10, 2016.
   www.itfglobal.org/en/transport-sectors/seafarers/in-focus/flags-of-conve-
   nience-campaign/.

Jayasuriya, Dinuk and Marie McAuliffe. 2013. Placing Recent Sri Lankan Maritime Arrivals in a Broader Migration Context. Occasional paper 02/2013, Irregular Migration Research Programme, Department of Immigration and Border Protection, Government of Australia, Canberra, October 2013. www.border.gov.au/ReportsandPublications/Documents/research/placing-recent-sri-lankan-maritime-arrivals-broader-migration-context.pdf.

Maley, Paul and Paige Taylor. 2010. Cuban Refugees from US Arriving Here in Exchange for Tamils. *The Australian*, April 6, 2010. www.theaustralian.com.au/archive/politics/cuban-refugees-from-us-arriving-here-in-exchange-for-tamils/story-e6frgczf-1225850083681.

Malta Independent, The. 2014. First MOAS Mission on Wednesday, Fisherman and Young Son Rescued. *The Malta Independent*, August 25, 2014. www.independent.com.mt/articles/2014-08-25/news/first-moas-private-migrant-rescue-mission-starts-on-wednesday-6341132288/.

McAuliffe, Marie and Victoria Mence. 2014. Global Irregular Maritime Migration: Current and Future Challenges. Occasional paper 07/2014, Irregular Migration Research Programme, Department of Immigration and Border Protection, Government of Australia, Canberra, April 2014. www.border.gov.au/ReportsandPublications/Documents/research/global-irregular-maritime-migration.pdf.

Minder, Rafael and Jim Yardley. 2013. Desperation Fuels Trips of Migrants to Spain. *The New York Times*, October 4, 2013. www.nytimes.com/2013/10/05/world/europe/as-desperation-mounts-more-migrants-cast-their-lot-on-a-troubled-sea.html.

Morrison, Scott E. 2014. Address by the Minister for Immigration and Border Protection, Australian Government, to the Lowy Institute for International Policy, "A New Force Protecting Australia's Borders, Sydney, Australia, May 9, 2014. www.lowyinstitute.org/news-and-media/audio/podcast-future-border-protection-scott-morrison-mp.

Moyer, Justin Wm. 2015. The Forgotten Story of How Refugees Almost Ended Bill Clinton's Career. *Washington Post,* November 17, 2015. http://washingtonpost.com/news/morning-mix/wp/2015/11/17/the-forgotten-story-of-how-refugees-almost-ended-bill-clintons-career/.

Muchler, Benno. 2014. Ethiopian Migrants Expelled by Saudis Remain in Limbo Back Home. *The New York Times,* January 7, 2014. www.nytimes.com/2014/01/08/world/africa/ethiopian-migrants-expelled-by-saudis-remain-in-limbo-back-home.html.

Nelson, Zed. 2014. Lampedusa Boat Tragedy: A Survivor's Story. *The Guardian*, March 22, 2014. www.theguardian.com/world/2014/mar/22/lampedusa-boat-tragedy-migrants-africa

Papastavridis, Efthymios. 2013. The Interception of Vessels on the High Seas: Contemporary Challenges to the Legal Order of the Oceans. Oxford, UK: Hart.

Pascouau, Yves and Pascal Schumacher. 2014. Frontex and the Respect of Fundamental Rights: From Better Protection to Full Responsibility. Policy Brief, European Policy Centre, Brussels, June 2014. www.epc.eu/pub_details.php?cat_id=3&pub_id=4512.

Plaintiff M70/2011 v. Minister for Immigration and Citizenship & Anor. 2011. 244 CLR 144, High Court of Australia. www.hcourt.gov.au/cases/case-m70/2011.

Popham, Peter. 2007. Tunisian Fishermen Face 15 Years' Jail Time in Italy for Saving Migrants from Rough Seas. *The Independent*, September 19, 2007. www.independent.co.uk/news/world/europe/tunisian-fishermen-face-15-years-jail-in-italy-for-saving-migrants-from-rough-seas-5329328.html.

Rittel, Horst W. J. and Melvin M. Webber. 1973. Dilemmas in a General Theory of Planning. *Policy Sciences* 4 (2): 155–69, 159.

Robinson, W. Courtland. 2004. The Comprehensive Plan of Action for Indochinese Refugees, 1989–1997: Sharing the Burden and Passing the Buck. *Journal of Refugee Studies* 17 (3): 319-33, www.jhsph.edu/research/centers-and-institutes/center-for-refugee-and-disaster-response/publications_tools/publications/additional_pdfs/Robinson2004-Indochinese_refugees.pdf.

Sale v. Haitian Centers Council, Inc. 1993. 509 U.S. Reports 155. https://supreme.justia.com/cases/federal/us/509/155/.

Saul, Heather. 2016. Yusra Mardini: Olympic Syrian Refugee Who Swam for Three Hours in Sea to Push Sinking Boat Carrying 20 to Safety. *The Independent*, August 5, 2016. www.independent.co.uk/news/people/yusra-mardini-rio-2016-olympics-womens-swimming-the-syrian-refugee-competing-in-the-olympics-who-a7173546.html.

Smith, Helena. 2015. Shocking Images of Drowned Syrian Boy Show Tragic Plight of Refugees. *The Guardian,* September 2, 2015. www.theguardian.com/world/2015/sep/02/shocking-image-of-drowned-syrian-boy-shows-tragic-plight-of-refugees.

Tan, Vivian. 2014. Tricked by Smugglers, It's Sink or Swim for Afghan Youth. UNHCR news release, May 16, 2014. www.unhcr.org/537618716.html.

Taylor, Rob. 2007. U.S. and Australia Strike Refugee Exchange Deal. Reuters, April 17, 2007. www.reuters.com/article/us-australia-refugees-idUSSYD26945620070418.

United Nations, Department of Economic and Social Affairs (UN DESA). 2016. *International Migration Report 2015: Highlights.* New York: United Nations. www.un.org/en/development/desa/population/migration/publications/migrationreport/docs/MigrationReport2015_Highlights.pdf

United Nations General Assembly. 1951. Convention Relating to the Status of Refugees, July 28, 1951. www.refworld.org/docid/3be01b964.html.

———. 1982. United Nation Convention on the Law of the Sea, Article 98 (1), December 10, 1982. www.refworld.org/docid/3dd8fd1b4.html.

———. 2000. Protocol against the Smuggling of Migrants by Land, Sea and Air, Supplementing the United Nations Convention against Transnational Organized Crime, Article 8. www.refworld.org/docid/479dee062.html

———. 2016. Outcome Document for 19 September 2016 High-Level Meeting to Address Large Movements of Refugees and Migrants, Draft for Adoption, July 29, 2016. www.un.org/pga/70/wp-content/uploads/sites/10/2015/08/HLM-on-addressing-large-movements-or-refugees-and-migrants-Draft-Declaration-5-August-2016.pdf.

United Nations High Commissioner for Refugees (UNHCR). 2002. Background Note on the Protection of Asylum-Seekers and Refugees Rescued at Sea, Section II (31). Background note, UNHCR, Geneva, March 18, 2002. www.unhcr.org/3e5f35e94.pdf.

———. 2013. Record Number of African Refugees and Migrants Cross the Gulf of Aden in 2012. Press briefing, UNHCR, Geneva, January 15, 2013. www.unhcr.org/50f5633c9.html.

———. 2014. Urgent European Action Needed to Stop Rising Refugee and Migrant Deaths at Sea. Press release, July 24, 2014. www.unhcr.org/en-us/news/press/2014/7/53d0cbb26/unhcr-urgent-european-action-needed-stop-rising-refugee-migrant-deaths.html.

———. 2014. *Central Mediterranean Sea Initiative: So Close, Yet So Far from Safety.* Geneva: UNHCR. www.unhcr.org/542c07e39.html.

———. 2014. Submission of the Office of the United Nations High Commissioner for Refugees – Seeking Leave to Intervene as Amicus Curiae. UNHCR submissions in the High Court of Australia in the Case of *CPCF v. Minister for Immigration and Border Protection and the Commonwealth of Australia*, September 15, 2014. www.refworld.org/docid/54169e8e4.html.

———. 2015. Joint Statement on Mediterranean Crossings. Press release, April 23, 2015. www.unhcr.org/5538d9079.html.

———. 2016. *Global Trends: Forced Displacement in 2015.* Geneva: UNHCR. www.unhcr.org/576408cd7.

UNHCR, Regional Office for South-East Asia. N.d. Mixed Maritime Movements in South-East Asia—2015. Accessed August 9, 2016. https://unhcr.atavist.com/mmm2015.

United Nations Office on Drugs and Crime (UNODC). 2011. *Issue Paper: Smuggling of Migrants by Sea.* Vienna: UNODC. www.unodc.org/documents/human-trafficking/Migrant-Smuggling/Issue-Papers/Issue_Paper_-_Smuggling_of_Migrants_by_Sea.pdf.

United Nations Secretary-General. 2008. *Oceans and the Law of the Sea.* New York: United Nations.

United States Citizenship and Immigration Services (USCIS). 2014. DHS to Implement Haitian Family Reunification Parole Program. News release, October 17, 2014. www.uscis.gov/news/dhs-implement-haitian-family-reunification-parole-program.

———. N.d. This Month in Immigration History: July 1979. Accessed September 21, 2016.

Weber, Leanne and Sharon Pickering. 2011. *Globalization and Borders: Death at the Global Frontier.* Basingstoke, UK: Palgrave Macmillan.

Willheim, Ernst. 2003. MV Tampa: The Australian Response. *International Journal of Refugee Law* 15 (2): 159-91.

CHAPTER TWO

UNAUTHORIZED MARITIME MIGRATION IN EUROPE AND THE MEDITERRANEAN REGION

By Elizabeth Collett

Introduction

Maritime migration across the Mediterranean Sea is not a new phenomenon; history has long connected the countries clustered around it. But there are few regions of the globe where such developmental and demographic disparities exist among geographically proximate countries. The delineation between European and African shores has been further emphasized in recent decades by the emergence of the European Union (EU) as a global economic and political power, and the accompanying creation of stronger, more coherent external border controls surrounding the bloc and a supranational legal framework for the management of migration.

Since the early 1990s, there has been a consistent flow of migrants across the Mediterranean from Africa and the Middle East (and sometimes further afield) undertaking dangerous, unauthorized sea journeys to reach European shores. The routes, volume, and composition of these flows have changed over time. However, the persistence of the movement over the past two decades, despite numerous policy interventions, hints at the intractable nature of the situation. Unauthorized maritime migration across the Mediterranean has long held a position on the European political agenda, but has now moved to the top.

The year 2014 saw an unprecedented rise in the number of people crossing the Mediterranean: more than 218,000 according to the

United Nations High Commissioner for Refugees (UNHCR).[1] The number of fatalities also reached a new high of at least 3,500.[2] But in 2015, the rate of arrivals on EU shores accelerated dramatically, particularly on the Greek islands in the Aegean that are only a short maritime crossing from the Turkish coast. By the end of 2015, more than 853,000 people had crossed the Aegean, placing European governments, and particularly Greece, under unparalleled pressure to take action.[3] With the intensification of both maritime flows and their political salience came a widespread perception of crisis across the European Union. Policies adopted by northern Mediterranean governments, and latterly the European Union itself, in response to these changes have met with varying degrees of success. The management of such flows is complicated by the interdependence of national and EU legal frameworks, the deep asymmetry between Member States with respect to their capacity to respond, and varying degrees of government stability across the southern basin.

Have the flows of fall 2015 signified a turning point in European reactions to maritime migration or have they merely pushed governments to double-down on existing policy approaches? This chapter looks at the nature and characteristics of Mediterranean flows over the past decade, and explores the intensifying policy responses of the European Union, its Member States, and critical transit countries. It investigates the particular challenges raised by the fact that the flows arriving in Europe include a significant number of asylum seekers, who must have their claims adjudicated according to international and EU law. This case study also looks at how EU policies may have created conditions that further complicate efforts to find a sustainable response. Finally, it looks at how policy responses are evolving in a tense political environment.

---

1 United Nations High Commissioner for Refugees (UNHCR), "UNHCR Urges Europe to Recreate a Robust Search and Rescue Operation on Mediterranean, as Operation Triton Lacks Resources and Mandate Needed for Saving Lives" (press release, February 12, 2015).

2 Ibid.

3 International Organization for Migration (IOM), *Mixed Migration Flows in the Mediterranean and Beyond: Compilation of Available Data and Information, Reporting Period 2015* (Geneva: IOM, 2015).

I. A Never-Ending Cycle? Shifts in Flow Since 2004

Since the early 1990s, the major maritime routes to Europe have shifted every few years. During the 1990s, the major flows were from Turkey to Greece, Albania to Italy, and Morocco to Spain (see Figure 1). More recent routes include those from West Africa to the Canary Islands (Spain), from and through Libya and Tunisia to Italy and Malta, and again from Turkey to Greece by sea or land. In any given year, migrants travel to Europe via all of these routes, but the popularity of each fluctuates in an imperfect cycle, dependent on a number of factors—not least the evolution of transit- and receiving-country border management and the geopolitical situation in the region.

Figure 1. Major Unauthorized Migration Routes into the European Union

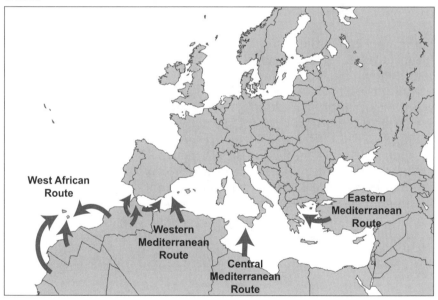

Source: Author's rendering.

Table 1. Unauthorized Entries Detected at EU Sea Borders, by Route

	Central Mediterranean	Eastern Mediterranean (by Sea)	Western Mediterranean (by Sea)	West African
2008	39,745	31,729	7,019	9,181
2009	10,236	28,848	5,003	2,244
2010	1,662	6,175	3,436	196
2011	59,002	1,467	5,103	340
2012	10,379	4,370	3,558	174
2013	40,304	11,831	2,609	283
2014	170,664	50,834	7,272	276
2015	153,946	885,386	7,164	874

Sources: Frontex, *Risk Analysis for 2016* (Warsaw: Frontex, 2016), 72; Frontex, *Annual Risk Analysis 2014* (Warsaw: Frontex, 2014), 31; Frontex, *General Report 2008* (Warsaw: Frontex, 2008), 13; Frontex, *Press Pack, May 2011* (Warsaw: Frontex, 2011), 7-9.

In the early 2000s, the routes from North Africa to Italy and Spain were the most significant, particularly the route from Libya to Sicily and the southern-most Italian island of Lampedusa. The number of migrants traveling this Central Mediterranean route has fluctuated year-on-year for much of the past decade, with notable surges during the Arab Spring of 2011 and again in 2014 and early 2015.[4] By 2007, a new flow of migrants had also emerged from West Africa (notably Senegal) to the Canary Islands. Then, by 2010, all other routes had been overtaken by those in the Eastern Mediterranean between Turkey and Greece (both by land and sea), which remain significant. Indeed, a review of headlines from the decade that focus on spontaneous maritime arrivals demonstrates a remarkably consistent sense of crisis; only the routes and destinations have changed.

---

4 For a detailed overview of routes, see the Dialogue on Mediterranean Transit Migration, "2014 Map on Mixed Migration Routes" (map, May 2014).

Box 1. A Note on Data and Context

A caution must be made with respect to data. Estimates of total border crossings have improved since the European Union (EU) border management agency
Frontex began to collate national data on detections of illegal external border
crossings in 2008. Search-and-rescue operations in the Mediterranean have also
likely contributed to more accurate counts of actual crossings and fatalities at
sea. However, the clandestine nature of entry means that numbers remain ap-
proximations at best.

Tragically, the death toll at sea is likely to be a significant underestimate. Between mid-2013 and mid-2016, a group of journalists aggregated all available
data on migrant fatalities on the routes to and through Europe, largely from
media reporting, and found that their calculations were 50 percent higher than
official estimations. Between January 1, 2000 and June 24, 2016, they estimated
that nearly 35,000 people had died or disappeared while trying to reach or
stay in Europe. Similarly, the International Organization for Migration (IOM)
Missing Migrants Project has collected data on dead and missing migrants
in the Mediterranean and elsewhere since 2014. The project uses data from
national authorities, survivor testimonies, and media reports, but acknowledges
that these data likely underestimate the true death toll.

It is also important to understand that the number of irregular maritime
migrants is only part of the total unauthorized population arriving in Europe.
Despite the dramatic surge in arrivals along the Eastern Mediterranean route
in 2015, sea arrivals constitute 57 percent of all detected illegal external
border crossings by land and sea. This figure does not include apprehensions
at EU airports. In addition, prior to the 2014–15 migrant and refugee crisis, the
majority of unauthorized migrants in Europe were thought to have arrived legally and subsequently overstayed their visas, though EU-wide data on overstay
remains patchy.

Note: The data collected by journalists in The Migrants' Files captured fatalities along all land, air,
and sea routes to and through Europe, and included deaths deemed to be linked to unauthorized status (for example, fatalities linked to poor detention conditions, which could include
suicides) or deportation.
Sources: The Migrants' Files, "The Human and Financial Cost of 15 Years of Fortress Europe,"
accessed August 30, 2016; The Migrants' Files, "Events during Which Someone Died Trying to
Reach or Stay in Europe," updated June 24, 2016; IOM, "Missing Migrants Project: Methodology,"
accessed August 29, 2016; Frank Laczko, Ann Singleton, Tara Brian, and Marzia Rango, "Migrant
Arrivals and Deaths in the Mediterranean: What Do the Data Really Tell Us?" *Forced Migra-
tion Review 51* (January 2016): 30–31; Frontex, *Risk Analysis 2016* (Warsaw: Frontex, 2016), 17;
European Commission, "Impact Assessment Report on the Establishment of an EU Entry Exit
System" (SWD [2016] 115 final, April 6, 2016).

The oscillating shifts in route across the Mediterranean speaks to the resilience, diversity, and pervasiveness of information networks, and the ability of smugglers and other facilitators to adjust their business models to find the path of least resistance at any given moment. Indeed, evidence on the "packages" that facilitators offer migrants suggests a complex, tiered pricing model,[5] even going so far as to charge migrants extra for food and water.

Geopolitical events have a clear impact on flows to Europe. In 2011, the Arab Spring led to local disruption and displacement throughout North Africa and, according to Frontex, the number of migrants traveling across the Central Mediterranean rose nearly fifteen-fold from 4,500 in 2010 to 65,000 in 2011.[6] This highlights the challenge European border agencies face in ensuring that sufficient resources are situated in the right locations at the right time.

With hindsight, the Arab Spring was merely a taste of the challenges to come. At the end of 2014, maritime migration was set to become more entrenched and critical to address. The spectacle of several large, decrepit freighters departing from Turkey during the winter of 2014–15—set adrift while holding hundreds of refugees (almost all from Syria)—highlighted demand for passage as both steady and increasing. Though Turkish authorities put an end to this smuggling tactic in short order, the strategy revealed the planning, execution, and resources of a highly organized operation, and a degree of collusion with port workers and officials. For those paying for a place on the ghost ships, the choice reflected the narrowing options for passage across the Central Mediterranean (with Libya increasingly unstable) as well as the challenges of remaining in Syria or the neighboring region.

By the beginning of 2015, it was clear to many observers that the number of migrants attempting passage was likely to increase over the year, exacerbated by large-scale displacement from Syria. For the first half of the year, focus remained squarely on the Central Mediterranean route. The cold and stormy winter months usually see a lull in unauthorized maritime crossings, but the winter of 2014–15 was an exception; there was a sharp increase in boat journeys originating in Libya, with 3,800 migrants arriving in Italy over a single weekend in early

---

5   United Nations Office on Drugs and Crime (UNODC), *Smuggling of Migrants into, through and from North Africa: A Thematic Review and Annotated Bibliography of Recent Publications* (New York: UNODC, 2010); Nektaria Stamouli, "Inside the Migrant-Smuggling Trade: Escapes Start at €1,000," *The Wall Street Journal*, March 29, 2016.

6   Frontex, *Annual Risk Analysis 2012* (Warsaw: Frontex, 2012).

2015.[7] A series of high-profile incidents also culminated in a record number of deaths in a single disaster on April 19, 2015, when up to 850 people died as their boat capsized off the coast of Libya.[8] This incident—following on similar disasters, intensifying media scrutiny, and increased public sympathy—finally catalyzed action from EU heads of state, who convened an extraordinary summit in Brussels to discuss a response (see Section V), including the establishment of a search and rescue operation to prevent further fatalities.

The chaotic high-profile flows in the Central Mediterranean obscured, during the first half of 2015, the upswing in journeys along the Eastern Mediterranean route from Turkey to Greece: smaller boats, shorter journeys, with less concentrated risk (though still dangerous). But as numbers increased sharply, the nature of the challenge facing EU policymakers shifted. This was no longer just an issue of saving lives, but of addressing a route that proved—within a matter of months—to be easily accessible to a far larger number of individuals. By mid-October 2015, arrivals on the Greek islands had reached 9,000 to 10,000 per day.[9]

For six months, the flows remained significant despite winter weather. Then, in March 2016, the border closures across the Western Balkans that impeded onward movement from Greece, coupled with the implementation of an unprecedented agreement between the European Union and the Turkish government to forcibly stem the flow, saw numbers drop precipitously. Within days, arrivals in Greece had dropped to just a few hundred per day, and crept lower through summer 2016.

Though many perceived this as heralding a definitive end to the crisis, in reality, the maritime migration flows merely reverted to their status 12 months earlier; large numbers were again arriving daily in Italy from North Africa, with some evidence of an emerging route from Egypt. Thus, at the time of writing, the Central Mediterranean had resumed its role as the dominant route. However, few of the underlying drivers impelling the large-scale movements of 2015 have receded.

---

7   IOM, "At Least 3,800 Migrants Rescued from Mediterranean since Friday: IOM" (press release, February 17, 2015).

8   Anthony Faiola, "U.N. Estimates That up to 850 Migrants Perished in Capsized Boat off Libya," *The Washington Post*, April 21, 2015.

9   UNHCR, "Greece Data Snapshot (8 Nov.)" (fact sheet, UNHCR, Geneva, November 2015).

II. Who Is Arriving? The Characteristics of Mixed Flows

The composition and motivations of those undertaking the journey is as fluid as the routes they take, and the term "mixed flows" refers directly to this fact.[10] Some are fleeing conflict and persecution, as demonstrated by the increase in recent Syrian, Iraqi, and Eritrean arrivals. Others have economic motivations, although research has highlighted key, yet understated, links between conflict and the economic and social instability that drive economic migration.[11] Further individuals have personal reasons for traveling, to join family members, for example. Some may have been displaced before choosing to make the journey: many of the Afghan nationals who crossed the Eastern Mediterranean in 2015–16 had spent significant time in either Pakistan or Iran prior to the journey, whilst a large proportion of Syrian nationals had spent time in neighboring countries, rather than making the journey directly.[12] The absence of sustainable living situations in many key refugee-hosting countries has thus impelled many to continue on in search of better options.[13]

Migrants and refugees arriving by sea tend not to be the most impoverished populations. Significant financial means and stamina are required to make the journey, and the poorest groups are often unable to pay their way. Instead, many of those who arrive are educated and well-resourced, or are capable of working in the transit region to earn sufficient funds to make the crossing.[14] Thus, conversations about reducing poverty to diminish motivation may be misplaced with respect to Mediterranean maritime movements.

---

10 Jacob Townsend and Christel Oomen, *Before the Boat: Understanding the Migrant Journey* (Brussels: Migration Policy Institute Europe, 2015).

11 Michael Collyer, "States of Insecurity: Consequences of Saharan Transit Migration" (working paper no. 31, Centre on Migration, Policy, and Security, University of Oxford, 2006).

12 UNHCR, "Profiling of Syrian Arrivals on Greek Islands in January 2016" (fact sheet, UNHCR, Geneva, January 2016); UNHCR, "Profiling of Syrian Arrivals on Greek Islands in February 2016" (fact sheet, UNHCR, Geneva, February 2016); UNHCR, "Profiling of Afghan Arrivals on Greek Islands in January 2016" (fact sheet, UNHCR, Geneva, January 2016); UNHCR, "Profiling of Afghan Arrivals on Greek Islands in February 2016" (fact sheet, UNHCR, Geneva, February 2016).

13 Adrian Edwards, "Seven Factors behind Movement of Syrian Refugees to Europe" (UNHCR press release, September 25, 2016).

14 UNODC, *Smuggling of Migrants into, through and from North Africa*; Hein de Haas, "The Myth of Invasion: The Inconvenient Realities of African Migration to Europe," *Third World Quarterly* 29, no. 7 (2009): 1305–22.

From 2013 onwards, the proportion of Syrian nationals making the journey rose dramatically—first across the Central Mediterranean, and subsequently between Turkey and Greece. However, it is notable that, while conflict and geopolitical changes were reflected through subsequent shifts in flows across the Mediterranean, the total number of migrants remained small compared to flows elsewhere, particularly within North Africa and the Middle East; UNHCR reported that just 5 percent of Syrian refugees had found protection within the European Union by the end of 2015.[15] Nonetheless, they were the dominant group among unauthorized maritime migrants by the end of 2014, with Eritreans in second place and Somalis close behind.[16] In 2015, the proportion of would-be asylum seekers amongst the flows further increased—notably from Syria, Iraq, and Afghanistan—tipping the balance heavily towards asylum-seeking groups. This shift added an additional layer of complexity for receiving countries tasked with addressing not just the rescue and safety of individuals, but also their protection needs.

However, the characteristics of those arriving differ greatly according to route and shift periodically. Most people who use the Central Mediterranean route are young men and generally come from countries in sub-Saharan Africa, such as Eritrea, Nigeria, and Somalia. While some are fleeing persecution or conflict (for example, those fleeing Somalia or Eritrea), others have economic motivations. In the first six months of 2016, most arrivals came from Nigeria (17 percent), Eritrea (13 percent), Gambia (8 percent), and Côte d'Ivoire (8 percent), with only a quarter from the top ten refugee-producing countries worldwide.[17] Between January and June 2016, men constituted between two-thirds and three-quarters of arrivals each month; relatively few women brave the journey, which has become fraught with exploitation and sexual violence. Almost all children who undertake the journey are unaccompanied.[18]

---

15 Migration Policy Institute (MPI) calculations using data from UNHCR, "Global Trends 2015—Table 5. Refugees and People in a Refugee-Like Situation, Excluding Asylum-Seekers, and Changes by Origin and Country of Asylum, 2015" (dataset accessed August 29, 2016).

16 Frontex, *Annual Risk Analysis 2015* (Warsaw: Frontex, 2015).

17 UNHCR, Regional Bureau Europe, "Refugees & Migrants Sea Arrivals in Europe" (fact sheet, UNHCR, Geneva, June 2016); UNHCR, *Global Trends: Forced Displacement in 2015* (Geneva: UNHCR, 2016), 16.

18 UNHCR, Regional Bureau Europe, "Refugees & Migrants Sea Arrivals in Europe;" Amnesty International, "Refugees and Migrants Fleeing Sexual Violence, Abuse, and Exploitation in Libya" (news release, July 1, 2016).

These characteristics are juxtaposed with those of migrants travel-ing the Eastern Mediterranean route, most of whom come from major refugee-producing countries. Syrians, Iraqis, and Afghans comprised 89 percent of flows between January and June 2016; smaller numbers of Pakistanis and Iranians also undertook the journey. The relatively less dangerous route (compared with the Central Mediterranean) has, from time to time, also attracted smaller numbers of migrants from North and sub-Saharan Africa, such as Somalis and Moroccans.[19] Though many young men travel this route, a significant number of family units do as well. Between January and June 2016, nearly two-thirds of those undertaking the journey were women or children.[20] This may be linked to restrictions on family reunion introduced in major destination countries such as Germany and Sweden from mid-2015 onward.[21]

Growing numbers of unaccompanied children have made the journey to Europe in recent years. In 2015, 88,000 unaccompanied children applied for asylum in the European Union: almost four times the number in 2014 (23,000) and almost seven times the number in 2013 (13,000).[22] The most common countries of origin were Afghanistan and Syria, whose nationals tend to use the Eastern Mediterranean route, and Eritrea, whose citizens tend to use the Central Mediter-ranean route. But as these data only capture children who register with authorities and apply for asylum, they likely underestimate the total number traveling through Europe. In turn, there are limited data on children who register but then abscond from reception facilities.[23] Many transit and destination countries have struggled to cope with this surge of unaccompanied children; often, the result is inadequate

---

19 UNHCR, "Greece Data Snapshot (24 Dec.)" (fact sheet, UNHCR, Geneva, December 2015); UNHCR, "Nationalities of Mediterranean Sea Arrivals to Greece – 2015 Monthly Breakdown, as of 30 November 2015" (dataset, November 30, 2015).

20 UNHCR, Regional Bureau Europe, "Refugees & Migrants Sea Arrivals in Europe."

21 Heaven Crawley, Franck Duvell, Nando Sigona, Simon McMahon, and Katharine Jones, "Unpacking a Rapidly Changing Scenario: Migration Flows, Routes and Trajectories across the Mediterranean" (research brief no. 1, Unravelling the Mediterranean Migration Crisis, March 2016), 9.

22 Eurostat, "Asylum Applicants Considered to be Unaccompanied Minors – Annual Data [tps00194]," updated August 11, 2016.

23 Reasons for these children absconding could include seeking reunification with family members in other countries, fear of a negative decision on their asylum application, or falling victim to human traffickers. See European Migration Network (EMN), *Policies, Practices, and Data on Unaccompanied Minors in the EU Member States and Norway* (Brussels: EMN, 2015), 7.

assessment and referral procedures, and a shortage of appropriate reception facilities.[24]

III. The Policy Response from Europe

Over the last several decades, both EU Member States and neighboring countries have made efforts to deter, rescue, or return those making the journey across the Mediterranean, with varying degrees of success. Often, success is measured in terms of the number of migrants taking a particular route following a particular initiative—although, as described above, deterrence in one part of the Mediterranean may lead, directly or indirectly, to an increase in traffic elsewhere.

National efforts take place under the umbrella of EU action and share the common goal of reducing the number of arrivals overall, which is arguably a greater challenge. As numbers have risen, the concept of EU solidarity has come under deep strain. Before turning to the complex interplay between so-called frontline states, such as Greece and Italy, and the overarching role of the European Union, it is useful to look at the policies that have been developed to address and manage the various routes across the Mediterranean. They are strikingly similar, wherever they have been applied, and though increased arrivals in 2015–16 catalyzed an intensification of EU political activity, the fundamental policies themselves have not changed.

A. Surveillance, Search, and Rescue

The core challenge of maritime migration is that the urgent humanitarian needs of those who find themselves in unsafe and overcrowded vessels overwhelm longer-term policy concerns, such as counter-smuggling. This means that ignoring a vessel, once identified, is not an option. The secondary challenge is then what to do with the boat and its occupants.

The approaches Southern European governments have taken to this second issue have fluctuated. Some have invested in joint patrols and early interdiction in the waters of countries of departure, preventing onward movement and escorting boats back to port. In the late

---

24 UNHCR, "Europe Refugee Emergency –Unaccompanied and Separated Children" (briefing note, October 9, 2015).

2000s, Spain made several agreements with countries in North and West Africa to establish joint patrols in Mauritanian, Moroccan, and Senegalese waters. These formed the basis for joint coordinated operations by Frontex (the EU border management agency) in support of the Spanish government. They have also become the blueprint for a series of Frontex surveillance operations at different points across the Mediterranean, under the aegis of a particular EU Member State.

Other approaches have focused on pushbacks from international waters that return individuals to their country of departure, or nearby. The most controversial of these was the short-lived Italian partnership with Libya. A series of largely confidential agreements, beginning in 2003, included collaboration on the pushback of migrants to Libya, payments (referred to as "reparations") in return for the right of the Italian government to patrol Libyan waters, and Italian financial support for detention camps in Libya.

Yet in parallel to these prevention policies, active search-and-rescue operations are undertaken that result in the transfer of intercepted migrants to EU shores. These tend to take place close to the European border or in nearby international waters. The most notable of these was Operation Mare Nostrum. Established by the Italian government in October 2013, it rescued approximately 100,000 migrants from boats in the Mediterranean before being disbanded a year later.[25] Two distinguishing characteristics of Mare Nostrum were that search and rescue was a core mandate and that it operated further south than the pre- and coexisting Frontex Joint Operations Hermes and Aeneas, which followed the Frontex surveillance model. Critics of the Italian initiative have suggested that, by operating closer to Libyan shores, it encouraged smugglers in Libya to send a greater number of boats, in more unstable condition, and more overloaded with passengers, with the expectation that swift rescue would follow.

These contrasting policies sit uncomfortably beside each other, particularly as the government that eventually receives the migrants (who may or may not be making claims for asylum) will, by law and necessity, take on further obligations. Search and rescue is often (though not always) simpler as the ship undertaking the rescue is expected to assume responsibility for those rescued. However, this has also been contested repeatedly, including under the banner of joint missions (as seen in longstanding disputes between Malta and Italy regarding

---

25 Duncan Robinson, "Alarm at Plan to End Italy's Mare Nostrum Rescue Operation," *Financial Times*, October 12, 2014.

disembarkation procedures for Frontex joint operations).[26] Interdiction and pushback may engender further humanitarian concerns if the country to which the individual is returned is not capable of offering such protection. The Italian partnership with Libya was cause for deep consternation from European governments, UNHCR, and NGOs alike given the lack of a national asylum system within Libya and concerns about the treatment of migrants in general.[27]

The preference for one approach over the other amongst European policymakers speaks not only to their interpretation of European and international legal frameworks, but also to changing national politics and public sympathies. It also reflects the stability of regional geopolitics: interdiction and return require the partnership and capacity of countries of departure, which may not be readily available. The Italian-Libyan partnership collapsed after the fall of the Gaddafi government, which led to concern about renewed flows from Libya to Lampedusa and elsewhere.

By contrast, search-and-rescue operations can be undertaken independently, and not only by official navy vessels. Alongside official Maltese government search and rescue operations, a charity, Migrant Offshore Aid Station (MOAS), began independent rescue operations in collaboration with Médecins sans Frontières (Doctors without Borders), led by the former commander of the Maltese Armed Forces, and rescued 11,600 people in 2014 and 2015.[28] In the Eastern Mediterranean, numerous independent operations sprang up in fall 2015, some

---

26 In 2010, the European Parliament approved new Frontex rules that required migrants to be disembarked in the search-and-rescue mission's host country, rather than the nearest port of call. Malta subsequently withdrew from future Frontex missions, citing concerns about rescued migrants undertaking longer journeys to access care and about additional migrants placing further pressure on Maltese reception services. When Frontex launched Operation Triton in 2014, Malta agreed to participate only in very exceptional circumstances. See Sergio Carrera and Leonhard den Hertog, "Whose *Mare?* Rule of Law Challenges in the Field of European Border Surveillance in the Mediterranean" (CEPS Paper in Liberty and Security in Europe no. 79, CEPS, Brussels, January 2015), 9; *Malta Independent,* "Malta to No Longer Host Frontex Missions... PN, PL MEPs Trade Blows after EP Vote," *Malta Independent,* March 26, 2010.
27 Emanuella Paoletti. "A Critical Analysis of Migration Policies in the Mediterranean: The Case of Italy, Libya and the EU" (RAMSES working paper no. 12/09, European Studies Centre, University of Oxford, 2009).
28 Migrant Offshore Aid Station (MOAS), "About MOAS," accessed August 29, 2016; Médecins sans Frontières, "MSF & MOAS to Launch Mediterranean Search, Rescue and Medical Aid Operation" (news release, April 10, 2015).

of which were funded by private actors.[29] Commercial vessels have also found themselves at the heart of rescue efforts, though not without contention. In 2014, it is thought that they were responsible for the rescue of more than 40,000 people traveling from Libya, one-quarter of the total that year, often being called upon by Italian authorities participating in Operation Mare Nostrum.[30] However, various shipping associations have highlighted the safety implications of ill-equipped vessels taking on this responsibility, as well as overall cost to the shipping industry.[31] Indeed, some of those who have taken on the responsibility have found themselves facing prosecution and imprisonment on grounds of facilitating unauthorized migration, and even smuggling. In 2007, for example, a group of Tunisian fishermen were placed on trial in Italy for rescuing 44 migrants in a small boat 40 miles south of Lampedusa.[32]

Bilateral and joint operations have proliferated over the past decade and have involved, at various moments, a large number of agencies—including coast guards, maritime authorities, border patrols, and naval vessels from all countries with a Mediterranean coastline. EU efforts to consolidate maritime management of boat arrivals have been slow to progress, not least due to the reluctance of EU Member States to cede authority on critical issues to the Frontex, limiting the agency to merely coordinating efforts between states.[33]

As will be discussed below, the current EU approach retains the tension between rescue-and-return approaches, with the development of both EU-led search and rescue missions alongside monitoring operations designed to address countersmuggling and promote the pullback of departing vessels. Yet there are also signs that EU Member States have come to terms with the fact that maritime border management is a collective responsibility, even if disagreement persists over ultimate responsibility for those intercepted at sea.

---

29 See, for example, Emergency Response Centre International, "ERCI: Emergency Response Centre International," accessed August 29, 2016.

30 Lorenzo Pezzani and Charles Heller, "'Sharing the Burden of Rescue': Illegalised Boat Migration, the Shipping Industry and the Costs of Rescue in the Central Mediterranean," Border Criminologies (blog), University of Oxford, November 2, 2015.

31 An investigation published by Reuters in September 2015 estimated that the loss of business incurred when ships conduct a rescue cost companies between US $10,000 and US $50,000 per day. See Jonathan Saul, "In Mediterranean, Commercial Ships Scoop up Desperate Human Cargo," Reuters, September 21, 2015.

32 Statewatch, "Criminalizing Solidarity, Part II—Italy/Tunisia: Fishermen on Trial for Rescuing Migrants," updated September 2007.

33 Henry Foy and Duncan Robinson, "Frontex Chief Welcomes Plan for More Powerful EU Border Force," Financial Times, December 13, 2015.

Box 2. Technological Developments

Beyond the physical patrolling and management of flows, governments have also developed technology to help identify potential migrant-smuggling boats. In 1999, the Spanish government developed and implemented an electronic surveillance network, known as SIVE, capable of early detection of migrants attempting to cross the sea. More recently, EU agencies are exploring the role of Remotely Piloted Aircraft Systems (or drones) to support coast guard activities, such as monitoring borders and ships. However, early detection is only useful as a deterrent if accompanied by the means to deal effectively with those who attempt passage (whether through an asylum procedure or return).

The European Union has also taken steps to coordinate border surveillance and share information among Member States. The European Border Surveillance System (Eurosur) aggregates information on border activities (including illegal crossings and crime) collected by a network of Member State National Coordination Centers (NCCs), European-level surveillance tools (e.g., satellites), and Frontex. Eurosur then provides analysis on the current situation at European borders and beyond. Similarly, the European Defence Agency's Maritime Surveillance System (Marsur)—launched in 2006 and operational from 2014—collects and shares maritime data (such as ship positions and tracks) among the navies of participating European states. The European Commission aims to introduce a Maritime Common Information Sharing Environment (CISE) by 2020 that will connect up these existing surveillance systems. The European Union has also tried to expand cooperation on surveillance through partnerships with third countries, most notably through its proposed Seahorse Mediterranean Network (which would share information between EU Mediterranean countries and North African countries like Libya), but this has been impeded by political instability and limited buy-in among partner countries.

Sources: Beth Stevenson, "EU Agencies Release Tenders for UAV Coastal Monitoring," FlightGlobal, August 17, 2016; Jørgen Carling and María Hernández-Carretero, "Protecting Europe and Protecting Migrants? Strategies for Managing Unauthorised Migration from Africa," *The British Journal of Politics and International Relations* 13, no. 1 (February 2011): 42–58; Frontex, "Eurosur," accessed August 29, 2016; European Defence Agency, "European Maritime Surveillance Network Reaches Operational Status" (news release, October 27, 2014); Sergio Carrera and Leonhard den Hertog, "Whose *Mare*? Rule of Law Challenges in the Field of European Border Surveillance in the Mediterranean" (CEPS Paper in Liberty and Security in Europe no. 79, CEPS, Brussels, January 2015); European Court of Auditors, *Special Report No. 9/2016: EU External Migration Spending in Southern Mediterranean and Eastern Neighbourhood Countries until 2014* (Luxembourg: European Court of Auditors, 2016).

B. Enforcement through Partnership

As detailed above, EU countries such as Spain and Italy recognized early on that cooperation with countries of departure would be critical in the effective management of maritime migration. In addition to partnering on surveillance and information sharing (see Box 2), European governments have developed a panoply of policies and approaches to both reduce the incidence of departure through deterrence and prevention and to ensure that those who do make the journey without authorization can be returned if necessary. Efforts have taken two broad forms: first, the negotiation of readmission agreements with key sending and transit countries; and second, the development of soft regional dialogue structures and broader partnership agreements that cover the full range of migration policy challenges, including legal migration and protection.

Return of unauthorized migrants is a core challenge of EU policy: the fear that individuals, once they have set foot in Europe, cannot be removed has catalyzed tough border management regimes and increasingly selective immigration policies. Many individuals cannot—and should not—be returned for reasons of safety. But others cannot be returned because the countries from which they originate, or through which they have passed, refuse to accept them. As a result, national governments and EU institutions have invested heavily in the promulgation of readmission agreements with key partner countries. As of August 2016, the European Union had 17 readmission agreements, while negotiations were ongoing with other third countries, such as Morocco.[34]

Given the difficulties of forging and maintaining agreements, European governments have made strategic choices on the basis of need. For example, the Spanish government has focused on neighboring nations in North Africa, such as Morocco and Mali. Meanwhile, arrivals to Italy stem largely from Libya, with a smaller number from as far away as Egypt. In order to address this, Italy has signed a number of bilateral readmission agreements with North African countries (including Algeria, Egypt, and Tunisia). The inclusion of some form of quid pro

---

34 The European Union has readmissions agreements with Azerbaijan (entered into force in 2014), Turkey (2014), Armenia (2014), Cape Verde (2014), Georgia (2011), Pakistan (2010), Moldova (2008), Serbia (2008), Bosnia and Herzegovina (2008), Montenegro (2008), Macedonia (2008), Ukraine (2008), Russia (2007), Albania (2006), Sri Lanka (2005), Macao (2004), and Hong Kong (2004). See European Council and Council of the European Union, "Agreements and Conventions," accessed August 29, 2016.

quo—from labor agreements through to additional development support—is a key characteristic of readmission agreements, whether national or EU-wide. Within the EU framework, the willingness of a third country to sign a readmission agreement is often influenced by the prospect of forging a visa-facilitation agreement to allow its nationals to travel to Europe more easily.

These agreements are politically sensitive for partner governments, and they often prefer to work quietly within informal frameworks —such as memoranda of understanding[35]—that marry political acceptability with a certain lack of transparency, rather than flag potentially inflammatory cooperation with the European Union to their citizens.[36] This is not an option available to EU institutions; readmission agreements have been high-profile, hard-fought endeavors, which have tended to underperform.[37] For third countries, the incentive to participate in such agreements may stem from the historical, political, or broader-based relationships with particular European states. This, coupled with the fact that brokering individual agreements with interested EU Member States can open multiple sources of financial and technical support, means many third countries prefer multiple direct relationships, rather than one overarching EU-led deal. Yet despite slow progress, the European Commission continues to prioritize readmission agreements as a core part of its strategy to effect return, as will be seen below.

C. Broader Engagement

A number of regional dialogues include an emphasis on migration, including the Union for the Mediterranean, the Rabat Process, and the 5+5 dialogue. These structures allow countries along the Southern Mediterranean rim to agree on common priorities for action together with EU Member States. To date, these dialogues have produced little in terms of concrete change in policy, but have contributed to network building across the Mediterranean and to the proliferation of support projects funded by the EU neighborhood and development programs.

---

35 Jean-Pierre Cassarino, "An Overview of North African Countries' Bilateral Cooperation on the Removal of Unauthorized Migrants: Drivers and Implications," Middle East Institute, May 4, 2012.

36 Jean-Pierre Cassarino, "Informalising Readmission Agreements in the EU Neighbourhood," *The International Spectator* 42, no. 2 (June 2007): 179–96.

37 European Commission, "Communication from the Commission to the European Parliament and the Council: Evaluation of the Readmission Agreements" (COM [2011] 76 final, February 23, 2011).

These investments are more proactive than reactive in nature, under-taken with the intention to deter unauthorized migration and, though still largely confined to rhetoric, provide alternative livelihoods to people who might otherwise feel compelled to travel to Europe.

This broader engagement has not yet paid dividends in terms of reducing migration flows across the Mediterranean, but reflects a more multifaceted approach to EU border management. However, challenges to this approach persist, not least in partner countries experiencing instability and government change, as with Libya. For example, the EU-Libya Border Management Assistance Programme currently operates from nearby Tunisia, and dialogue with Libya is, for the time being, limited to core security and border management issues.

Following the Arab Spring in 2011, the European Commission rein-vigorated its strategy of partnership with the southern Mediterranean states in an effort to bolster the positive changes that the uprising her-alded. As part of this, the European Union began to pursue a series of mobility partnership agreements with North African countries. Mobility partnerships are a flagship initiative of the EU Global Approach to Migration (first developed in 2005), bringing interested Member States together with third countries to negotiate a series of principles and projects to foster a comprehensive approach to migration management, which theoretically includes facilitation of legal migration. Though these more focused agreements have been reached with a number of Mediterranean states,[38] it is unclear whether they have brought about significant change. Rather, they often become the umbrella agree-ment under which pre-existing EU and bilateral projects are collated. However, the existence of an agreement that requires broad-based dialogue on a regular basis should, in theory, improve overall relation-ship management.

D. Southern Investments

Countries to the south of the Mediterranean, notably Algeria, Libya, Morocco, and Tunisia, have also developed migration management policies in recent years. Many have been developed in collaboration with, or been supported by, the European Union (or individual Member

---

38 The European Union has signed mobility partnerships with Moldova and Cape Verde (2008); Georgia (2009); Armenia (2011); Morocco, Azerbaijan, and Tunisia (2013); and Jordan (2014). See Paula García Andrade, Iván Martín, Viorica Vita, and Sergo Mananashvili, *EU Cooperation with Third Countries in the Field of Migration* (Brussels: European Parliament, 2015), 31.

States), and have included upstream efforts to stem irregular entry into these countries from further south. The fact that EU development funds have been used to support border management initiatives has been criticized by a number of actors.[39]

In the past few years, it has become clear to several southern Mediterranean governments that their countries are gradually becoming destinations as well as points of transit. As a result, some have moved to develop more comprehensive approaches to the management of migration, which may have a concomitant effect on migration through these countries to Europe. For example, the Moroccan government announced several measures in 2013 and 2014, including a regularization scheme for unauthorized migrants in the country and the development of an immigrant integration policy, which would include language and job training.[40]

IV. An Emerging EU and Euro-Mediterranean Response

Responses to maritime migration have been complicated by the realities of the European Union. The concept of solidarity, heralded as a core principle of EU policy, implies that should one Member State experience a large-scale crisis, all others should rally around it in support.[41] Similarly, the nature of EU collaboration on mobility—and specifically the unfinished nature of current systems—means a structural weakness in one country quickly becomes a structural weakness for all.

---

39 See, for example, Oxfam, "EU Ministers Must Change Course on Migration Cooperation with Africa" (press release, May 11, 2016).

40 Anna Jacobs, "King Mohammed VI Calls on the Government to Preserve the Right of Immigrants in Morocco," *Morocco World News*, September 10, 2013; Katharina Natter, "Almost Home? Morocco's Incomplete Migration Reforms," *World Politics Review*, May 5, 2015.

41 The concept of solidarity is laid out in Article 222 of the Treaty of Lisbon: "The Union and its Member States shall act jointly in a spirit of solidarity if a Member State is the object of a terrorist attack or the victim of a natural or man-made disaster. The Union shall mobilise all the instruments at its disposal, including the military resources made available by the Member States, to.... assist a Member State in its territory, at the request of its political authorities." See European Union, "Treaty of Lisbon Amending the Treaty on European Union and the Treaty Establishing the European Community," December 13, 2007.

This became painfully evident in 2015, though warning signs had existed for many years.[42] As detailed above, there were two main destinations for migration flows across the Mediterranean in 2015: Italy and Greece. While the two countries experienced very different flows, they posed a singular challenge for the European Union. To understand this, one must understand interstate cooperation within the European Union, as well as the deeply variable positions and capacity of its Member State.

The Knock-On Effects of Maritime Migration within the European Union

EU Member States are fundamentally intertwined. The signing of the Schengen Convention in 1985 led to the removal of internal borders between the majority of EU Member States. The six nonparticipating states are Bulgaria, Ireland, Romania, the United Kingdom and, critically for matters of maritime migration, Cyprus and Malta. To ensure the internal security of the Schengen area, EU Member States developed a range of legal and operational instruments to improve coherence and cooperation at external EU borders, and to harmonize national asylum systems, visa policies, and measures to address irregular migration.

Common border management thus developed as a corollary to the Schengen Agreement, based on the premise that the external borders of the European Union are only as strong as the weakest link. Initially, cooperation was limited to capacity building and the development of a Common Border Code, but by 2005, the European Union had established its own border management agency, Frontex, to support closer coordination between Member States. Critically, Frontex has no direct responsibility for the actions undertaken during these operations, or for border management writ large, which remains with the Member States involved. Since 2005, Frontex has grown significantly—from a budget of 6.28 million euros in 2005 to 87.92 million euros in 2010 (a 14-fold increase in five years) and a projected budget of 254 million euros in 2016.[43] In the beginning, it relied heavily on specific offers of technical, infrastructural, and financial support from Member States. In 2011, new legislation was passed to further expand the mandate and

---

42 Elizabeth Collett, "The Asylum Crisis in Europe: Designed Dysfunction" (MPI commentary, September 2015).

43 Frontex, *Beyond the Frontiers – Frontex: The First Five Years* (Warsaw: Frontex, 2010); Frontex, "Budget 2016" (budget tables, December 24, 2015).

powers of the agency to buy and maintain its own equipment, though it remained deeply reliant on Member State engagement.[44]

The capacity of each EU Member State to fulfil its national obligations regarding external border management depends on two key factors: geography and resources. Several governments, such as Luxembourg and Austria, have no external land or sea borders, and several of those that do, such as Sweden and Denmark, are clustered in regions surrounded by peer Member States. At the other extreme, Greece has had to contend with a near-impossible border management proposition: an extensive land border with Turkey and a sea border characterized by multiple archipelagos of small islands.

As mixed flows of migrants and asylum seekers fluctuated between Greek land and sea borders in the late 2000s, Frontex offered support in the form of joint operations. However, it became clear that there were broad deficiencies in the Greek government's approach to border management as well as in the reception processes for those who arrived. For example, along the Greek-Turkish land border, the central Greek response was to erect a 10.5-kilometer wall at the most porous point, supplemented by teams of border officials from across the European Union to bolster the Greek-led teams. However, efforts to secure one part of the border led to increased arrivals elsewhere—in particular a diversion from land to sea crossings. In January 2014, a boat being towed by a Greek coast guard vessel capsized, leading to 12 deaths[45] and raising questions about the Greek capacity to undertake maritime search and rescue. The absence of national migration and asylum infrastructure within the country, combined with limited national financial resources to redress this, led Greece to become deeply reliant on the European Union and other Member States to finance investments in border management and the development of an asylum system. The situation in Italy, though less acutely deficient, faces similar geographic and resource limitations.

---

44 "Regulation No 1168/2011 of the European Parliament and of the Council Amending Council Regulation (EC) No 2007/2004 Establishing a European Agency for the Management of Operational Cooperation at the External Borders of the Member States of the European Union," *Official Journal of the European Union* 2011 L 304/1, November 22, 2011.
45 UNHCR, "UNHCR—Statement on Boat Incident off Greece Coast" (press release, January 21, 2014).

Box 3. The Development of the Common European Asylum System

Over the past three decades, the EU Member States have come together to develop a series of systems to manage the movement of people, whether travelers, migrants, or asylum seekers. In developing a common travel area, referred to as the Schengen system, it quickly became clear to all participating governments that a common policy baseline for immigration and asylum across the European Union was needed. The foundation for this is the Dublin Convention, which states that asylum seekers should have their protection claims adjudicated in the country through which they first enter the European Union. One Member State can send asylum seekers back to another if it can prove that they first entered there. This has become the cornerstone of the Common European Asylum System (CEAS), which outlines minimum standards on reception, adjudication, return, and the creation of a coordinating agency—the European Asylum Support Office.

The creation of the CEAS has had uneven effects across the European Union. Although first-arrival countries must deal with initial reception, many migrants who land there avoid fingerprinting so as to be able to move onward through Europe and claim asylum elsewhere without triggering the Dublin obligation to return them to their first point of entry. In the move toward harmonization, the role of the European Union itself remains somewhat uncertain. Though the collaborative frameworks are regulated, and (ideally) monitored, by EU institutions, most of the actual power remains with its Member States. Each monitors its own borders and, beyond meeting EU-determined minimum standards, makes decisions about the functioning of its own national asylum systems. While the only sustainable long-term solutions are likely to be found through coordinated EU action, this will require a political consensus that will be extremely difficult to establish.

As a result, the European Court of Human Rights (ECHR) and the European Court of Justice (ECJ) have slowly become more active in the area of immigration policy. Although the courts have slightly different remits—the ECHR rules on violations of human rights, and the ECJ rules on infractions of EU law—they have both demonstrated an activist approach to monitoring Member State activities in the Mediterranean and elsewhere.

As a result of the 2012 ECHR ruling in *Hirsi vs. Italy* that pushbacks to North Africa were a violation of European human-rights law, even if they occurred outside Member States' territorial waters, the European Union agreed new rules on interception. Subsequent legislation clarified that individuals should not be "forced to, conducted to, or otherwise handed over to" unsafe countries, where there is a serious risk of death, torture, or other inhuman or degrading treatment—nor should they be handed over to ostensibly safe countries that might then hand them over to unsafe countries.

Rulings on the function of CEAS itself, specifically the Dublin Convention, can have a knock-on effect for the management of external borders. In the case of *Tarakhel vs. Switzerland*, the ECHR ruled that an Afghan asylum-seeking family could not be returned to Italy, their first country of entry into the European Union, over concerns about reception conditions there for families with children. This may expand the grounds for preventing returns under the Dublin Convention, meaning that Member States cannot return migrants to countries of first arrival if standards of protection are not being met there.

Sources: Hirsi Jamaa and Others v. Italy, Application No. 27765/09 (European Court of Human Rights, 2012); "Regulation (EU) No 656/2014 of the European Parliament and of the Council of 15 May 2014 Establishing Rules for the Surveillance of the External Sea Borders in the Context of Operational Cooperation Coordinated by the European Agency for the Management of Operational Cooperation at the External Borders of the Member States of the European Union," *Official Journal of the European Union* 2014 L189/93, June 27, 2014; Steve Peers, *New Rules on Maritime Surveillance: Will They Stop the Deaths and Push-Backs in the Mediterranean?* (London: Statewatch, 2014); *Tarakhel v. Switzerland*, Application No. 29217/12 (European Court of Human Rights, 2014).

Why should other EU Member States get involved? In theory, the dual concepts of solidarity and equitable responsibility sharing—frequently invoked by Mediterranean states[46] and repeated in endless EU documents—should be sufficient. But these concepts remain poorly defined and are thus easy to ignore. In reality, motivations have been more complex, and certainly not without reservation. While other, more remote EU Member States recognize the extraordinary position of the Mediterranean-adjacent states, they are equally aware that many, if not most, arrivals to these states do not intend to remain there. Instead, the majority seek to move on to other EU Member States, predominantly in Northwestern Europe. Many of these arrivals also claim asylum at their final destination, despite the existence of EU rules, specifi-

---

46 Notably via the statements of the Quadro Group, a regional bloc composed of Cyprus, Greece, Italy, and Malta.

cally the Dublin Regulation, delineating the country of first arrival as the one responsible for such claims (see Box 3). Despite being on the frontline of irregular maritime arrivals, Italy and Greece received just 8 percent of all first-time EU asylum applications in 2015 (7 percent, and 1 percent, respectively), while Germany received 35 percent of all applications.[47]

This secondary movement across the European Union has proved the greater catalyst for action amongst EU Member States that do not directly receive maritime arrivals. These states see onward movement as a security risk, as well as evidence of southern states passing on the responsibility to provide asylum by not systematically registering and fingerprinting all arrivals. However, for the most part onward movement was seen as a manageable irritant, largely confined to technical discussions between EU Member States.

The 2011 Arab Spring highlighted how quickly this irritant could transform into a political issue: although the 20,000 Tunisian nationals that arrived on European shores constituted a small proportion of those displaced by the unrest, the decision by the Italian government to offer them temporary residence permits catalyzed a dispute between Italy and France, and led to the temporary reintroduction of border controls between the two countries.[48] Similarly, in 2011 the European Court of Human Rights ruled that returning asylum seekers to Greece from elsewhere in the European Union—as mandated by the Dublin Convention for those who first arrived in the country—would amount to a violation of their rights, given poor reception conditions in Greece. This left northern Member States with no other option than to take primary responsibility for secondary arrivals.[49]

Given the mutual frustration between northern and southern Member States concerning their relative levels of responsibility for arrivals, it is easy to assume that the entire European Union has a stake in managing maritime migration. However, this is not so: a number of countries, notably those to the east, have been largely unaffected and have less experience managing large-scale asylum systems. However, the lack of capacity in these countries—many of which had long been relatively passive bystanders during EU discussions of asylum responsibility-

---

47 Eurostat, "Asylum and First-Time Asylum Applicants by Citizenship, Age and Sex. Annual Aggregated Data (Rounded) [migr_asyappctza]," updated March 18, 2016.

48 MPI, "Top 10 of 2011 – Issue #1: Arab Spring and Fear of Migrant Surge Expose Rift in EU Immigration Policy Circles," *Migration Information Source*, December 1, 2011.

49 *M.S.S. v. Belgium and Greece*, Application No. 30696/09 (European Court of Human Rights, 2011).

sharing—is also cause for concern. A number of countries beyond Greece, such as Bulgaria and Hungary, have been found wanting in terms of their implementation of EU minimum standards regarding border management, asylum reception, and processing claims. This is not just an issue of political will and implementation, but also the ability of less well-resourced countries to create spare capacity to deal with fluctuations in arrival numbers. For example, the number of asylum applications Bulgaria received increased by 467 percent between 2012 and 2013 (from 1,230 to 6,980), placing enormous strain on the national systems and necessitated a swift European response.

V.   2014 Onwards: Crisis Escalation

Between 2014 and 2016, European policy responses to the escalating sense of crisis had two distinct phases: first, policy responses to mounting fatalities along the Central Mediterranean route dominated until mid-2015, spurred by the activism of the Italian government; second, efforts to address the exponential rise in flows from Turkey to the poorly resourced Aegean islands of Greece from mid-2015 through to March 2016. At the time of writing, a distinct phase three is yet to materialize; many observers note that few of the drivers impelling individuals to undertake these dangerous journeys have subsided, and efforts to address differences within the European Union itself have not yet resolved fundamental challenges. The locus of activity has now swung back to the Central Mediterranean, with flows in 2016 matching those of 2015 (see Figure 2). However, political perceptions of crisis are not static, nor are they a precise reflection of on-the-ground conditions; following the extraordinary flows across the Eastern Mediterranean in late 2015, and despite the high number of registered fatalities in 2016, there is now a pervading sense that the Central Mediterranean route is manageable.

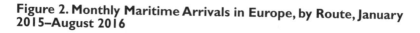

Figure 2. Monthly Maritime Arrivals in Europe, by Route, January 2015–August 2016

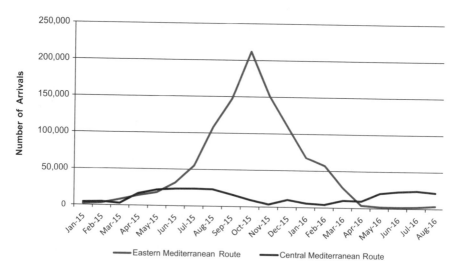

Source: UNHCR, "Refugees/Migrants Emergency Response, Mediterranean—Demographic Data" (dataset accessed September 13, 2016).

A. The Central Mediterranean

It is a sad truth that the majority of policy responses regarding the Central Mediterranean over the past three years have been catalyzed by visceral televised images of individual loss of life. In October 2013, around 368 (mostly Somali and Eritrean) migrants traveling from Libya to Italy drowned off the coast of Lampedusa.[50] Within days, the Italian government commenced Operation Mare Nostrum, calling on the European Union and other Member States to support it.[51]

Instead, the European Commission convened a Task Force on the Mediterranean (TFM), cochaired by the Italian government, to bring together relevant officials from EU Member States, the European Commission, EU agencies, and international organizations. In December

---

50 BBC News, "Italy Boat Sinking: Hundreds Feared Dead off Lampedusa," BBC News, October 3, 2013; Barbara Molinario, "Eritrean Survivor of Lampedusa Tragedy Returns to Honour the Dead, Meet Pope Francis" (UNHCR news release, October 2, 2014).

51 The European Union contributed 1.8 million euros in emergency funding to Mare Nostrum. At the national level, the Slovenian government was the only one to respond to the call for support, by offering a ship.

2014, the TFM issued a report outlining the measures the European Union intended to take with respect to migrant flows across the Mediterranean. The initial report offered very little that was new, but rather reviewed current activity.[52] This may have been a result of "too many cooks" in the room: a dozen policy portfolios (Directorates General) with differing priorities and 28 EU Member States with a broad range of interests, coupled with limited political focus and will to resolve the issue among all but the core southern states.

In June 2014, heads of state outlined EU priorities for the next phase of policy development, but mentioned the Mediterranean only obliquely. The resulting strategic guidelines offered few concrete ways forward, particularly on the issue of EU solidarity. More detailed ideas emerged outside of the spotlight, notably a proposal from the Austrian government outlining an EU humanitarian initiative on refugee resettlement,[53] which the Commission began to further develop. Meanwhile, in October 2014, Interior Ministers agreed on a set of operational priorities, including deeper cooperation with third countries, and floated the possibility of creating asylum processing centers in transit countries.[54]

Eventually, and largely in response to the Italian threat to cease Mare Nostrum operations, 22 Member States reluctantly agreed in October 2014 to contribute to Operation Triton, a Frontex-led border protection operation with a narrower geographical remit and mandate than Mare Nostrum. Critically, Triton does not include an explicit search-and-rescue component, although its patrol vessels do rescue people in distress if they encounter them, which is typically what then occurs. However, this more passive approach still relies on the engagement of the Italian navy and others to offer an active search component.

As Central Mediterranean crossings increased during the first months of 2015, the now-familiar cycle of crisis and policy reaction reached a new high. In mid-April, two large and overcrowded boats capsized; the second of these resulted in the largest single loss of life during a crossing to Europe, with around 650 fatalities. The scale of the disasters,

---

52 European Commission, "Communication from the Commission to the European Parliament and the Council on the Work of the Task Force Mediterranean" (COM [2014] 869 final, December 4, 2013).

53 Austrian Delegation to the Strategic Committee on Immigration, Frontiers, and Asylum, "EU Resettlement Initiative – 'Save Lives'" (discussion paper, Council of the European Union, September 7, 2014).

54 Council of the European Union, "Council Conclusions on Taking Action to Manage Migratory Flows" (conclusions following a Justice and Home Affairs Council meeting, Luxembourg, October 10, 2014).

combined with the accelerating pace of arrival, finally spurred a political response commensurate to the challenge: the Council convened the first extraordinary EU summit on migration, bringing together European heads of state to discuss the challenge.[55]

A ten-point plan, hastily drafted by the European Commission and the European External Action Service, called for increased resources from EU Member States for Operation Triton, though notably omitted any explicit reference to a search-and-rescue mandate.[56] Much of the discussion, and division, focused on whether the Italian Mare Nostrum initiative had itself increased, rather than reduced, the incidence of boat journeys across the Central Mediterranean. Despite this, the humanitarian imperative to prevent further loss of life outweighed concerns about the new operation becoming a similar pull factor.

The ten-point plan also focused squarely on disrupting the smuggling operations that facilitate maritime migration and on preventing further movement—a move that was heavily criticized by several UN agencies and many nongovernmental observers for focusing on security rather than humanitarian concerns. Notably, the plan called for a military operation under the auspices of the EU Common Security and Defence Policy (CDSP) to board, search, and seize boats intercepted in the Mediterranean. This operation—known formally as EU NAVFOR (and later christened Operation Sophia)—was launched in July 2015, and had several phases of implementation. The first phase, intelligence gathering, was largely uncontroversial and lasted until October of that same year. The second and third phases focused on the operational goal of seizing and destroying boats leaving Libya and arresting any smugglers found aboard, initially in international waters and latterly in Libyan waters, subject to the permission of the Libyan government and a UN Security Council resolution. A final phase then envisaged pursuit of the same goal on Libyan soil prior to departure. Twenty-two EU Member States contributed to the operation with vessels personnel.

The operation has been controversial in a number of ways, notably whether an EU coercive operation would be allowed to operate in Libyan waters. In the first months of the operation, there was no Libyan government in place to give approval, and the UN Security Council expressed grave concerns about the nature of the operation and, crucially, whether it would open the legal door to other more incursive

---

55 European Council, "Special Meeting of the European Council, 23/04/2015," updated April 23, 2015.

56 European Commission, "Joint Foreign and Home Affairs Council: Ten Point Action Plan on Migration" (press release, April 20, 2015).

operations elsewhere. Eventually, however, a UN Security Council resolution was passed in October 2015 to allow the force to operate in international waters.[57] At the time of writing, neither the new Libyan Government of National Accord nor the United Nations had given permission for the mission to extend into Libyan waters.

Beyond the legal mandate, a number of NGOs and human-rights groups expressed concern that by focusing on countersmuggling rather than the migrants aboard the boat, the operation would endanger lives. In practice, the responsibilities imposed by international law have meant that interceptions typically also result in the rescue of the individuals on board. Indeed, in the intelligence-gathering phase alone, EU NAVFOR vessels rescued more than 3,000 individuals. From the operational side, there were concerns that the patrols might become a pull factor (similar to the concern expressed about Mare Nostrum) and that they might change the calculus of smugglers involved in the industry, reducing the overall efficacy of the operation. A leaked report of the first six months of the operation conceded that smugglers did seem to be responding quickly to the new reality, and that the operation would slowly lose efficacy if limited to the high seas, as smugglers were learning to operate from within Libyan waters, fueling boats just enough to travel a very small distance from the Libyan coast into international waters.[58]

In June 2016, additional responsibilities were added to the EU NAVFOR mandate, including the training and capacity building of the Libyan border and coast guard.[59] This represented an exit strategy for the European Union in that fully capable Libyan forces would be able to identify, intercept, and "pullback" boats independently, negating the need for EU-led operations that resulted in rescue and transfer to Europe. However, given the fragility of the current government, the continued instability and violence across much of the country, and the reportedly dire refugee-reception conditions,[60] this is considered to be both a long-term strategy and one that may result in worsened conditions for a stranded migrant population.

---

57 United Nations Security Council, "Resolution 2240 (2015)," October 9, 2015.

58 European External Action Service (EEAS), "EU NAVFOR MED Operation Sophia – Six Monthly Report for the Period 22 June-31 December 2015" (working document, EEAS, Brussels, January 2016).

59 European Council and Council of the European Union, "EUNAVFOR MED Operation Sophia: Mandate Extended by One Year, Two New Tasks Added" (press release, June 20, 2016).

60 Amnesty International, "EU Risks Fuelling Horrific Abuse of Refugees and Migrants in Libya" (news release, June 14, 2016).

What is clear in the short term is that, despite these investments, flows across the Central Mediterranean and fatalities at sea have yet to decrease. Naval operations are, and can only be, one small part of the overall solution. Beyond these headline initiatives, designed to deal with immediate humanitarian challenges, a number of other priorities have been articulated to address the broader drivers of mixed migration outside the European Union and to strengthen internal cooperation to manage the large number of arrivals at Europe's external borders (see Section VI in this chapter).

B. The Eastern Mediterranean

It took some time for media outlets and other observers to recognize the dramatically increasing number of migrants crossing from the Turkish coast to the Greek islands. The number of arrivals had been gradually increasing from April 2015, but it was not until August when more than 100,000 migrants and asylum seekers began arriving per month on the scattered islands that the Eastern Mediterranean route received serious attention.

The islands of the Aegean are remote, poorly resourced, and unequal to the task of receiving large-scale inflows. In the early stages, disparate groups of volunteers and small NGOs operated ad hoc search and rescue and provided initial shelter amid a chaotic set of interventions from the Greek government. Larger international organizations and agencies slowly arrived during the summer of 2015, but it took time to set up infrastructure. This was in part due to internal concerns amongst many agencies, notably UNHCR, that initial reception and support should be the primary responsibility of the Greek government, rather than overstretched humanitarian organizations. Despite strong encouragement from the European Commission and the increasingly desperate lack of basic resources, officials in Greece were reluctant to invoke the Civil Protection Mechanism (typically used for disaster relief following flooding, earthquakes, or forest fires).

There are several reasons for the slow response. The swift upswing in arrivals would have taxed even the most well-resourced of nations; indeed, further north, asylum seekers quickly overwhelmed the reception capacities of Germany, the Netherlands, and Sweden. The basic lack of capacity in the Greek immigration and asylum system was a pre-existing problem, further compounded by the fact that the Greek government had extremely limited emergency resources in the wake of deep recession and austerity measures that drastically cut government spending and shrunk the public sector since 2010. Political will also played a role. While in the Central Mediterranean the primary challenge was characterized as one of search and rescue, to the east, the challenge was one of reception and onward movement. Recognizing that few arrivals wished to remain in Greece, the primary goal of the Greek government was to transfer arrivals from the islands to the mainland, where they could continue their journey north via the Western Balkans—not developing robust domestic reception capacity.

By the end of 2015, after more than 800,000 people had arrived via the Eastern Mediterranean route, with thousands more arriving each day, a sense of political panic was growing, particularly in the northern European countries dealing with escalated numbers of asylum claims. This was particularly the case for Germany that received more than one-third of all asylum claims within the European Union in 2015, and a domestic increase of 155 percent from the previous year.[61] With little opportunity to prevent departures from the Turkish coast, inadequate development of registration and reception centers on the Aegean islands, and Western Balkans states adopting a "wave through" policy for migrants and asylum seekers traveling across the Greek border, EU heads of state began to consider more drastic options to stem the flow, and turned to the Turkish government.

Following the publication of an EU-Turkey Action Plan by the European Commission in October 2015, a series of negotiations over the winter led to a seminal, and controversial, deal struck with the Turkish government on March 18, 2016. Full implementation came just two days later. The agreement aimed to address the overwhelming flow of smuggled migrants and asylum seekers traveling from Turkey to the Greek islands by tasking the Turkish coast and border guard with preventing departures, and allowing Greece to return to Turkey "all new irregular migrants" arriving after March 20. In exchange, EU Member States pledged to increase resettlement of Syrian refugees residing in Turkey,[62] accelerate visa liberalization for Turkish nationals, and significantly boost existing financial support for the refugee population in Turkey.[63] The deal was met with substantial criticism, notably concerning the way the deal would be implemented and whether the

---

61 Eurostat, "Record Number of Over 1.2 Million First Time Asylum Seekers Registered in 2015" (news release, March 4, 2016).

62 For every Syrian national returned to Turkey from the Greek islands under the deal, one Syrian national residing in Turkey would be resettled to the European Union under a "one-for-one" formula.

63 European Council and Council of the European Union, "EU-Turkey Statement, 18 March 2016" (press release, March 18, 2016).

treatment of individual asylum seekers would meet legal and human rights standards.

Despite this criticism, the deal served its purpose, and from a political perspective, it was seen as a necessary intervention to reduce rising levels of chaos and public anxiety. The reduction in flows has been a result of swift action from the Turkish government, coupled with the message sent to would-be arrivals by closing the routes out of Greece. Implementation on the European side, by contrast, has been haphazard, particularly on the simpler aspects of the deal, such as reception conditions. On the Greek islands, open reception centers designed for short-term stays have been poorly converted into overcrowded, closed centers with reportedly dire conditions, and policymakers show little impetus to address this.[64] Registration and processing of cases remain slow and, as predicted by many observers, few individuals have actually been returned to Turkey under the terms of the deal.[65] As a result, thousands sit in limbo on the Aegean islands.

At the time of writing, the EU-Turkey deal remains in place, though politically fragile. The failure of the European Union to deliver on its side of the deal—notably on visa liberalization for Turkish nationals— could lead to an abrupt end of the partnership. Furthermore, it is not clear that the European Union has thought through the consequences of any future collapse of the agreement, or a longer-term sustainable strategy for managing large-scale flows to the European Union upon which its Member States can agree.

VI. Intensifying, Yet Uneven, Collaboration

One of the key complexities for European policymakers seeking to address maritime migration has been disaggregating status and motivation: those fleeing conflict and persecution share boats with those traveling to find employment or join family members. The challenge is now one of status. Syrians, for example, are categorized as prima facie

---

64 UNHCR, Regional Bureau Europe, "Weekly Report (27 May – 2 June)" (weekly report, June 3, 2016).

65 Elizabeth Collett, "The Paradox of the EU-Turkey Refugee Deal" (MPI commentary, March 2016).

refugees by neighboring countries and UNHCR.[66] Once on European territory, however, they become asylum seekers again, subject to national asylum processes framed by CEAS rules. The European institutions have made a number of proposals to reform and address what have become obvious deficiencies in existing EU policy on immigration and asylum, with varying degrees of success.

The EU policy response to maritime migration has not dramatically shifted and still broadly utilizes the policy toolbox that existed before 2014. The issue has, however, intensified in terms of political salience and become a pan-European concern. However, one should not mistake shared concern for a unified response. The policies proposed and adopted between 2014 and 2016 are characterized by deep discord and persistent imbalances in the capacity and political will of each government to respond. This section outlines the main policy trends—beyond immediate emergency response—as well as the longer-term approaches that are likely to emerge in the coming years.

A. *Sharing Responsibility and Shoring Up Internal Weaknesses*

As detailed above, continued imbalances in pressure and responsibility across the European Union have placed core immigration projects— notably Schengen—in jeopardy. During fall 2015, a series of unilateral decisions by EU Member States to close sections of their national borders to stem flows of asylum seekers and migrants raised concerns that, without some more equitable distribution of responsibility, not only would this lead to a collapse of the Schengen system, but that the stress placed on particular national asylum systems would lead to domestic chaos and potential political upheaval. These anxieties have also been overlaid with a security concern that, in the absence of robust identification and registration upon arrival, potential terrorists would have increased opportunity to travel to Europe to perpetrate attacks, a fear realized in November 2015 with a large-scale assault in Paris. Several of the attackers were later found to have traveled through Turkey and Greece.

While a number of proposals have been tabled since spring 2015 to address these challenges, the European Commission has shied away

---

66 The term "prima facie" refers to individuals who, due to the severity of conditions in their country of origin (or, in the case of stateless persons, their county of habitual residence), are granted status without undergoing an individual refugee status determination process.

from a fundamental rethink: proposals follow the logic of existing EU policies to shape and support national systems, in large part due to the reluctance of many governments to countenance a stronger role for the European Union itself. One distinct innovation, however, has been the acceleration away from a purely legal and regulatory approach to one that promotes practical, operational cooperation in key domains. The following subsections describe the three main facets of this approach.

I. Rethinking the Redistribution and Relocation of Asylum Seekers

In May 2015, the European Commission published the European Agenda on Migration following commitments made during the extraordinary summit of EU heads of state.[67] One of the agenda's flagship initiatives was a proposal to activate emergency clauses contained in the Lisbon Treaty, and support those countries most affected by maritime migration—Greece and Italy—through the relocation of up to 40,000 asylum seekers from Syria, Iraq, and Eritrea across the European Union.[68] This was later revised upwards to the potential relocation of 160,000 asylum seekers from Greece and Italy, with a reserve number for any Member State that comes under pressure in the future.[69]

The core innovation within the proposal, aside from heralding a new level of cooperation within the Common European Asylum System, is the development of a distribution key to allocate specific numbers of both refugees and asylum seekers to individual EU Member States. Critically, the initial proposal intended the scheme to be mandatory though this was deeply contested by a number of governments. Following tense negotiations in September 2015, the emergency scheme was agreed on a voluntary basis, and set in place.

Despite significant political and operational investment, relocation processes in both Greece and Italy remain sluggish with just over 4,000

---

67 European Commission, "Communication from the Commission to the European Parliament, the Council, the European Economic and Social Committee and the Committee of the Regions: A European Agenda on Migration" (COM [2015] 240 final, May 13, 2015).

68 Eligibility for relocation would be based on an EU-average recognition rate of 75 percent for claims made by a particular nationality, and updated on a quarterly basis according to the latest available statistics. See European Commission, "Communication from the Commission to the European Parliament, the European Council and the Council: First Report on Relocation and Resettlement" (COM [2016] 165 final, March 16, 2016).

69 The reserve relocation was initially earmarked for Hungary, which subsequently refused the offer. See Eszter Zalan, "Hungary Rejects EU Offer to Take Refugees," *EU Observer*, September 11, 2015.

of the 160,000 promised relocations completed in the first of its two years of operation.[70] Lack of capacity and infrastructure in the southern European countries, combined with limited and/or overstretched capacity in receiving states has contributed to the slow progress. Many refugees selected for relocation have also been reluctant to move to countries with which they were unfamiliar, such as Bulgaria or Luxembourg.[71] In addition, despite formally agreeing to the scheme, several EU Member States (notably Hungary) remain deeply opposed to relocation. As of the end of August 2016, nearly 60,000 asylum seekers were residing in Greece, many awaiting relocation. With scarce facilities for vulnerable migrants, including unaccompanied minors, there is simmering pressure to find a solution.

Relocation is a worthy ambition, and one that acknowledges the weaknesses of the existing Dublin system. However, implementing relocation as an emergency response was always likely to founder compared to the high expectations of EU policymakers and publics. Previous experiences of relocation—notably a pilot scheme implemented to support Malta in 2009—highlighted a lack of will and capacity amongst other states, resulting in a low number of refugees eventually relocated.[72] Despite this, in 2016, the Commission incorporated the principles of relocation into a proposed reform of the Dublin Regulation, which would allow for redistribution when a particular country exceeds a predetermined number of asylum claims in a given year.[73]

The European Commission has also proposed expanding the mandate of the European Asylum Support Office (EASO)—an EU agency designed to provide information and support to EU Member States.[74] Renamed the European Union Agency for Asylum, it would have several new responsibilities, such as ensuring greater uniformity of asylum application assessment, managing the relocation process, and assisting Member States (for example, by deploying asylum support teams).

---

70 European Commission, "Member States' Support to Emergency Relocation Mechanism," updated September 1, 2016.

71 Duncan Robinson and Kerin Hope, "Refugees in Greece Refuse to Relocate across EU," *Financial Times,* May 16, 2016.

72 European Asylum Support Office (EASO), *EASO Fact Finding Report on Intra-EU Relocation Activities from Malta* (Malta: EASO, 2012).

73 European Commission, "Proposal for a Regulation of the European Parliament and of the Council Establishing the Criteria and Mechanisms for Determining the Member State Responsible for Examining an Application for International Protection Lodged in One of the Member States by a Third-Country National or a Stateless Person (Recast)" (COM [2016] 270 final, May 4, 2016).

74 European Commission, "Proposal for a Regulation of the European Parliament and of the Council on the European Union Agency for Asylum and Repealing Regulation (EU) No 439/2010" (COM [2016] 271 final, May 4, 2016).

2. Enhancing Border Management and Support at First Entry

Though the mandate and budget of Frontex have expanded significantly since inception, the fact that it is reliant on the willingness of EU Member States to provide human, technical, and physical resources has become a critical weakness. In recognition of this, the European Commission tabled a proposal for a European border and coast guard in December 2015, with the intention of creating a more integrated approach to border management through an agency with a standing pool of border guards and other operational experts. A critical feature of the proposal was that the border force would have a right to intervene (at the behest of the European Commission) if a particular country demonstrated a continued inability to manage a crisis situation. This element speaks directly to the frustrations experienced in Greece, where the national authorities were unable to manage the situation but reluctant to allow other countries to support them.

The proposal was fast-tracked through the first half of 2016, and agreed in record time by the 28 Member States, though the unilateral right to intervene was dropped from the final agreement, as it was seen as too deep an incursion into national sovereignty. As of August 2016, the new European border and coast guard was in the early stages of implementation.[75]

Another challenge highlighted by the recent spike in arrivals at concentrated points along the external EU border has been the need to respond quickly and with sufficient resources. This has two characteristics: first, the absence of sufficient personnel and infrastructure to identify and register arrivals and to offer them the opportunity to make an asylum claim; second, the weak coordination and interoperability between key national and EU agencies, notably Frontex, EASO, Europol, and the various information-sharing databases that exist in the area of border management and asylum. For example, the European Commission estimated that during September 2015, when more than 100,000 people arrived from Turkey, just 8 percent were fingerprinted as they transited through Greece,[76] and there was limited capacity to address document fraud.

In an effort to redress this, the European Commission proposed the creation of hotspots at key points along the external border, notably

---

75 European Parliament, "MEPs Back Plans to Pool Policing of EU External Borders" (press release, July 6, 2016).

76 European Commission, "Implementing the European Agenda on Migration: Commission Reports on Progress in Greece, Italy and the Western Balkans" (press release, February 10, 2016).

in Greece and Italy. In theory, the hotspots would be the locations at which migrants and officials first interact, offering a one-stop shop for identification, fingerprinting, document checks, and information about asylum procedures, with multiple EU agencies working together for the first time to exchange information. In practice, the implementation was ad hoc and slow: by December 2015, hotspots had yet to be constructed in key locations such as the Greek islands of Kos and Samos, or completed in Lesvos, Leros, and Chios.[77] Following the implementation of the EU-Turkey deal, the role of the Greek hotspots changed significantly from sites of first reception, where individuals were expected to remain just a few days, to centers where they are detained on an indefinite basis. This may help an overstretched administration ensure registration and identification, but it has led to significant overcrowding and poor living conditions. Meanwhile, in Italy, it is estimated that a significant number of arrivals manage to circumvent the hotspots entirely, leading to questions about their efficacy in terms of both security concerns and protection needs.

Fostering effective cooperation between agencies has also proved challenging, particularly efforts to ensure that information exchange is timely and accurate. Following the November 2015 attacks in Paris, EU Member States developed a roadmap to improve the interoperability of different surveillance systems and encourage national law enforcement agencies to share information more systematically.[78]

3. Reinforcing Emergency Response

The crisis uncovered an additional operational weakness within the European Union: the effective deployment of on-the-ground resources in a timely manner. The European Commission has the capacity to earmark emergency funding for particular countries but, as became clear in Greece, Hungary, and other countries, sending money to states with limited human resources and relevant expertise does not resolve a problem that ultimately requires specialized knowledge and planning

---

77 European Commission, "Annex 2 to the Communication from the Commission to the European Parliament and the Council on the State of Play of Implementation of the Priority Actions under the European Agenda on Migration—Greece State of Play Report" (COM [2016] 85 final, February 10, 2016).

78 Council of the European Union, "Draft Roadmap to Enhance Information Exchange and Information Management Including Interoperability Solutions in the Justice and Home Affairs Area" (working document, May 13, 2016). This roadmap was subsequently endorsed by the Justice and Home Affairs (JHA) Council in June 2016. See Council of the European Union, "Justice and Home Affairs Council, 09-10/06/2016," updated June 9, 2016.

to transform cash into usable support. In the early months of the crisis, volunteers and NGOs filled the gap left by overstretched government administration. Similarly, the EU Civil Protection mechanism designed to provide support following a disaster depends upon the willingness of the affected Member State to activate it. In Greece, as noted above, there was initially reluctance to do this, despite its use by Bulgaria several years earlier, following an increase in arrivals at the Turkish-Bulgarian border,[79] and by Hungary in 2015.[80] Even when Greece finally invoked the mechanism, the response from other Member States was lackluster as many had themselves become overwhelmed.

The expansion of the mandates of EASO and Frontex (soon to be the European border and coast guard) aims in part to address this sluggish delivery of emergency support by ensuring that these agencies have their own resources to deploy on short notice. In addition, the European Union passed legislation in early 2016 to allow humanitarian funds to be deployed directly to international agencies and NGOs operating within an EU Member State. In April 2016, 83 million euros were disbursed to UNHCR and seven international NGOs in Greece to support the development reception capacity for the large numbers stranded in the country.[81] This reflected the bizarre reality that, as of late 2015, support could be provided to neighboring non-EU states of the Western Balkans far more efficiently than to those with EU membership.

B. A New Era of Migration Partnership

Beyond internal mechanisms to redistribute responsibility across the European Union, there is a new emphasis on the foreign policy dimension of EU action.

From underestimating the role of migration in foreign policy in recent years, policymakers have now put migration and asylum issues at the top of the agenda. In doing so, there has been renewed focus on the factors driving individuals to make these journeys, from armed conflict and political instability that carry the threat of persecution, to persistent disparities in income and the active facilitation of smuggling networks. As a result, the European Union is beginning to invest

---

79 European Commission, "European Assistance to Help Bulgaria Face the Refugee Crisis" (press release, October 23, 2013).
80 European Commission, "EU's Civil Protection Mechanism Helps Hungary Cope with Refugee Influx" (news release, September 14, 2015).
81 European Commission, "EU Provides €83 Million to Improve Conditions for Refugees in Greece" (press release, April 19, 2016).

more deeply in understanding the nature of the smuggling and trafficking industries, including their networks, routes, and motivations. This is a very difficult endeavor, and experienced policymakers admit that knowledge is largely based on assumption rather than significant evidence.

At the same time, a conversation is emerging about enhanced protection for refugees in their region of origin and how to address the root causes of migration, including through poverty reduction. Partnership agreements with Jordan and Lebanon, for example, focus on improving conditions for refugees in country, in return for efforts to improve trade relationship with the European Union.[82] The approach to protection in the region of origin is largely encapsulated through the Regional Protection Programmes (RPPs) piloted in the African Great Lakes region and Eastern Europe. The challenges to the success of these programs were multiple: some were already obsolete prior to implementation (the humanitarian crises had moved elsewhere), and limited financing meant that most of the measures had little real effect compared to the more robust work undertaken by UNHCR. An effort to revive the concept, in modified and expanded form, is now being undertaken, with three Regional Development and Protection Programmes (RDPPs) developed for the Middle East, Horn of Africa, and North Africa regions. Led by coalitions of EU Member States, with strong support and financing from the European Commission, these programs hope to learn from the weaknesses of earlier RPPs.

More broadly, although all actors agree that it is necessary to address root causes, few specific ideas of how to do so have emerged, and most policymakers are skeptical as to the likelihood of success. Thus, calls to strengthen partnerships with countries of origin and transit to reduce either the propensity or the ability of individuals to begin a journey to the European Union have been renewed in 2015–16. These calls have backtracked from the more holistic rhetoric of the Global Approach to Migration and emphasize the need for third countries to manage migration flows, to counter smuggling networks, and to reinforce their border controls. In addition to the launch of the RDPPs, the EU committed to a joint summit of leaders from the European and African Unions to discuss shared migration issues (the Valletta Conference, held in November 2015).

---

82 European Commission, "EU-Jordan: Towards a Stronger Partnership" (press release, July 20, 2016).

The results of the conference were underwhelming. An action plan was published, outlining dozens of specific projects and ambitions, and the European Union launched a 1.8 billion euro Emergency Trust Fund for Africa. However, African Union states criticized the EU approach for its focus solely on a European agenda to the exclusion of African priorities and noted that the 1.8 billion euros was a small sum when spread across the continent. There was also a sense that, given the strength of flows across the Aegean in late 2015, the conference was addressing the wrong geography at the wrong moment. Parallel negotiations with the Turkish government—resulting in the March 2016 EU-Turkey deal—were of greater importance to most of the European actors at the table.

Despite the increased focus on partnership approaches during 2015, it is the EU-Turkey deal that truly reflects the changed EU approach to partnership with non-EU countries. The transactional nature of the deal—focused squarely on migration management, rather than migration and development—and its high price tag have sent a message to other non-EU countries that their cooperation on migration is a commodity that is rapidly increasing in value. In early 2016, the Italian government proposed a more focused approach—the migration compact,[83] which has now been adapted into a more comprehensive EU-led partnership framework.[84] In June 2016, heads of state mandated that the EU foreign policy chief, Federica Mogherini, forge similar deals with a priority list of countries and be willing to withhold funding for countries that do not comply with EU migration management priorities.[85]

Efforts to pay off non-EU countries to manage migration have not yielded strong positive outcomes for EU governments to date, unless these are linked to the broader common interests of the third countries in question. The EU-Turkey deal, for many reasons, is unlikely to be replicable elsewhere. But with public confidence in governments' ability to manage migration lower than a year ago, the political pressure to achieve tangible results is higher than ever.

---

83 Matteo Renzi, "Migration Compact: Contribution to an EU Strategy for External Action on Migration" (non-paper, April 2016).

84 European Commission, "Communication from the Commission to the European Parliament, the European Council and the European Investment Bank on Establishing a New Partnership Framework with Third Countries under the European Agenda on Migration" (COM [2016] 385 final, June 7, 2016).

85 European Council, "European Council Meeting (28 June 2016) Conclusions" (press release, June 28, 2016).

VII. Looking Forward: Crisis Over?

Efforts to address maritime migration in the Mediterranean have intensified since 2014, both at the national and the EU level. Despite this effort, it is not clear that any sustainable collaborative solutions have been found to date; many of the fundamental drivers and policy challenges that have fueled the phenomenon remain as strong as ever, and EU Member States have struggled to find consensus on all but the most straightforward of solutions. As a result, the European Union has focused on treating the symptoms rather than addressing the underlying causes of maritime migration.

Efforts to strengthen EU collaboration suffer in two key ways. First, fault lines between the political positions of the governments involved inhibit consensus. The framing of Mediterranean migration as a European problem, has led to a dichotomy between EU Member States and third countries. Though countries to both the north and south of the Mediterranean are experiencing similar challenges, the invisible yet critical EU external border has limited some discussions. Similarly, the EU and non-EU blocs are not, themselves, regionally coherent. Within the European Union, northern, southern, and eastern Member States have differing priorities, and there are splits even within these blocs; alliances are also fluid depending on the policy under negotiation and the political salience of specific migration issues domestically. The "beggar thy neighbor" instinct that prevails within Europe significantly limits progress in updating EU frameworks. To the south, North African countries have few ideological or political affinities with the European Union, and many are more concerned with domestic stability than regional cooperation.

Second, it has become increasingly clear that a comprehensive approach cannot be found in the application of immigration and asylum policies alone. Within the European Union, a broad range of policy frameworks have relevance, from the Common Security and Defence Policy and the Maritime Security Strategy, through to the implementation of broad foreign policy, development, and humanitarian priorities. To date, there is little coherence among these policy frameworks and fundamental differences in terms of core philosophy, though efforts to bring ministries and departments together have accelerated dramatically in recent years. A more holistic approach to maritime migration will be difficult to come by, but is essential.

While the need for a comprehensive approach is increasingly accepted by all actors in theory, absolute solutions remain elusive and crisis management has become the "new normal" for the European Union. The proposals tabled following the April 2015 summit have proved extraordinarily divisive as EU governments focus on their own national crises, while also falling far short of what is needed. As broader EU mechanisms, including the Schengen system, come under pressure, Mediterranean maritime migration has become more than just a humanitarian crisis—it is also a symbol of collaborative dysfunction in Europe. Unless the political will is found to fundamentally rethink core EU immigration and asylum policies, they risk collapse.

Works Cited

Amnesty International. 2016. EU Risks Fuelling Horrific Abuse of Refugees and Migrants in Libya. News release, June 14, 2016. www.amnesty.org/en/latest/news/2016/06/eu-risks-fuelling-horrific-abuse-of-refugees-and-migrants-in-libya.

———. 2016. Refugees and Migrants Fleeing Sexual Violence, Abuse, and Exploitation in Libya. News release, July 1, 2016. www.amnesty.org/en/latest/news/2016/07/refugees-and-migrants-fleeing-sexual-violence-abuse-and-exploitation-in-libya/.

Austrian Delegation to the Strategic Committee on Immigration, Frontiers, and Asylum. 2014. EU Resettlement Initiative – "Save Lives." Discussion paper, Council of the European Union, September 7, 2014. www.europarl.europa.eu/meetdocs/2014_2019/documents/libe/dv/18_resettlement_save_lifes_/18_resettlement_save_lifes_en.pdf.

BBC News. 2013. Italy Boat Sinking: Hundreds Feared Dead off Lampedusa. BBC News, October 3, 2013. www.bbc.com/news/world-europe-24380247.

Carling, Jørgen and María Hernández-Carretero. 2011. Protecting Europe and Protecting Migrants? Strategies for Managing Unauthorised Migration from Africa. *The British Journal of Politics and International Relations* 13 (1): 42–58.

Carrera, Sergio and Leonhard den Hertog. 2015. Whose *Mare?* Rule of Law Challenges in the Field of European Border Surveillance in the Mediterranean. CEPS Paper in Liberty and Security in Europe no. 79, CEPS, Brussels, January 2015. www.ceps.eu/system/files/LSE_79.pdf.

Cassarino, Jean-Pierre. 2007. Informalising Readmission Agreements in the EU Neighbourhood. *The International Spectator* 42 (2): 179–96. www.europarl.europa.eu/meetdocs/2009_2014/documents/droi/dv/67_cassarinoarticle_/67_cassarinoarticle_en.pdf.

———. 2012. An Overview of North African Countries' Bilateral Cooperation on the Removal of Unauthorized Migrants: Drivers and Implications. Middle East Institute, May 4, 2012. www.mei.edu/content/overview-north-african-countries-bilateral-cooperation-removal-unauthorized-migrants-drivers.

Collett, Elizabeth. 2015. The Asylum Crisis in Europe: Designed Dysfunction. Migration Policy Institute commentary, September 2015. www.migrationpolicy.org/news/asylum-crisis-europe-designed-dysfunction.

———. 2016. The Paradox of the EU-Turkey Refugee Deal. Migration Policy Institute commentary, March 2016. www.migrationpolicy.org/news/paradox-eu-turkey-refugee-deal.

Collyer, Michael. 2006. States of Insecurity: Consequences of Saharan Transit Migration. Working paper no. 31, Centre on Migration, Policy, and Security, University of Oxford, 2006. www.compas.ox.ac.uk/2006/wp-2006-031-collyer_saharan_transit_migration.

Council of the European Union. 2014. Council Conclusions on Taking Action to Manage Migratory Flows. Conclusions following a Justice and Home Affairs Council meeting, Luxembourg, October 10, 2014. www.consilium.europa.eu/uedocs/cms_data/docs/pressdata/en/jha/145053.pdf.

———. 2016. Draft Roadmap to Enhance Information Exchange and Information Management Including Interoperability Solutions in the Justice and Home Affairs Area. Working document, May 13, 2016. www.statewatch.org/news/2016/may/eu-council-jha-info-8437-16.pdf.

———. 2016. Justice and Home Affairs Council, 09-10/06/2016. Updated June 9, 2016. www.consilium.europa.eu/en/meetings/jha/2016/06/9-10/.

Crawley, Heaven, Franck Duvell, Nando Sigona, Simon McMahon, and Katharine Jones. 2016. Unpacking a Rapidly Changing Scenario: Migration Flows, Routes and Trajectories across the Mediterranean. Unravelling the Mediterranean Migration Crisis research brief no. 1, March 2016. www.compas.ox.ac.uk/media/PB-2016-MEDMIG-Unpacking_Changing_Scenario.pdf.

de Haas, Hein. 2009. The Myth of Invasion: The Inconvenient Realities of African Migration to Europe. *Third World Quarterly* 29 (7): 1305–22.

Dialogue on Mediterranean Transit Migration. 2014. 2014 Map on Mixed Migration Routes. Map, May 2014. www.imap-migration.org/fileadmin/Editor/Visualisations/MTM/i-Map_poster_14.05_ENGLISCH_Screen_reduced.pdf.

Edwards, Adrian. 2016. Seven Factors behind Movement of Syrian Refugees to Europe. UNHCR press release, September 25, 2016. www.unhcr.org/news/briefing/2015/9/560523f26/seven-factors-behind-movement-syrian-refugees-europe.html.

Emergency Response Centre International. N.d. ERCI: Emergency Response Centre International. Accessed August 29, 2016. www.ercintl.org.

European Asylum Support Office (EASO). 2012. *EASO Fact Finding Report on Intra-EU Relocation Activities from Malta.* Malta: EASO. www.refworld.org/pdfid/52aef8094.pdf.

European Commission. 2011. Communication from the Commission to the European Parliament and the Council: Evaluation of the Readmission Agreements. COM (2011) 76 final, February 23, 2011. http://eur-lex.europa.eu/legal-content/EN/TXT/PDF/?uri=CELEX:52011DC0076&from=EN.

———. 2013. Communication from the Commission to the European Parliament and the Council on the Work of the Task Force Mediterranean. COM (2014) 869 final, December 4, 2013. http://ec.europa.eu/dgs/home-affairs/what-is-new/news/news/docs/20131204_communication_on_the_work_of_the_task_force_mediterranean_en.pdf.

———. 2013. European Assistance to Help Bulgaria Face the Refugee Crisis. Press release, October 23, 2013. http://europa.eu/rapid/press-release_IP-13-993_en.htm.

———. 2015. Communication from the Commission to the European Parliament, the Council, the European Economic and Social Committee and the Committee of the Regions: A European Agenda on Migration. COM (2015) 240 final, May 13, 2015. http://ec.europa.eu/dgs/home-affairs/what-we-do/policies/european-agenda-migration/background-information/docs/communication_on_the_european_agenda_on_migration_en.pdf.

———. 2015. EU Provides €83 Million to Improve Conditions for Refugees in Greece. Press release, April 19, 2016. http://europa.eu/rapid/press-release_IP-16-1447_en.htm.

———. 2015. EU's Civil Protection Mechanism Helps Hungary Cope with Refugee Influx. News release, September 14, 2015. http://ec.europa.eu/echo/news/EUCPM-helps-Hungary-cope-with-refugee-influx_en.

———. 2015. Joint Foreign and Home Affairs Council: Ten Point Action Plan on Migration. Press release, April 20, 2015. http://europa.eu/rapid/press-release_IP-15-4813_en.htm.

———. 2016. Annex 2 to the Communication from the Commission to the European Parliament and the Council on the State of Play of Implementation of the Priority Actions under the European Agenda on Migration—Greece State of Play Report. COM [2016] 85 final, February 10, 2016. http://ec.europa.eu/dgs/home-affairs/what-we-do/policies/european-agenda-migration/proposal-implementation-package/docs/managing_the_refugee_crisis_state_of_play_20160210_annex_02_en.pdf.

———. 2016. Communication from the Commission to the European Parliament, the European Council and the Council: First Report on Relocation and Resettlement. COM (2016) 165 final, March 16, 2016. http://ec.europa.eu/dgs/home-affairs/what-we-do/policies/european-agenda-migration/proposal-implementation-package/docs/20160316/first_report_on_relocation_and_resettlement_en.pdf.

———. 2016. Communication from the Commission to the European Parliament, the European Council and the European Investment Bank on Establishing a New Partnership Framework with Third Countries under the European Agenda on Migration. COM (2016) 385 final, June 7, 2016. http://ec.europa.eu/dgs/home-affairs/what-we-do/policies/european-agenda-migration/proposal-implementation-package/docs/20160607/communication_external_aspects_eam_towards_new_migration_ompact_en.pdf.

———. 2016. EU-Jordan: Towards a Stronger Partnership. Press release, July 20, 2016. http://europa.eu/rapid/press-release_IP-16-2570_en.htm.

———. 2016. Impact Assessment Report on the Establishment of an EU Entry Exit System. SWD (2016) 115 final, April 6, 2016. http://eur-lex.europa.eu/legal-content/EN/TXT/?qid=1473790957354&uri=CELEX:52016SC0115.

———. 2016. Implementing the European Agenda on Migration: Commission Reports on Progress in Greece, Italy and the Western Balkans. Press release, February 10, 2016. http://europa.eu/rapid/press-release_IP-16-269_en.htm.

———. 2016. Member States' Support to Emergency Relocation Mechanism. Updated September 1, 2016. http://ec.europa.eu/dgs/home-affairs/what-we-do/policies/european-agenda-migration/press-material/docs/state_of_play_-_relocation_en.pdf.

———. 2016. Proposal for a Regulation of the European Parliament and of the Council Establishing the Criteria and Mechanisms for Determining the Member State Responsible for Examining an Application for International Protection Lodged in One of the Member States by a Third-Country National or a Stateless Person (Recast). COM (2016) 270 final, May 4, 2016. http://ec.europa.eu/dgs/home-affairs/what-we-do/policies/european-agenda-migration/proposal-implementation-package/docs/20160504/dublin_reform_proposal_en.pdf.

————. 2016. Proposal for a Regulation of the European Parliament and of the Council on the European Union Agency for Asylum and Repealing Regulation (EU) No 439/2010. COM (2016) 271 final, May 4, 2016. http://ec.europa.eu/dgs/home-affairs/what-we-do/policies/european-agenda-migration/proposal-implementation-package/docs/20160504/easo_proposal_en.pdf.

European Council. 2015. Special Meeting of the European Council, 23/04/2015. Updated April 23, 2015. www.consilium.europa.eu/en/meetings/european-council/2015/04/23/.

————. 2016. European Council Meeting (28 June 2016) Conclusions. Press release, June 28, 2016. www.consilium.europa.eu/en/press/press-releases/2016/06/28-euco-conclusions/.

European Council and Council of the European Union. 2016. EU-Turkey Statement, 18 March 2016. Press release, March 18, 2016. www.consilium.europa.eu/en/press/press-releases/2016/03/18-eu-turkey-statement/.

————. 2016. EUNAVFOR MED Operation Sophia: Mandate Extended by One Year, Two New Tasks Added. Press release, June 20, 2016. www.consilium.europa.eu/en/press/press-releases/2016/06/20-fac-eunavfor-med-sophia.

————. N.d. Agreements and Conventions. Accessed August 29, 2016. www.consilium.europa.eu/en/documents-publications/agreements-conventions/search-results/?dl=EN&title=readmission&from=0&to=0.

European Court of Auditors. 2016. *Special Report No. 9/2016: EU External Migration Spending in Southern Mediterranean and Eastern Neighbourhood Countries until 2014.* Luxembourg: European Court of Auditors. www.euractiv.com/wp-content/uploads/sites/2/2016/03/SR-Migration-EN.pdf.

European Defence Agency. 2014. European Maritime Surveillance Network Reaches Operational Status. News release, October 27, 2014. www.eda.europa.eu/info-hub/press-centre/latest-news/2014/10/27/european-maritime-surveillance-network-reaches-operational-status.

European External Action Service (EEAS). 2016. EU NAVFOR MED Operation Sophia – Six Monthly Report for the Period 22 June-31 December 2015. Working document, January 27, 2016.

European Migration Network (EMN). 2015. *Policies, Practices, and Data on Unaccompanied Minors in the EU Member States and Norway.* Brussels: EMN. http://ec.europa.eu/dgs/home-affairs/what-we-do/networks/european_migration_network/reports/docs/emn-studies/emn_study_policies_practices_and_data_on_unaccompanied_minors_in_the_eu_member_states_and_norway_synthesis_report_final_eu_2015.pdf.

European Parliament. 2016. MEPs Back Plans to Pool Policing of EU External Borders. Press release, July 6, 2016. www.europarl.europa.eu/news/en/news-room/20160701IPR34480/meps-back-plans-to-pool-policing-of-eu-external-borders.

European Union. 2007. Treaty of Lisbon Amending the Treaty on European Union and the Treaty Establishing the European Community. December 13, 2007. www.refworld.org/docid/476258d32.html.

Eurostat. 2016. Asylum and First-Time Asylum Applicants by Citizenship, Age and Sex. Annual Aggregated Data (Rounded) [migr_asyappctza]. Updated March 18, 2016. http://ec.europa.eu/eurostat/.

————. 2016. Asylum Applicants Considered to be Unaccompanied Minors – Annual Data [tps00194]. Updated August 11, 2016. http://ec.europa.eu/eurostat/.

————. 2016. Record Number of Over 1.2 Million First Time Asylum Seekers Registered in 2015. News release, March 4, 2016. http://ec.europa.eu/eurostat/documents/2995521/7203832/3-04032016-AP-EN.pdf.

Faiola, Anthony. 2015. U.N. Estimates That up to 850 Migrants Perished in Capsized Boat off Libya. *The Washington Post,* April 21, 2015. www.washingtonpost.com/world/un-says-between-800-and-850-migrants-died-in-boat-capsizing-off-libya/2015/04/21/a8383770-e803-11e4-9767-6276fc9b0ada_story.html.

Foy, Henry and Duncan Robinson. 2015. Frontex Chief Welcomes Plan for More Powerful EU Border Force. *Financial Times,* December 13, 2015. www.ft.com/cms/s/0/7bd81ad4-a02b-11e5-beba-5e33e2b79e46.html.

Frontex. 2008. *General Report 2008.* Warsaw: Frontex. http://frontex.europa.eu/assets/About_Frontex/Governance_documents/Annual_report/2008/frontex_general_report_2008.pdf.

————. 2010. *Beyond the Frontiers – Frontex: The First Five Years.* Warsaw: Frontex. http://frontex.europa.eu/assets/Publications/General/Beyond_the_Frontiers.pdf.

————. 2011. *Press Pack, May 2011.* Warsaw: Frontex. http://frontex.europa.eu/assets/Media_centre/Frontex_Press_Pack.pdf.

————. 2012. *Annual Risk Analysis 2012.* Warsaw: Frontex. http://frontex.europa.eu/assets/Attachment_Featured/Annual_Risk_Analysis_2012.pdf.

————. 2014. *Annual Risk Analysis 2014.* Warsaw: Frontex. http://frontex.europa.eu/assets/Publications/Risk_Analysis/Annual_Risk_Analysis_2014.pdf.

————. 2015. *Annual Risk Analysis 2015.* Warsaw: Frontex. http://frontex.europa.eu/assets/Publications/Risk_Analysis/Annual_Risk_Analysis_2015.pdf.

————. 2015. Budget 2016. Budget tables, December 24, 2015. http://frontex.europa.eu/assets/About_Frontex/Governance_documents/Budget/Budget_2016.pdf.

————. 2016. *Risk Analysis for 2016.* Warsaw: Frontex. http://frontex.europa.eu/assets/Publications/Risk_Analysis/Annula_Risk_Analysis_2016.pdf.

————. N.d. Eurosur. Accessed August 29, 2016. http://frontex.europa.eu/intelligence/eurosur/.

García Andrade, Paula, Iván Martín, Viorica Vita, and Sergo Mananashvili. 2015. *EU Cooperation with Third Countries in the Field of Migration.* Brussels: European Parliament. www.europarl.europa.eu/RegData/etudes/STUD/2015/536469/IPOL_STU(2015)536469_EN.pdf.

Hirsi Jamaa and Others v. Italy. 2012. Application No. 27765/09. European Court of Human Rights. http://hudoc.echr.coe.int/eng?i=001-109231.

International Organization for Migration (IOM). 2015. At Least 3,800 Migrants Rescued from Mediterranean since Friday: IOM. Press release, February 17, 2015. www.iom.int/news/least-3800-migrants-rescued-mediterranean-friday-iom.

———. 2015. *Mixed Migration Flows in the Mediterranean and Beyond: Compilation of Available Data and Information, Reporting Period 2015.* Geneva: IOM. http://doe.iom.int/docs/Flows%20Compilation%202015%20Overview.pdf.

———. N.d. Missing Migrants Project: Methodology. Accessed August 29, 2016. http://missingmigrants.iom.int/methodology.

Jacobs, Anna. 2013. King Mohammed VI Calls on the Government to Preserve the Right of Immigrants in Morocco. *Morocco World News*, September 10, 2013. www.moroccoworldnews.com/2013/09/104254/king-mohammed-vi-calls-on-the-government-to-preserve-the-right-of-immigrants-in-morocco/.

Laczko, Frank, Ann Singleton, Tara Brian, and Marzia Rango. 2016. Migrant Arrivals and Deaths in the Mediterranean: What Do the Data Really Tell Us?" *Forced Migration Review* 51: 30–31. www.fmreview.org/destination-europe/laczko-singleton-brian-rango.html.

Malta Independent. 2010. Malta to No Longer Host Frontex Missions... PN, PL MEPs Trade Blows after EP Vote. *Malta Independent*, March 26, 2010. www.independent.com.mt/articles/2010-03-26/news/malta-to-no-longer-host-frontex-missions-pn-pl-meps-trade-blows-after-ep-vote-272208/.

Médecins sans Frontières. 2015. MSF & MOAS to Launch Mediterranean Search, Rescue and Medical Aid Operation. News release, April 10, 2015. www.msf.org/article/msf-moas-launch-mediterranean-search-rescue-and-medical-aid-operation.

Migrant Offshore Aid Station (MOAS). N.d. About MOAS. Accessed August 29, 2016. www.moas.eu/about/.

Migrants' Files, The. 2016. Events during Which Someone Died Trying to Reach or Stay in Europe. Updated June 24, 2016. https://docs.google.com/spreadsheets/d/1YNqIzyQfEn4i_be2GGWESnG2Q80E_fLASffsXdCOftI/edit#gid=1085726718.

———. N.d. The Human and Financial Cost of 15 Years of Fortress Europe. Accessed August 30, 2016. www.detective.io/detective/the-migrants-files.

Migration Policy Institute. 2011. Top 10 of 2011 – Issue #1: Arab Spring and Fear of Migrant Surge Expose Rift in EU Immigration Policy Circles. *Migration Information Source*, December 1, 2011. www.migrationpolicy.org/article/top-10-2011-issue-1-arab-spring-and-fear-migrant-surge-expose-rift-eu-immigration-policy.

Molinario, Barbara 2014. Eritrean Survivor of Lampedusa Tragedy Returns to Honour the Dead, Meet Pope Francis. UNHCR news release, October 2, 2014. www.unhcr.org/en-us/news/latest/2014/10/542d0ece5/eritrean-survivor-lampedusa-tragedy-returns-honour-dead-meet-pope-francis.html.

M.S.S. v. Belgium and Greece. 2011. Application No. 30696/09. European Court of Human Rights. http://hudoc.echr.coe.int/eng?i=001-103050.

Natter, Katharina. 2015. Almost Home? Morocco's Incomplete Migration Reforms. *World Politics Review*, May 5, 2015. www.worldpoliticsreview.com/articles/15691/almost-home-morocco-s-incomplete-migration-reforms.

Oxfam. 2016. EU Ministers Must Change Course on Migration Cooperation with Africa. Press release, May 11, 2016. www.oxfam.org/en/pressroom/press-releases/2016-05-11/eu-ministers-must-change-course-migration-cooperation-africa.

Paoletti, Emanuella. 2009. A Critical Analysis of Migration Policies in the Mediterranean: The Case of Italy, Libya and the EU. RAMSES working paper no. 12/09, European Studies Centre, University of Oxford, 2009. www.sant.ox.ac.uk/esc/ramses/ramsespaperPaoletti.pdf.

Peers, Steve. 2014. *New Rules on Maritime Surveillance: Will They Stop the Deaths and Push-Backs in the Mediterranean?* London: Statewatch. www.statewatch.org/analyses/no-237-maritime-surveillance.pdf.

Pezzani, Lorenzo and Charles Heller. 2015. "Sharing the Burden of Rescue": Illegalised Boat Migration, the Shipping Industry and the Costs of Rescue in the Central Mediterranean. Border Criminologies (blog), University of Oxford, November 2, 2015. www.law.ox.ac.uk/research-subject-groups/centre-criminology/centreborder-criminologies/blog/2015/10/sharing-burden.

Regulation (EU) No 656/2014 of the European Parliament and of the Council of 15 May 2014 Establishing Rules for the Surveillance of the External Sea Borders in the Context of Operational Cooperation Coordinated by the European Agency for the Management of Operational Cooperation at the External Borders of the Member States of the European Union. *Official Journal of the European Union* 2014 L189/93, June 27, 2014. http://data.europa.eu/eli/reg/2014/656/oj.

Regulation No 1168/2011 of the European Parliament and of the Council Amending Council Regulation (EC) No 2007/2004 Establishing a European Agency for the Management of Operational Cooperation at the External Borders of the Member States of the European Union. *Official Journal of the European Union* 2011 L 304/1, November 22, 2011. http://eur-lex.europa.eu/eli/reg/2011/1168/oj.

Renzi, Matteo. 2016. Migration Compact: Contribution to an EU Strategy for External Action on Migration. Non-paper, April 2016. www.governo.it/sites/governo.it/files/immigrazione_0.pdf.

Robinson, Duncan. 2014. Alarm at Plan to End Italy's Mare Nostrum Rescue Operation. *Financial Times*, October 12, 2014. www.ft.com/cms/s/0/ec9edf84-508e-11e4-8645-00144feab7de.html.

Robinson, Duncan and Kerin Hope. 2016. Refugees in Greece Refuse to Relocate across EU. *Financial Times,* May 16, 2016. www.ft.com/cms/s/0/826f1bf2-1b75-11e6-b286-cddde55ca122.html.

Saul, Jonathan. 2015. In Mediterranean, Commercial Ships Scoop up Desperate Human Cargo. Reuters, September 21, 2015. www.reuters.com/investigates/special-report/europe-migrants-ship/.

Stamouli, Nektaria. 2016. Inside the Migrant-Smuggling Trade: Escapes Start at €1,000. *The Wall Street Journal*, March 29, 2016. www.wsj.com/articles/european-border-crackdown-kick-starts-migrant-smuggling-business-1459260153.

Statewatch. 2007. Criminalizing Solidarity, Part II—Italy/Tunisia: Fishermen on Trial for Rescuing Migrants. Updated September 2007. www.statewatch.org/news/2007/sep/07italy-tunisia-fishermen.htm.

Stevenson, Beth. 2016. EU Agencies Release Tenders for UAV Coastal Monitoring. FlightGlobal, August 17, 2016. www.flightglobal.com/news/articles/eu-agencies-release-tenders-for-uav-coastal-monitori-428588/.

Tarakhel v. Switzerland. 2014. Application No. 29217/12. European Court of Human Rights. http://hudoc.echr.coe.int/eng?i=001-148070.

Townsend, Jacob and Christel Oomen. 2015. *Before the Boat: Understanding the Migrant Journey*. Brussels: Migration Policy Institute Europe. www.migrationpolicy.org/research/boat-understanding-migrant-journey.

United Nations High Commissioner for Refugees (UNHCR). 2014. UNHCR—Statement on Boat Incident off Greece Coast. Press release, January 21, 2014. www.unhcr.org/en-us/news/press/2014/1/52df83d49/unhcr-statement-boat-incident-greece-coast.html.

———. 2015. Europe Refugee Emergency – Unaccompanied and Separated Children. Briefing note, October 9, 2015. http://reliefweb.int/sites/reliefweb.int/files/resources/Europerefugeecrisis-briefingnoteonunaccompaniedandseperatedchildren.pdf.

———. 2015. Greece Data Snapshot (8 Nov.). Fact sheet, UNHCR, Geneva, November 2015. http://data.unhcr.org/mediterranean/download.php?id=140.

———. 2015. Greece Data Snapshot (24 Dec.). Fact sheet, UNHCR, Geneva, December 2015. http://data.unhcr.org/mediterranean/download.php?id=329.

———. 2015. Nationalities of Mediterranean Sea Arrivals to Greece – 2015 Monthly Breakdown, as of 30 November 2015. Dataset, November 30, 2015. http://data.unhcr.org/mediterranean/download.php?id=244.

———. 2015. UNHCR Urges Europe to Recreate a Robust Search and Rescue Operation on Mediterranean, as Operation Triton Lacks Resources and Mandate Needed for Saving Lives. Press release, February 12, 2015. www.unhcr.org/en-us/news/press/2015/2/54dc80f89/unhcr-urges-europe-recreate-robust-search-rescue-operation-mediterranean.html.

———. 2016. *Global Trends: Forced Displacement in 2015*. Geneva: UNHCR. www.unhcr.org/576408cd7.pdf.

———. 2016. Profiling of Afghan Arrivals on Greek Islands in February 2016. Fact sheet, UNHCR, Geneva, February 2016. https://data.unhcr.org/mediterranean/download.php?id=875.

———. 2016. Profiling of Afghan Arrivals on Greek Islands in January 2016. Fact sheet, UNHCR, Geneva, January 2016. http://data.unhcr.org/mediterranean/download.php?id=726.

———. 2016. Profiling of Syrian Arrivals on Greek Islands in February 2016. Fact sheet, UNHCR, Geneva, February 2016. https://data.unhcr.org/mediterranean/download.php?id=874.

———. 2016. Profiling of Syrian Arrivals on Greek Islands in January 2016. Fact sheet, UNHCR, Geneva, January 2016. http://data.unhcr.org/mediterranean/download.php?id=725.

———. N.d. Global Trends 2015—Table 5. Refugees and people in a Refugee-Like Situation, Excluding Asylum-Seekers, and Changes by Origin and Country of Asylum, 2015. Dataset, accessed August 29, 2016. www.unhcr.org/globaltrends/2015-GlobalTrends-annex-tables.zip.

———. N.d. Refugees/Migrants Emergency Response, Mediterranean—Demographic Data. Dataset, accessed September 13, 2016. http://data.unhcr.org/mediterranean/regional.php.

United Nations High Commissioner for Refugees, Regional Bureau Europe. 2016. Refugees & Migrants Sea Arrivals in Europe. Fact sheet, UNHCR, Geneva, June 2016. http://data.unhcr.org/mediterranean/download.php?id=1782.

———. 2016. Weekly Report (27 May – 2 June). Weekly report, June 3, 2016. https://data.unhcr.org/mediterranean/download.php?id=1436.

United Nations Office on Drugs and Crime (UNODC). 2010. *Smuggling of Migrants into, through and from North Africa: A Thematic Review and Annotated Bibliography of Recent Publications.* New York: UNODC. www.unodc.org/documents/human-trafficking/Migrant_smuggling_in_North_Africa_June_2010_ebook_E_09-87293.pdf.

United Nations Security Council. 2015. Resolution 2240 (2015). October 9, 2015. www.un.org/en/ga/search/view_doc.asp?symbol=S/RES/2240(2015).

Zalan, Eszter. 2015. Hungary Rejects EU Offer to Take Refugees. EU Observer, September 11, 2015. https://euobserver.com/migration/130217.

CHAPTER 3

MARITIME MIGRATION IN THE BAY OF BENGAL, ANDAMAN SEA, AND STRAITS OF MALACCA

By Kathleen Newland

Introduction[1]

A s a vast region with myriad islands, peninsulas, and ancient sea routes, Asia has an enduring tradition of maritime migration. In recent decades, this movement has become increasingly contentious, as refugees and irregular migrants traverse the region by sea and complicate the attempts of governments in the Asia-Pacific region to control their borders, regulate immigration, and fulfill their obligations under international law. Migrant workers from Asian countries are seeking work within the region in greater numbers (even as the Middle East and West remain important destinations). Meanwhile, refugees fleeing persecution and conflict travel by land, air, and sea—sometimes all three within the same journey—in search of asylum, preferably in a country where they also have a prospect of making a living.

These flows of people have persisted in the region for decades. But the spring of 2015 marked the beginning of a period of crisis as waves of migrants and refugees, most departing from ports in Myanmar and Bangladesh, crossed or attempted to cross the Bay of Bengal to reach Southeast Asia. Malaysia, with its 4 percent unemployment rate and predominantly Muslim culture, was the desired end point for most. The number of maritime migrants on this route tripled between 2012

---

1 This chapter updates and expands an earlier brief by the author published by the Migration Policy Institute (MPI) and the International Organization for Migration (IOM), "Irregular Maritime Migration in the Bay of Bengal: The Challenges of Protection, Management, and Cooperation" (MPI and IOM Issue in Brief No. 13, Washington, DC and Bangkok, 2015).

and 2014, reaching 63,000 in 2014 and more than 8,000 per month in the first quarter of 2015.[2] By the end of 2015, however, the surge had tapered off, with only about 1,000 migrants crossing the Bay of Bengal in the last quarter.[3] The total number of migrants to travel the Bay of Bengal route to Southeast Asia in 2015 amounted to about 33,600, reflecting the collapse of traffic in the second half of the year.[4]

A report released by the United Nations High Commissioner for Refugees (UNHCR) in December 2015 estimated that fatality rates for migrants moving across the Bay of Bengal and the Andaman Sea were three times higher than those of migrants involved in the 2015 Mediterranean crisis: 12 in every 1,000 migrants on the Asian route were thought to have perished before reaching land.[5]

This chapter attempts to put the crisis of 2014–15 into the broader context of maritime migration in the Bay of Bengal/Andaman Sea/ Straits of Malacca (BAM) region, before concluding with several recommendations for policymakers in the region and a consideration of what recent history has to teach us about responses to maritime migration crises.

I.   Irregular Maritime Movements in the Context of Asian Migration

Irregular maritime movements in Asia are driven by both economic dynamism and disparity, in some cases with the added impetus of violence, repression, and ethnic discrimination.

Divergent economic and population growth trajectories could, in the not too distant future, transform some Asian countries that are mainly countries of migrant origin at present (as listed in Table 1) into destinations themselves. While Malaysia and Thailand continue to send

---

2   United Nations High Commissioner for Refugees (UNHCR), IOM, and United Nations Office on Drugs and Crime (UNODC), *Bay of Bengal and Andaman Sea: Proposals for Action* (Geneva and Vienna: UNHCR, IOM, and UNODC, 2015).

3   Statement by Volker Türk, UNHCR Assistant High Commissioner for Protection, at the 2nd Special Meeting on Irregular Migration in the Indian Ocean, UNHCR, Bangkok, December 3-4, 2015.

4   UNHCR Regional Office for South-East Asia, "Mixed Maritime Movements in South-East Asia—2015," accessed August 9, 2016.

5   Ibid.

some migrant workers abroad,[6] the rapid growth of their economies now draws growing numbers of immigrants. In addition to constant change, Asian migration is also characterized by extreme diversity. It encompasses forced and voluntary movements; regular and irregular migration; north-south, south-south, and south-north trajectories; and both permanent and temporary flows in all migration categories. Two distinctive (and related) features of Asian migration are the large and growing proportion of women migrants, and the significant challenges posed by migrant smuggling and human trafficking.

Table 1. Major Countries of the South and Southeast Asian Migration System

Countries Primarily of Migrant Origin	Countries and Territories Primarily of Migrant Destination	Countries of Both Origin and Destination
Bangladesh*	Brunei	Malaysia*
Cambodia	Hong Kong SAR (Special Administrative Region of China)	Thailand*
China	Republic of Korea	India
Indonesia*	Singapore	
Lao People's Democratic Republic	Taiwan Province of China	
Myanmar*	Maldives	
Nepal		
Pakistan		
Philippines		
Sri Lanka		
Vietnam		

* Countries most involved in the maritime migration crisis of 2014–15
Source: Graeme Hugo, "The New International Migration in Asia: Challenges for Population Research," *Asian Population Studies* 1, no. 1 (2005): 93–120; updated using data from Migration Policy Institute (MPI) Data Hub, "International Migrant Population by Country of Origin and Destination," accessed August 1, 2016.

---

6 Ji-Ping Lin, "Tradition and Progress: Taiwan's Evolving Migration Reality," *Migration Information Source,* January 24, 2012.

The economic dynamism of Brunei, Malaysia, Singapore, and Thailand attracts migrants from around the BAM region and farther afield.[7] Almost half of the population of Singapore and about one-quarter of the population of Brunei are foreign born.[8] However, immigration into these two city-states is tightly and quite effectively controlled. On the other hand, large proportions of the immigrant populations in Thailand and Malaysia—both among the top 25 destination countries for international migrants worldwide—do not have legal status.[9] Thailand had an estimated 3.9 million foreign-born residents (6 percent of its population) in 2015.[10] The vast majority, about 3.5 million, came from the neighboring countries of Myanmar (1.98 million), the Lao People's Democratic Republic (969,000), and Cambodia (805,000).[11] Almost all were active in the labor market, but only about half were registered or had started the registration process that would give them permission to work legally.[12] Similarly, Malaysia was host to 2.5 million migrants (8 percent of its population) in 2015.[13] Slightly more than 1 million were from Indonesia, a significant share of whom were unauthorized, as about half the flow of migrants from Indonesia is irregular.[14] Other major countries of origin were Bangladesh (358,000), Myanmar (252,000), and Nepal (205,000).[15]

Most migrants traveling to Thailand traverse its land borders with the Lao People's Democratic Republic, Cambodia, and eastern Myanmar. In

---

7 Malaysia's fairly liberal travel policy made it possible for travelers from Muslim countries, such as Iran and Iraq, to travel to Malaysia without a visa. The country has thus become both an attractive destination and a transit county in which irregular migrants can make arrangements for onward travel to, for example, Australia.

8 United Nations Department of Economic and Social Affairs (UNDESA) Population Division, *International Migration Report 2015: Highlights* (New York: UNDESA Population Division, 2016), 29.

9 UNHCR, *Maritime Interception Operations and the Processing of International Protection Claims: Legal Standards and Policy Considerations with Respect to Extraterritorial Processing* (Geneva: UNHCR, 2010), 15–7, 55–9; MPI Data Hub, "Top 25 Destination Countries for Global Migrants over Time," accessed August 15, 2016.

10 UNDESA, *International Migration Report 2015*, 29.

11 UNDESA Population Division, "Trends in International Migrant Stock 2015—by Destination and Origin" (dataset POP/DB/MIG/Stock/Rev.2015, December 2015).

12 Jerry Huguet, Aphichat Chamratrithirong, and Claudia Natali, *Thailand at a Crossroads: Challenges and Opportunities in Leveraging Migration for Development* (Washington, DC and Bangkok: MPI and IOM, 2012).

13 UNDESA, *International Migration Report 2015*, 29.

14 UNDESA Population Division, "International Migrant Stock 2015;" Graeme Hugo, "The New International Migration in Asia: Challenges for Population Research," *Asian Population Studies* 1, no. 1 (2005): 93–120.

15 UNDESA Population Division, "Trends in International Migrant Stock 2015."

recent decades, Thailand has also been an important country of transit for maritime migrants from western Myanmar and Bangladesh who are smuggled through Thailand to Malaysia. Up until the third quarter of 2013, Malaysia itself was a significant country of transit as migrants continued their journeys through to Indonesia, where many hoped to take to the sea again in order to reach Australia. But significant shifts in Australian policy that took effect after the general election of September 2013, including denial of entry to all irregular maritime arrivals regardless of refugee status, disrupted the final leg of that route.[16]

Figure 1. Southeast Asia Migration Routes

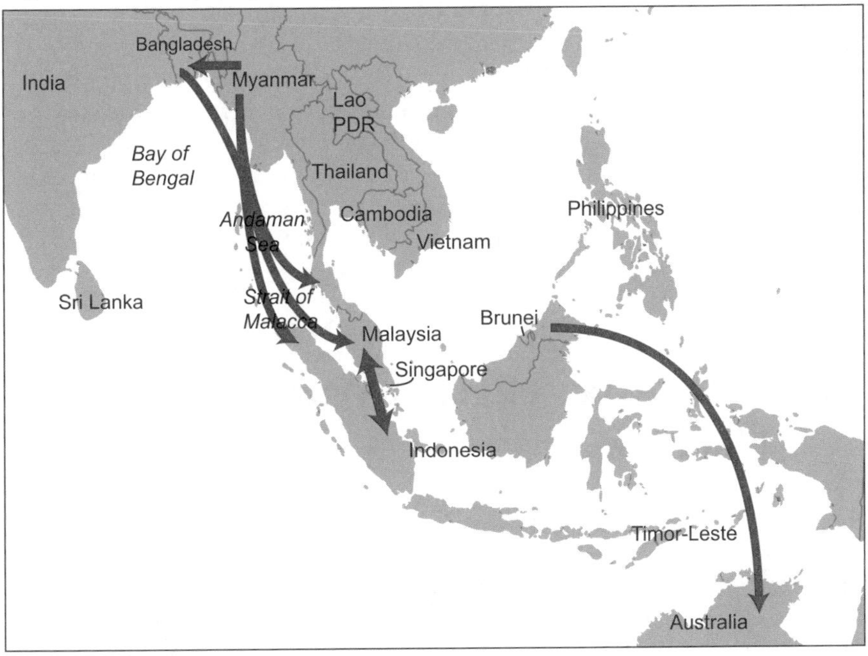

Source: Author's rendering.

In 2014–15, the arc from Bangladesh, at the northern apex of the Bay of Bengal, around to Myanmar, Thailand, Malaysia, and Indonesia was the epicenter of intense, complex, irregular maritime flows. The people traveling include voluntary labor migrants, refugees fleeing conflict or persecution, stateless persons, victims of trafficking, unaccompanied children, and migrants impelled to leave their homes by severe poverty. Virtually all used smugglers, who commonly collect people in

16 For an analysis of irregular maritime migration to Australia, see Chapter 5 in this volume.

small boats and transport them to larger ocean-going vessels capable of holding hundreds of migrants.[17] The initial fee to board a ship was affordable, as low as US $50. But many migrants got part of the way to their destination only to find that they were being held for ransom under grim conditions; to gain release and delivery to the final destination, they or their families had to pay an additional fee of hundreds or even thousands of dollars.[18]

The protection needs of these migrants differ. Many of the categories listed above—refugees, children, the stateless, and the trafficked—are the subject of special provisions in international law that aim to protect them from being returned to dangerous situations. But protection of the fundamental human rights of migrants trying to escape poverty and hopelessness is much less developed. Destination governments, meanwhile, are understandably concerned with controlling their borders and preventing public services from being overwhelmed, as well as preventing public backlash against migrants and the officials perceived to be responsible for any loss of control over who enters and who remains inside national borders. In this context, the fundamental human rights of migrants of all types too often go unprotected.

II.   Indonesian Migrant Workers to Malaysia

As irregular migration from Myanmar across the Bay of Bengal built toward crisis in 2015, a separate, large flow of irregular maritime migrants proceeded without notable drama in the same region. Malaysia is the main country of destination for both authorized and unauthorized migrant workers from Indonesia. Indonesian men work in the plantation sector, timber, construction, and manufacturing, while Indonesian women are predominantly in domestic work and other service-sector jobs.[19] Irregular Indonesian migrant workers travel to Malaysia across the Straits of Malacca in large numbers, often on small

---

17 UNHCR Regional Office for South-East Asia, "Irregular Maritime Movements in South-East Asia—2014," accessed August 9, 2016.

18 Ibid.

19 IOM, *Labour Migration from Indonesia: An Overview of Indonesian Migration to Select Destinations in Asia and the Middle East* (Jakarta: IOM, 2010).

overcrowded boats and at considerable risk.[20] They also make the same journey in reverse, to visit or resettle at home. Casualties are common. For example, in September 2015, more than 60 irregular Indonesian migrants perished when their boat foundered and sank off the coast of Malaysia.[21]

Indonesians constitute about half of authorized migrant workers in Malaysia, and are thought to make up an even larger proportion of unauthorized workers; although data are very poor, one study estimated that Indonesian workers comprised 70 percent of unauthorized laborers in Malaysia.[22] Demand for low-waged labor is high in Malaysia, and affinities of language, culture, and ethnicity make absorption into the labor force relatively easy for Indonesians. Proximity and the high volume of traffic between the two countries also facilitate unauthorized movement. Passage by ferry from Batam, Indonesia across to ports in southwestern, western, and eastern Malaysia is relatively easy: workers could enter as tourists simply by showing that they had 1,000 Malaysian shillings—about US $320—in their possession.[23] Others used false documents.[24]

The large number of Indonesian migrants who work legally in Malaysia suggests that those who choose to migrate illegally do so because there are benefits to using unauthorized channels. One important factor that encourages unauthorized migration is the high cost of regular migration. To migrate from Indonesia to Malaysia through legal channels, individuals are required to furnish complicated and extensive documentation, which takes a long time to procure. Private recruiters manage the process throughout the region, including placing workers with an employer. Their fees amount to three or four times the monthly wage for a worker going to Hong Kong, and as much as 14 times the monthly wage one for going to Taiwan.[25] It is much easier and cheaper—but riskier—for Indonesian migrants to hop a ferry or a

20 Marie McAuliffe and Victoria Mence, "Global Irregular Maritime Migration: Current and Future Challenges" (Occasional Paper Series 07/2014, Government of Australia, Department of Immigration and Border Protection, Irregular Migration Research Programme, April 2014).
21 Reuters, "Indonesian Migrant Boat Death Toll Rises to 61," Reuters, September 7, 2015.
22 IOM, Labour Migration from Indonesia.
23 Graeme Hugo, "Indonesia's Labor Looks Abroad," Migration Information Source, April 1, 2007.
24 Ibid.
25 Hugo, "The New International Migration in Asia."

fishing boat to Malaysia and to use their networks to find a job.[26] Unlike many other irregular migration flows, this one is not controlled by smugglers, so the costs of irregular journeys remain low.[27] Malaysian migration law also contributes, inadvertently, to the lure of irregular migration, as it ties the migrant to a specific employer. In accordance with a Memorandum of Understanding (MOU) signed between the governments of Indonesia and Malaysia, an employer may hold a migrant's travel and identity documents.[28] Thus, a migrant going through formal channels may find it extremely difficult to leave an employer who is abusive, deceptive, or doesn't pay wages owed. An irregular migrant has much greater flexibility.[29]

Periodic crackdowns from both the country of origin and destination have also encouraged irregularity. In 2009, after a series of well-publicized cases of abuse of Indonesian domestic workers, the government of Indonesia banned domestic workers from going to Malaysia[30]—a move that only drove migration into irregular channels. The Indonesian government extended the ban in 2015 to apply to migrants headed to the Middle East and North Africa.[31] Malaysia, for its part, has had several large-scale campaigns to legalize irregular migrants, including in 1993, 1996, and 2002.[32] These efforts regularized hundreds of thousands of migrant workers, although usually for a limited period of time. But Malaysia has also had periodic campaigns to punish and deport irregular migrant workers, particularly those who did not take the opportunity to adjust to legal status.

Enforcement policies became harsher after a new migration law was passed in 2002, with fines, canings, and arrests (including by a citizens' vigilante group empowered by the government[33]). After a delay in implementation following the 2004 tsunami, a new campaign began in March 2004 that drove some 400,000 Indonesian migrants to leave the country. The motivation to leave clandestinely, by sea, was increased by a fine of about US $226 charged to unauthorized migrants who departed through official channels, even if voluntarily. Another immigration amnesty took place between September 2011 and January 2014,

26 Hugo, "Indonesia's Labor Looks Abroad."

27 Ibid.

28 IOM, *Labour Migration from Indonesia.*

29 Ibid.

30 Ibid.

31 Hilary Whiteman, "Indonesia Maid Ban Won't Work in Mideast, Migrant Groups Say," CNN, May 6, 2015.

32 Hugo, "Indonesia's Labor Looks Abroad."

33 IOM, *Labour Migration from Indonesia.*

during which 1.3 million migrant workers registered to get documents. By the time the campaign ended, 500,000 were successful and 330,000 were deported, while others continued to wait for an outcome.[34] As with earlier regularizations, a crackdown on irregular foreign workers followed the end of the amnesty period.

In November 2015, the International Labor Organization (ILO) convened a binational workshop in Jakarta to ensure that Indonesian domestic migrant workers in Malaysia, many of whom are unauthorized, would have greater opportunities to move through legal channels. Amid declarations of greater cooperation in the future, a spokesman from the Indonesian Ministry of Manpower claimed that the government would take a greater role in the recruitment process of Indonesian migrant workers, thereby driving out unscrupulous middlemen and improving the protection and working conditions of migrant workers.[35]

Despite measures to staunch it, the flow of unauthorized migrants from Indonesia to Malaysia persists as one of the largest in the world. Since most other large unauthorized flows, such as those from Mexico to the United States and from Bangladesh to India, take place mostly over land, Indonesia-Malaysia is likely the world's largest bilateral corridor for irregular maritime migration.

III. The Migration Crisis of 2014–15 in the BAM Region

As noted in the introduction to this chapter, UNHCR estimates that 63,000 people crossed the Bay of Bengal in 2014—nearly three times as many as in 2012 and up 12 percent from 2013. An additional 25,000 set out during the first quarter of 2015, threatening a new record.[36] Between January 2014 and December 2015, more than 1,600 migrants

---

34 Jason Ng, "Malaysia Gets Tough on Illegal Immigrants as Amnesty Program Expires," Indonesia Real Time (blog), *The Wall Street Journal*, January 21, 2014.

35 International Labor Organization, "Indonesia and Malaysia Discussed Ways to Improve Protection of Domestic Migrant Workers in Malaysia" (press release, November 3, 2015).

36 UNHCR Regional Office for South-East Asia, "Mixed Maritime Movements in South-East Asia—2015."

are estimated to have died on their journeys,[37] the vast majority of them at sea in the BAM region, from dehydration, starvation, or abuse at the hands of smugglers. However, there was a dramatic reduction in migrant flows in the second half of 2015, and by the end of the year, the numbers of migrants to travel the Bay of Bengal tallied 33,600.[38] The migration crisis ended swiftly, but was a long time in the making.

Members of the Rohingya minority in western Myanmar have suffered extreme poverty and discrimination since the end of British colonial rule and the establishment of the modern state of Burma (whose name was changed to Myanmar in 1989). Like other religious and ethnic minorities in Myanmar, conflict with the dominant Buddhist culture and the state that embraces it has been a persistent thread in the lives of the Muslim population of Rakhine State, the majority of whom identify as Rohingya. Myanmar authorities portray the Rohingya as illegal immigrants from Bangladesh or the descendants of Bengalis who illegitimately settled in Myanmar under colonial rule.

A history of communal tensions goes back to the colonial period and the turmoil of World War II, when Muslim volunteers in what is now Rakhine State were armed by the British to fight the Japanese and used their weapons both in the war and in conflicts with rival ethnic groups in the state.[39] These volunteers were branded as traitors by many who fought for the liberation of Myanmar from the British, a perception that was compounded when Rohingya leaders petitioned to join parts of Rakhine State with East Pakistan in 1947 and, later, to join the newly created state of Bangladesh.[40] In both cases, they were rebuffed, and the Rohingya remained pariahs within Myanmar. Discrimination against them became official with Myanmar's adoption of the *Nationality Act of 1982*. "Rohingya" was not recognized as an indigenous ethnic group, and those without such classification were denied citizenship, rendering them effectively stateless.

About 180,000 people were affected by communal violence between Muslims and Buddhists in Rakhine State in June 2012 and again four

37 IOM, Global Migration Data Analysis Center, "Dangerous Journeys: International Migration Increasingly Unsafe in 2016" (data briefing series, issue no. 4, August 2016).

38 UNHCR Regional Office for South-East Asia, "Mixed Maritime Movements in South-East Asia—2015."

39 Aye Chan, "The Development of a Muslim Enclave in Arakan (Rakhine) State of Burma (Myanmar)," *SOAS Bulletin of Burma Research* 3, no. 2 (2005): 396–420.

40 Human Rights Watch (HRW), *Malaysia/Burma: Living in Limbo: Burmese Rohingyas Living in Malaysia* (New York: HRW, 2000).

months later, according to the United Nations Office for the Coordination of Humanitarian Affairs.[41] Some Rohingya fled to join impoverished communities in neighboring Bangladesh. At least 200,000 Rohingya are reckoned to live in Bangladesh, where 32,600 have been recognized as refugees.[42]

In 2014, about 140,000 people, almost all stateless Rohingya, remained displaced within Myanmar as a result of the violence.[43] Most were required to stay in squalid camps for internally displaced persons (IDPs), where they had no access to education or medical care, limited access to work, and many other limitations on their personal freedom. Although almost all were living in precarious circumstances, local and national authorities took no actions to make it possible for them to resume their former lives. Under these conditions, thousands left Myanmar. UNHCR reported that in the two years following the outbreak of violence (from June 2012 to June 2014), 87,000 people embarked on irregular maritime journeys across the Bay of Bengal from ports in Myanmar and Bangladesh. The vast majority were Rohingya, along with a much smaller proportion of Bangladeshi labor migrants.[44]

These journeys resulted in more than 1,600 known deaths between January 2014 and the end of 2015.[45] The distances traveled were great, and many boats may have been lost at sea without ever being detected. From Rakhine State to Malaysia, for example, is 1,500 nautical miles. Some boats traveled still farther: one was intercepted by the Sri Lankan navy off the east coast of Sri Lanka in February 2013. It had lost its way and been at sea for two months. Ninety people on board had died of dehydration and starvation; 30 survivors were rescued.[46] In 2012–13, some 1,600 Rohingya managed to reach Australia—a distance of more than 3,000 nautical miles—and others have been found as far away as the coasts of Indonesia and Timor-Leste.[47]

41 United Nations Office for the Coordination of Humanitarian Affairs (UNOCHA), "Humanitarian Bulletin: Myanmar, June 2013" (issue brief, June 2013).
42 Chris Buckley and Austin Ramzy, "Migrants Flooding into Malaysia and Indonesia Trade One Nightmare for Another," *The New York Times*, May 25, 2015.
43 UNOCHA, "Humanitarian Bulletin: Myanmar."
44 Adrian Edwards, "More than 20,000 People Risk All on Indian Ocean to Reach Safety: UNHCR Report" (UNHCR news release, August 22, 2014).
45 IOM, "Missing Migrants Project—Latest Global Figures," updated August 25, 2016.
46 Andrej Mahecic, "UNHCR Calls for Urgent Action to Prevent Rohingya Boat Tragedies" (UNHCR news release, February 22, 2013).
47 McAuliffe and Mence, "Global Irregular Maritime Migration."

The most common destination for the Muslims leaving Rakhine State, however, remains Malaysia, drawn by its relative prosperous and predominantly Muslim culture. As many as 500,000 migrants from Myanmar are believed to live in Malaysia, although many may have migrated before the 2012 anti-Rohingya violence in Myanmar.[48] As of the end of 2015, UNHCR counted 156,342 persons of concern residing in Malaysia, 92 percent of whom originated from Myanmar, and most of whom were Rohingya.[49] Most of the Rohingya in Malaysia work in the informal sector (in agriculture, construction, and domestic service, for example) without petitioning for asylum.

Migrants from western Myanmar and the neighboring coastal area of Bangladesh most often leave the shore on small boats and are then transferred to larger vessels with a capacity of 100 to 800 passengers. With passengers ultimately paying a total of US $1,600 to USD $2,400 each in upfront and backend fees, smugglers in the region made more than US $100 million in 2014.[50] Smugglers routinely take people to Thailand by boat, before proceeding overland to Malaysia.

The journey can be harrowing; once migrants reach the Thailand-Malaysia border, smugglers often demand more money to take them further. Those who are unable to pay are beaten, forced to work without pay, trafficked, and in some cases killed.[51] The discovery in April and May 2015 of smuggler camps on both sides of the Thailand-Malaysia border showed the critical dangers migrants traveling this route faced. Barbed-wire pens, watchtowers, cages, and dozens of graves marked the sites where smugglers held their human cargo for ransom.[52]

Reports of the grim findings at the camps, first brought to light in Thailand, prompted the Royal Thai Government to crack down on smugglers. As is so often the case with phenomena as complex as maritime migration, a straightforward policy seems to have triggered unintended consequences. Smugglers fearful of encountering Thai law enforcement abandoned migrant-filled vessels at sea. The ill-provisioned boats drifted, in some cases for months, as their passengers became more

---

48 Thomas Fuller, "Asian States Say They'll Focus on Causes of Migrant Crisis," *The New York Times*, May 29, 2015.

49 UNHCR, "Global Focus: Malaysia," accessed August 9, 2016.

50 UNHCR Regional Office for South-East Asia, "Irregular Maritime Movements in South-East Asia—2014."

51 IRIN, "In Search of a Regional Rohingya Solution," IRIN, July 26, 2013.

52 Chris Buckley and Thomas Fuller, "Jungle Camp in Malaysia Yields Graves and Signs of Migrant Abuse," *The New York Times*, May 26, 2015.

and more desperate. Denied permission to land, and in some cases pushed back out to sea,[53] an unknown number—believed to be upwards of 1,000—died of starvation, dehydration, or violence aboard the boats. Hundreds were rescued by local fishermen in Indonesia.[54] In the face of a growing humanitarian disaster, on May 20, 2015 Malaysia and Indonesia, both of which had initially replicated Thai policy in pushing migrant vessels back to sea, agreed to receive the migrants on a temporary basis, pending resettlement or repatriation.[55]

Some irregular migrants who reached Malaysia moved on to Indonesia in the hopes of reaching Australia. As Australia's zero-tolerance policy for boat arrivals was revived in 2013 and shut off that destination, some found themselves stuck in Indonesia, either awaiting resettlement to another country or looking for a chance to return to Malaysia.

The crisis that unfolded in April and May 2015 had multiple causes, both distant and proximate. The roots of the problem lay in the violence and discrimination experienced by Muslim communities in Myanmar, particularly in the 2012 destruction of Rohingya communities in Rakhine State, and the grinding poverty of Rohingya communities in Bangladesh. Poverty in the border region also drives some Bangladeshi citizens to become customers of migrant smugglers. The foreign secretary of Bangladesh estimated that perhaps one-third of the maritime flow in the BAM region in 2015 consisted of Bangladeshi nationals.[56] Unlikely to be recognized as refugees, Bangladeshi migrants intercepted at arrival or rescued at sea are eligible for Assisted Voluntary Return programs administered by the International Organization for Migration (IOM). Bangladesh continues to cooperate with the other countries in the BAM region to take back unauthorized Bangladeshi migrants.

If poverty, human-rights violations, and statelessness are the root causes of the flows across the Bay of Bengal, the proximate causes of the 2015 crisis were a sharp escalation in the numbers of people attempting the voyage, public revelations of the smugglers' brutal methods, smuggler reaction to the Thai campaign against them,

---

53 UNHCR, "UNHCR Alarmed at Reports of Boat Pushbacks in South-East Asia" (press release, May 13, 2015).

54 Joe Cochrane, "Indonesia and Malaysia Agree to Care for Stranded Migrants," *The New York Times*, May 20, 2015.

55 Ibid.

56 Fuller, "Asian States Say They'll Focus on Causes of Migrant Crisis."

and the corrupt officials who facilitated (and profited from) their operations.[57]

As smugglers sought to avoid Thailand, the numbers of migrants in Malaysian and Indonesian waters escalated sharply in the first two weeks of May; thousands were stranded at sea with inadequate food, fuel, and water. In the spring of 2015, an estimated 5,000 migrants were abandoned in the Bay of Bengal on seaborne vessels without adequate supplies by smugglers who had been paid to traffic them to Malaysia, Thailand, or further afield. This led to an estimated 370 deaths.[58] Indonesia and Malaysia announced at that time that they would not permit the boats to land and would turn them away unless, in the case of Malaysia, the boats were sinking. Some migrant boats were turned away from the coast after being furnished with food, water, and fuel to continue their search for a destination.[59]

Strong expressions of international concern ensued, including a rare public statement issued jointly on May 19, 2015 by the United Nations Secretary-General's Special Representative for International Migration, the United Nations High Commissioner for Refugees, the United Nations High Commissioner for Human Rights, and the Director-General of IOM. It called for the leaders of Indonesia, Malaysia, and Thailand "to facilitate safe disembarkation, and to give priority to saving lives, protecting rights, and respecting human dignity."[60] The statement urged states in the region and beyond to implement nine action points, including scaled-up search-and-rescue operations, an end to pushbacks, safe and predictable disembarkation of people rescued at sea, and expanded legal channels for safe and orderly migration (including labor migration). Following a meeting of the Indonesian, Malaysian, and Thai foreign ministers on May 20, 2015, Indonesia and Malaysia agreed to

---

57 Australian Broadcasting Corporation, "Malaysia to Follow Indonesia in Turning Back Migrant Boats; Thousands May Face Starvation at Sea," Australian Broadcasting Corporation, May 13, 2015.

58 UNHCR Regional Office for South-East Asia, "Mixed Maritime Movements in South-East Asia—2015."

59 Eileen Ng, "Malaysia to Push Back Rohingya Unless Boats Are Sinking," The Jakarta Post, May 12, 2015.

60 UNHCR, Office of the United Nations High Commissioner for Human Rights (OHCHR), IOM, and Special Representative of the Secretary-General (SRSG) for Migration and Development, "Search and Rescue at Sea, Disembarkation, and Protection of the Human Rights of Refugees and Migrants Now Imperative to Save Lives in the Bay of Bengal and Andaman Sea" (joint statement issued in New York and Geneva, May 19, 2015).

take in migrants stranded at sea on a temporary basis, pending resettlement or repatriation. The Philippines also announced that it would not turn away any migrant boats that reached its territorial waters.[61]

By late May 2015, rescue-at-sea operations had been expanded and refugee processing established. Boat arrivals in the BAM region appeared to be tapering off.[62] Some migrants had been rescued and allowed to remain in Indonesia or Malaysia, while others had decided to return home. The majority remained stuck in legal limbo as they awaited a decision on their case for remaining in a destination country. By mid-December 2015 there were about 2,500 Rohingya in detention, more than 53 percent more than at the same time a year previously.[63] And as of April 2016, more than 370 of these migrants remained in Belantik detention center in northern Malaysia. UNHCR officials were unable to access migrants at the center to evaluate their status from May until August 2015, by which point many had fallen ill with tuberculosis, further complicating the arduous asylum process. UNHCR had thus far failed to convince the Malaysian government to allow them to settle in one of the existing Rohingya communities in the country, although the Malaysian authorities did agree to work with UNHCR to establish a pilot program allowing 300 Rohingya with refugee status to work. Undocumented Rohingya already living in these Malaysian neighborhoods report that prospects are bad and life is unsafe as smugglers and debt collectors live nearby.[64]

As of February 2016, more than 1,000 Rohingya remained in Indonesia.[65] By April 2016, many of the Rohingya rescued off the coast of Indonesia a year earlier had disappeared from the camps that hosted them; presumably, many made their way to Malaysia, with or without the help of smugglers, and work in the informal economy. A UNHCR official confirmed that a significant proportion of those who initially made landfall in Indonesia had managed to reach Malaysian shores.[66]

---

61 Cochrane, "Indonesia and Malaysia Agree to Care for Stranded Migrants."

62 Michael Forsythe, "Migrant Crisis in Southeast Asia Shows Signs of Ebbing," *The New York Times*, May 27, 2015.

63 UNHCR Regional Office for South-East Asia, "Mixed Maritime Movements in South-East Asia—2015."

64 Jonathan Vit, "Where Are the Rohingya Boat Survivors Now?" IRIN, April 15, 2016.

65 Wahyudi Soeriaatmadja, "Trapped in Indonesia Refugee Camp for Years after Failing to Reach Australia," *The Straits Times*, February 1, 2016.

66 Vit, "Where Are the Rohingya Boat Survivors Now?"

IV. International and Regional Responses to Crisis

The humanitarian crisis surrounding the migrant boats adrift in the BAM region cast the challenges facing regional cooperation into sharp relief. The initial reactions of the three destination countries revealed the paucity of legal and institutional resources for a regional response (see Box 1 and Table 2). Although the Association of Southeast Asian Nations (ASEAN) includes among its members four of the five countries most affected by the crisis (Indonesia, Malaysia, Myanmar, and Thailand—only Bangladesh, in the South Asian region, is not a member), ASEAN remained mostly silent during the most acute phase of the crisis. It was, perhaps, bound by a strong collective commitment to the principle of noninterference in the internal affairs of other Member States (including vis-à-vis the treatment of minority groups)—a principle that handicapped it as a platform for coordinating regional responses.

Malaysia, in its capacity as ASEAN chair, called the tripartite meeting of the Indonesian, Malaysian, and Thai foreign ministers on May 20, 2015 to discuss the crisis—a meeting that set the stage for further regional discussions but produced no direct action. Two months later, in Kuala Lumpur, there was an emergency ASEAN Ministerial Meeting on Transnational Crime Concerning Irregular Movement of Persons in Southeast Asia, which made recommendations for the creation of a joint task force and funding to respond to the movements of refugees and migrants. The committee also resolved to use the Treaty on Mutual Legal Assistance on Criminal Matters to improve prosecution of those involved in human trafficking and to strengthen law enforcement by means of information and intelligence sharing, amongst other measures.[67]

---

67 Association of Southeast Asian Nations (ASEAN), "Emergency ASEAN Ministerial Meeting on Transnational Crime Concerning Irregular Movement of Persons in Southeast Asia" (chairman's statement, Kuala Lumpur, July 2, 2015). However, this meeting did not address issues of protection, prevention, or root causes of the crisis. See Marie McAuliffe, *Resolving Policy Conundrums: Enhancing Humanitarian Protection in Southeast Asia* (Washington, DC: MPI, forthcoming).

Box 1. The International Legal and Institutional Framework in the Region

The Association of Southeast Asian Nations (ASEAN) has no common agreements on migration except for a nascent process for mutual recognition of the qualifications of highly skilled professionals in certain fields. Among the ten ASEAN Member States, only two—Cambodia and the Philippines—are parties to the United Nations Refugee Convention. Neither Indonesia nor Malaysia are members of the International Organization for Migration (IOM), the largest multilateral institution dealing with migration, though Indonesia is an observer. Myanmar, the major source of irregular maritime migrants in the region, has refused to acknowledge any responsibility for the Rohingya, denying that they are citizens. As a result, there is little common ground when dealing with the mixed flows of migrants and refugees that affects multiple ASEAN countries but in different ways.

There are, however, two bodies of international law to which most ASEAN countries are party: international law focused on transnational crime and international maritime law. Most have signed the antitrafficking and antismuggling protocols to the United Nations Convention against Transnational Organized Crime. Similarly, most have signed the International Convention for Safety of Life at Sea (SOLAS), as amended, and to a lesser extent the International Convention on Maritime Search and Rescue (SAR) (see Table 2). Membership in the International Maritime Organization (IMO) and the Bali Process is almost universal in the region. These endorsements may offer a pathway to stronger regional cooperation on migration at sea, focused on the twin priorities of saving lives and countering smuggling. As the events of April and May 2015 showed, however, one-dimensional approaches may bring undesirable and unintended consequences. A crackdown on smugglers may leave migrants exposed to greater danger; expanded maritime search and rescue without a plan for dealing with persons rescued may cause tensions among the states involved.

Table 2. Asia-Pacific States and International Frameworks

	1951 Refugee Convention[a]	1974 SOLAS Convention	1978 SOLAS Protocol[b]	1988 SOLAS Protocol[b]
Bangladesh		X		X
Brunei*		X	X	
Cambodia*	X	X	X	X
China	X			
Indonesia*		X	X	
India		X	X	X
Malaysia*		X	X	X
Myanmar*		X	X	X
Philippines*	X			
Singapore*		X	X	X
Sri Lanka				
Thailand*		X		
Vietnam*		X	X	X

IMO = International Maritime Organization; IOM = International Organization for Migration; SAR = International Convention on Maritime Search and Rescue; SOLAS = International Convention for Safety of Life at Sea

[a] United Nations Convention relating to the Status of Refugees

[b] Amendments to SOLAS

[c] Protocol against the Smuggling of Migrants by Land, Sea and Air, supplementing the United Nations Convention against Transnational Organized Crime

[d] Protocol to Prevent, Suppress and Punish Trafficking in Persons, Especially Women and Children, supplementing the United Nations Convention against Transnational Organized Crime

[e] With reservation

* ASEAN Member State

Table 2. (Continued)

1979 SAR Convention	Bali Process Member	IOM Member	IMO Member	Anti-Smuggling Protocol[c]	Anti-Trafficking Protocol[d]
X	X	X	X		
	X		X		
	X	X	X	X	X
	X	(Observer)	X		X
X	X	(Observer)	X	X[e]	X[e]
X	X	X	X	X	X
X	X		X		X[e]
X	X	X	X	X[e]	X[e]
	X	X	X	X	X
X	X		X		X
	X	X	X		X
X	X	X	X	X	X[e]
X	X	X	X		X[e]

Generally, regional mechanisms remained remarkably passive in the face of the 2014–15 crisis despite mandates that seem tailor-made to address it. A prime example is the Bali Process on People Smuggling, Trafficking in Persons, and Related Transnational Crime. Its 48 members include most of the countries in the Asia-Pacific region as well as UNHCR, IOM, and the United Nations Office on Drugs and Crime (UNODC). The Bali Process is a voluntary, nonbinding Regional Consultative Process. Its objectives include promoting intelligence and information-sharing among members, combating people-smuggling and trafficking networks, assisting their victims, and reducing irregular migration in the region by promoting implementation of a Regional Cooperation Framework.[68] This framework, established by a ministerial meeting of the Bali Process in 2011, is meant "to enable interested Bali Process members to establish practical arrangements aimed at enhancing the region's response to irregular movement through consistent processing of asylum claims, durable solutions for refugees, the sustainable return of those not owed protection and targeting of people smuggling enterprises."[69] The governments involved in the 2014–15 crisis chose not to use this or other regional mechanism immediately, perhaps because they are not designed to be emergency responses mechanisms and do not have the personnel or the resources needed for crisis management.[70] However, the Bali Process and other regional structures were invoked as follow-up mechanisms later in the year as regional and international actors sought to address the longer-term effects of the crisis and to prevent a recurrence.[71]

Almost a year after the crisis, on March 23, 2016, the Sixth Ministerial Conference of the Bali Process laid out a "comprehensive regional approach." It highlighted the importance of coordinating procedures for rescue at sea and disseminating information about the dangers of irregular maritime journeys to at-risk populations. It also stressed the value of information sharing and welcomed the establishment of a

---

68 The Bali Process, "About the Bali Process," accessed July 20, 2016.
69 Ibid.
70 Other regional processes include the Manila Process and the Asia-Pacific Consultations on Refugees, Displaced Persons, and Migrants, both established in 1996.
71 At a November 2015 roundtable meeting of the Jakarta Declaration on Addressing the Irregular Movement of Persons, representatives of governments in South and Southeast Asia discussed strengthening the Bali Process as one possible mechanisms to combat future flows. See UNHCR Regional Office for South-East Asia, "Mixed Maritime Movements in South-East Asia—2015."

Working Group on the Disruption of Criminal Syndicates.[72] The Ministerial Conference attributed the reduction in migrant flows across the Bay of Bengal in the second half of 2015 to policies enacted in the affected countries that aimed to disrupt international smuggling and trafficking networks.[73] Following the conference, UNHCR welcomed the commitment made by ministers in attendance to take a regional approach to managing future mixed migration flows and expressed the hope that greater cooperation would lead policymakers to address the underlying causes of displacement, smuggling, and trafficking. In particular, the organization hoped that regional cooperation might open a path towards a tripartite agreement between Thailand, Myanmar, and UNHCR that would lead to the repatriation of the stranded Rohingya to Myanmar.[74]

The most acute phase of the 2014–15 maritime migration crisis inevitably brought to mind the massive outpouring of people from Indochina in the years following the Vietnam War (see Box 2). In both cases, although on a different scale, an international conference marked the beginning of more systematic international efforts to cooperate with the countries most immediately affected to manage the outflows and find a suitable resolution for the migrants and refugees caught up in the crisis.

---

72 The Bali Process, "Sixth Ministerial Conference of the Bali Process on People Smuggling, Trafficking in Persons, and Related Transnational Crime" (co-chairs' statement, Bali, Indonesia, March 23, 2016).
73 Ibid.
74 UNHCR, "UNHCR Welcomes Ministerial Declaration in Bali, Calls for New Compact to Absorb Refugees in Region" (press release, March 23, 2016).

Box 2. Resolving a Maritime Migration Crisis: The "Boat People" of Vietnam, 1979–89

If Southeast Asia highlights the difficulties of a contemporary maritime migration crisis, its experiences also point to one path toward resolution. The aftermath of the Vietnam War in 1975 saw a massive outpouring of people from Vietnam, the Lao People's Democratic Republic, and Cambodia. With the exception of the 140,000 who were evacuated alongside the departing American forces and about 250,000 who crossed the land border into China, most Vietnamese moved by boat without permission to disembark in another country. By 1979, 200,000 people had been resettled and 350,000 remained in the region, but the rate of arrivals was three times the rate of departures in first-asylum countries. In June 1979, the five member countries of ASEAN declared that they could not accept further new arrivals. Boats bearing refugees were pushed back out to sea by national authorities.

The United Nations Secretary-General convened an international conference in July 1979, in a remarkably successful effort to address the humanitarian and political crisis. Ultimately, some 623,800 people were resettled in 20 countries outside the region between July 1979 and July 1982 as a result of commitments made at the conference.

The 65 governments that attended the conference agreed on a variety of measures that brought the number of refugees in the region down to manageable levels: worldwide resettlement offers of 260,000, an Orderly Departure Program (ODP), and regional processing centers in Indonesia and the Philippines for refugees being resettled. First-asylum countries were assured that no refugees would remain with them permanently and therefore agreed to stop pushing back boats. As all these measures were implemented, the numbers of boat arrivals fell, although they did not stop.

After nearly ten years of success, arrivals again mounted in 1987-88 and pushbacks resumed. But this time, the resettlement countries were not willing to accept all those leaving Vietnam as prima facie refugees. A second international conference was held in 1989. The resulting Comprehensive Plan of Action (CPA) stands out as an example of international cooperation to resolve a major mixed flow of refugees and migrants while preserving first asylum and stemming boat departures. It was also the first such plan to include the country of origin. Countries of first asylum in the region resumed temporary protection for boat arrivals, the vast majority from Vietnam. All were given access to a full refugee status-determination process, with a resettlement guarantee for those found to be refugees. Nonrefugees were repatriated and given some reintegration assistance. The CPA was in effect until 1997. During that period, more than 109,000 Vietnamese returned home, ODP departures increased sharply, and another roughly 107,000 Vietnamese "boat people" were resettled.

For all the resettlement successes that resulted from the 1979 and 1989 international conferences, the Indochinese migration crisis came with a terrible, incalculable human toll: As many as 10 percent of all those who originally set out on boats died during the journey, most from drowning, dehydration, or pirate attacks.

Sources: W. Courtland Robinson, *Terms of Refuge: The Indonchinese Exodus and the International Response* (New York: Zed Books, 1998); United Nations High Commissioner for Refugees (UN-HCR), *The State of the World's Refugees 2000: Fifty Years of Humanitarian Action* (Geneva: UNHCR, 2000).

Convening a New International Forum

As regional mechanisms proved ineffective throughout the spring of 2015, some 20 governments and several international institutions attended a Special Meeting on Irregular Migration in the Indian Ocean in Bangkok on May 29, 2015 at the invitation of the Thai government. Having at first announced that it would not attend the conference, Myanmar did so and absorbed little direct criticism of its treatment of the Rohingya. UNHCR was one of the few voices to explicitly call for "the full assumption of responsibility by Myanmar towards all people on its territory."[75] The official summary issued at the end of the meeting, however, contained oblique references to country-of-origin responsibility. For example, it called for "full respect for human rights and adequate access of people to basic rights and services such as housing, education, and health care," and "emphasized the need for relevant countries and the international community to resolve irregular maritime migration . . . by addressing the root causes and other contributing factors."[76] In addition to country-of-origin responsibility, the other major sticking point at the Bangkok conference was resettlement. The three main receiving countries in the region continued to insist that no residual caseload could remain within their borders, and that all those allowed to disembark should be resettled elsewhere.

75 Statement by Volker Türk, UNHCR Assistant High Commissioner for Protection, at the Special Meeting on Irregular Migration in the Indian Ocean, Bangkok, May 29, 2015.
76 Ibid.

UNHCR pleaded for realism on this subject, noting that "in the light of several major crises around the world, rising numbers of refugees and asylum seekers and urgent needs everywhere, the capacity of a number of states to offer places is limited."[77]

The weeks surrounding the conference saw several other governments from within and outside the region pledge to support efforts to help the displaced. The problem of disembarkation was resolved by the Philippines and Indonesia, which agreed to host processing centers for the boat arrivals. The United States pledged to lead any multicountry resettlement initiative for those determined to be refugees. Turkey pledged funds to IOM and UNHCR for emergency operations, while Saudi Arabia and the United Arab Emirates agreed in principle to contribute to a humanitarian fund for migrants and refugees stranded at sea.[78] In a bizarre coda, the tiny West African country of Gambia said it would take all the refugees, although its capacity to do so was far from clear.[79]

IOM, UNHCR, and UNODC committed to supporting the governments in the region on humanitarian migration procedures and antismuggling efforts. To address the crisis more broadly they submitted a ten-point proposal for action (see Box 3), noting that "only a coordinated effort by the source, transit, and destination countries in the region can provide protection for those who need it and successfully prosecute the perpetrators of this misery and death."[80]

---

77 Ibid.

78 Zuhrin Azam Ahmad, "Riyahd to Chip in for Rohingya," *The Star*, June 8, 2015.

79 Agence France-Presse, "Gambia Offers to Resettle All Rohingya Refugees," *The Guardian*, May 20, 2015.

80 UNHCR, IOM, and UNODC, *Bay of Bengal and Andaman Sea*.

Box 3. Ten-Point Proposal for Action in the Bay of Bengal and Andaman Sea

In May 2015, in response to increased migratory flows across the Bay of Bengal and the Andaman Sea, the United Nations High Commissioner for Refugees (UNHCR), International Organization for Migration (IOM), and United Nations Office on Drugs and Crime (UNODC) issued a call for coordination among source, transit, and destination countries on the following ten items:

1. Strengthen search-and-rescue (SAR) operations.

2. Establish effective, predictable disembarkation to a place of safety.

3. Establish or enhance reception facilities.

4. Identify those people in need of international protection and determine how to meet their needs.

5. Facilitate solutions for persons in need of international protection.

6. Support the return of those not in need of international protection.

7. Reinforce the gathering, sharing, analysis, and use of information related to movements by sea.

8. Build capacity in countries of transit and first asylum.

9. Expand legal alternatives to dangerous movements.

10. Address humanitarian, human rights, and particularly development needs in migrant-source countries.

Source: UNHCR, IOM, and UNODC, Bay of Bengal and Andaman Sea: Proposals for Action (Geneva and Vienna: UNHCR, IOM, and UNODC, 2015).

In December 2015, the countries that participated in the May 29 Bangkok meeting reconvened for a follow-up meeting. Here, Thailand laid out a draft of an "Action Agenda" for steps that would carry forward the policy proposals from the May 29 special meeting.[81] At the December meeting, the Thai government announced that it intended to provide IOM with US $100,000 to carry out these initiatives.[82]

---

81 UNHCR Regional Office for South-East Asia, "Mixed Maritime Movements in South-East Asia—2015."

82 Ministry of Foreign Affairs of the Kingdom of Thailand, "Result of the 2nd Special Meeting on Irregular Migration in the Indian Ocean," updated December 4, 2015.

V.   Recommendations and Conclusions

As in other regions of the world affected by unauthorized maritime migration, better collection and sharing of data are needed to solidify the evidence base for policymaking. An Asia-Pacific facility dedicated to collecting, organizing, and analyzing information on migration in the region could also identify the gaps in knowledge that need to be filled. The Regional Mixed Migration Secretariat (RMMS) for the Horn of Africa–Yemen region, established in 2011, is a useful model for organizing data collection and research on regional migration, including migration by sea.

Better evidence and analysis of the causes of maritime migration, including the involvement of organized crime in the smuggling industry, would help to define the nature of the problem. War, poverty, and repression are undoubtedly root causes, but the patterns of boat departures do not map to them as closely as one might expect. The profiles and motivations of migrants also need closer study. The decision to make a dangerous, illegal voyage is complex. In addition to their own personal situations, migrants take into account the nature of border protection regimes, the costs of clandestine travel, the danger of the voyage, the presence of a known community (perhaps including family or friends) at the intended destination, the availability of rescue, the chances of being allowed to stay, and the likelihood of being able to earn a living. The accuracy of information potential migrants have about these and other factors is highly variable. Understanding the information sources on which migrants rely is an important part of understanding the dynamics of migration.

Along with better data and analysis, more active use of forums for collaboration among countries in the region could help to support the development and management of migration policies. This is crucial, as emerging Asian economies that need labor must coexist alongside poorer countries that hope to supply it. The sea lanes of Asia have always been crucial to its dynamism, and people will continue to use them. The future prospects of the region will be enhanced if they can do so safely, legally and profitably.

Works Cited

Agence France-Presse. 2015. Gambia Offers to Resettle All Rohingya Refugees. *The Guardian*, May 20, 2015. www.theguardian.com/world/2015/may/21/south-east-asia-migrant-crisis-gambia-offers-to-resettle-all-rohingya-refugees.

Ahmad, Zuhrin Azam. 2015. Riyahd to Chip in for Rohingya. *The Star*, June 8, 2015. www.thestar.com.my/News/Nation/2015/06/08/Riyadh-to-chip-in-for-Rohingya-Saudi-Arabia-positive-towards-Msia-proposal-for-humanitarian-fund/.

Association of Southeast Asian Nations (ASEAN). 2015. Emergency ASEAN Ministerial Meeting on Transnational Crime Concerning Irregular Movement of Persons in Southeast Asia. Chairman's statement, Kuala Lumpur, July 2, 2015. http://reliefweb.int/sites/reliefweb.int/files/resources/Chairman-Statement-Emergency-ASEAN-Ministers-Meeting-on-Transnational-Crime-2-July-2015-1.pdf.

Australian Broadcasting Corporation. 2015. Malaysia to Follow Indonesia in Turning Back Migrant Boats; Thousands May Face Starvation at Sea. Australian Broadcasting Corporation, May 13, 2015. http://abc.net.au/news/2015-05-13/malaysia-to-turn-back-migrant-boats/6466726.

Bali Process, The. 2016. Sixth Ministerial Conference of the Bali Process on People Smuggling, Trafficking in Persons, and Related Transnational Crime. Co-chairs' statement, Bali, Indonesia, March 23, 2016. www.baliprocess.net/UserFiles/baliprocess/File/BPMC%20Co-chairs%20Ministerial%20Statement_with%20Bali%20Declaration%20attached%20-%2023%20March%202016_docx.pdf.

———. N.d. About the Bali Process. Accessed July 20, 2016. www.baliprocess.net/.

Buckley, Chris and Thomas Fuller. 2015. Jungle Camp in Malaysia Yields Graves and Signs of Migrant Abuse. *The New York Times*, May 26, 2015. www.nytimes.com/2015/05/27/world/asia/jungle-camp-in-malaysia-yields-graves-and-signs-of-migrant-abuse.html.

Buckley, Chris and Austin Ramzy. 2015. Migrants Flooding into Malaysia and Indonesia Trade One Nightmare for Another. *The New York Times*, May 25, 2015. www.nytimes.com/2015/05/26/world/asia/migrants-flooding-into-malaysia-trade-one-nightmare-for-another.html.

Chan, Aye. 2005. The Development of a Muslim Enclave in Arakan (Rakhine) State of Burma (Myanmar). *SOAS Bulletin of Burma Research* 3 (2): 396–420. www.soas.ac.uk/sbbr/editions/file64388.pdf.

Cochrane, Joe. 2015. Indonesia and Malaysia Agree to Care for Stranded Migrants. *The New York Times*, May 20, 2015. www.nytimes.com/2015/05/21/world/asia/indonesia-malaysia-rohingya-bangladeshi-migrants-agreement.html?_r=2.

Edwards, Adrian. 2014. More than 20,000 People Risk All on Indian Ocean to Reach Safety: UNHCR Report. United Nations High Commissioner for Refugees (UNHCR) news release, August 22, 2014. www.unhcr.org/en-us/news/latest/2014/8/53f741fc9/20000-people-risk-indian-ocean-reach-safety-unhcr-report.html.

Forsythe, Michael. 2015. Migrant Crisis in Southeast Asia Shows Signs of Ebbing. *The New York Times*, May 27, 2015. www.nytimes.com/2015/05/27/world/asia/myanmar-bangladesh-rohingya-migrant-crisis-shows-signs-of-ebbing.html.

Fuller, Thomas. 2015. Asian States Say They'll Focus on Causes of Migrant Crisis. *The New York Times*, May 29, 2015. www.nytimes.com/2015/05/30/world/asia/myanmar-deflects-un-criticism-over-rohingya.html.

Hugo, Graeme. 2005. The New International Migration in Asia: Challenges for Population Research. *Asian Population Studies* 1 (1): 93–120.

———. 2007. Indonesia's Labor Looks Abroad. *Migration Information Source*, April 1, 2007. www.migrationpolicy.org/article/indonesias-labor-looks-abroad.

Huguet, Jerry, Aphichat Chamratrithirong, and Claudia Natali. 2012. *Thailand at a Crossroads: Challenges and Opportunities in Leveraging Migration for Development*. Washington, DC and Bangkok: Migration Policy Institute and International Organization for Migration. www.migrationpolicy.org/research/Thailand-Leveraging-Migration.

Human Rights Watch (HRW). 2000. Malaysia/Burma: Living in Limbo: Burmese Rohingyas Living in Malaysia. New York: HRW. www.hrw.org/report/2000/08/01/malaysia/burma-living-limbo-burmese-rohingyas-malaysia.

International Labor Organization. 2015. Indonesia and Malaysia Discussed Ways to Improve Protection of Domestic Migrant Workers in Malaysia. Press release, November 3, 2015. www.ilo.org/jakarta/info/public/pr/WCMS_421579/lang--en/index.htm.

International Organization for Migration (IOM). 2010. *Labour Migration from Indonesia: An Overview of Indonesian Migration to Select Destinations in Asia and the Middle East*. Jakarta: IOM. www.iom.int/jahia/webdav/shared/shared/mainsite/published_docs/Final-LM-Report-English.pdf.

———. 2016. Missing Migrants Project—Latest Global Figures. Updated August 25, 2016. https://missingmigrants.iom.int/latest-global-figures.

International Organization for Migration, Global Migration Data Analysis Center. 2016. Dangerous Journeys: International Migration Increasingly Unsafe in 2016. Data briefing series, issue no. 4, August 2016. https://missingmigrants.iom.int/sites/default/files/gmdac_data_briefing_series_issue4.pdf.

IRIN. 2013. In Search of a Regional Rohingya Solution. IRIN, July 26, 2013. www.irinnews.org/report/98477/analysis-search-regional-rohingya-solution.

Lin, Ji-Ping. 2012. Tradition and Progress: Taiwan's Evolving Migration Reality. *Migration Information Source,* January 24, 2012. www.migrationpolicy.org/article/tradition-and-progress-taiwans-evolving-migration-reality.

Mahecic, Andrej. 2013. UNHCR Calls for Urgent Action to Prevent Rohingya Boat Tragedies. UNHCR news release, February 22, 2013. www.unhcr.org/512756df9.html.

McAuliffe, Marie. Forthcoming. *Resolving Policy Conundrums: Enhancing Humanitarian Protection in Southeast Asia*. Washington, DC: Migration Policy Institute.

McAuliffe, Marie and Victoria Mence. 2014. Global Irregular Maritime Migration: Current and Future Challenges. Occasional Paper Series 07/2014, Government of Australia, Department of Immigration and Border Protection, Irregular Migration Research Programme, April 2014. www.border.gov.au/ReportsandPublications/Documents/research/global-irregular-maritime-migration.pdf.

Migration Policy Institute (MPI) Data Hub. N.d. International Migrant Population by Country of Origin and Destination. Accessed August 1, 2016. www.migrationpolicy.org/programs/data-hub/charts/international-migrant-population-country-origin-and-destination?width=1000&height=850&iframe=true.

———. N.d. Top 25 Destination Countries for Global Migrants over Time. Accessed August 15, 2016. www.migrationpolicy.org/programs/data-hub/charts/top-25-destination-countries-global-migrants-over-time?width=1000&height=850&iframe=true.

Ministry of Foreign Affairs of the Kingdom of Thailand. 2015. Result of the 2nd Special Meeting on Irregular Migration in the Indian Ocean. Updated December 4, 2015. www.mfa.go.th/main/en/media-center/28/62757-Result-of-the-2nd-Special-Meeting-on-Irregular-Mig.html.

Newland, Kathleen. 2015. Irregular Maritime Migration in the Bay of Bengal: The Challenges of Protection, Management, and Cooperation. MPI and IOM Issue in Brief No. 13, Washington, DC and Bangkok, July 2015. www.migrationpolicy.org/research/irregular-maritime-migration-bay-bengal-challenges-protection-management-and-cooperation.

Ng, Eileen. 2015. Malaysia to Push Back Rohingya Unless Boats Are Sinking. *The Jakarta Post*, May 12, 2015. www.thejakartapost.com/news/2015/05/12/malaysia-push-back-rohingya-unless-boats-are-sinking.html.

Ng, Jason. 2014. Malaysia Gets Tough on Illegal Immigrants as Amnesty Program Expires. Indonesia Real Time (blog), *The Wall Street Journal*, January 21, 2014. http://blogs.wsj.com/indonesiarealtime/2014/01/21/malaysia-gets-tough-on-illegal-immigrants-as-amnesty-program-expires/.

Reuters. 2015. Indonesian Migrant Boat Death Toll Rises to 61. Reuters, September 7, 2015. www.reuters.com/article/us-malaysia-boat-capsized-idUSKC-N0R70EI20150907.

Robinson, W. Courtland. 1998. *Terms of Refuge: The Indonchinese Exodus and the International Response.* New York: Zed Books.

Soeriaatmadja, Wahyudi. 2016. Trapped in Indonesia Refugee Camp for Years after Failing to Reach Australia. *The Straits Times*, February 1, 2016. www.straitstimes.com/asia/se-asia/trapped-in-indonesia-refugee-camp-for-years-after-failing-to-reach-australia.

Türk, Volker. 2015. Statement by the UNHCR Assistant High Commissioner for Protection at the 2nd Special Meeting on Irregular Migration in the Indian Ocean, UNHCR, Bangkok, December 3–4, 2015. www.unhcr.org/566165a412.pdf.

———. 2015. Statement by the UNHCR Assistant High Commissioner for Protection at the Special Meeting on Irregular Migration in the Indian Ocean, UNHCR, Bangkok, May 29, 2015. www.unhcr.org/556ef3c39.pdf.

United Nations Department of Economic and Social Affairs (UNDESA) Population Division. 2015. Trends in International Migrant Stock 2015—by Destination and Origin. Dataset, POP/DB/MIG/Stock/Rev.2015, December 2015. www.un.org/en/development/desa/population/migration/data/estimates2/estimates15.shtml.

———. 2016. *International Migration Report 2015: Highlights.* New York: UNDESA Population Division. www.un.org/en/development/desa/population/migration/publications/migrationreport/docs/MigrationReport2015_Highlights.pdf.

United Nations High Commissioner for Refugees (UNHCR). 2000. *The State of the World's Refugees 2000: Fifty Years of Humanitarian Action.* Geneva: UNHCR. www.unhcr.org/en-us/publications/sowr/4a4c754a9/state-worlds-refugees-2000-fifty-years-humanitarian-action.html.

———. 2010. *Maritime Interception Operations and the Processing of International Protection Claims: Legal Standards and Policy Considerations with Respect to Extraterritorial Processing.* Geneva: UNHCR. www.refworld.org/docid/4cd12d3a2.html.

———. 2015. UNHCR Alarmed at Reports of Boat Pushbacks in South-East Asia. Press release, May 13, 2015. www.unhcr.org/news/press/2015/5/555345959/unhcr-alarmed-reports-boat-pushbacks-south-east-asia.html.

———. 2016. UNHCR Welcomes Ministerial Declaration in Bali, Calls for New Compact to Absorb Refugees in Region. Press release, March 23, 2016. www.unhcr.org/en-us/news/press/2016/3/56f259336/unhcr-welcomes-ministerial-declaration-bali-calls-new-compact-absorb-refugees.html.

———. N.d. Global Focus: Malaysia. Accessed August 9, 2016. http://reporting.unhcr.org/node/2532#_ga=1.28183996.1804866093.1466447949.

United Nations High Commissioner for Refugees, Regional Office for South-East Asia. N.d. Irregular Maritime Movements in South-East Asia—2014. Accessed August 9, 2016. http://storybuilder.jumpstart.ge/en/unhcr-imm.

———. N.d. Mixed Maritime Movements in South-East Asia—2015. Accessed August 9, 2016. https://unhcr.atavist.com/mmm2015.

United Nations High Commissioner for Refugees, International Organization for Migration, and United Nations Office on Drugs and Crime (UNODC). 2015. *Bay of Bengal and Andaman Sea: Proposals for Action.* Geneva and Vienna: UNHCR, IOM, and UNODC. www.UNHCR.org/55682d3b6.html.

United Nations High Commissioner for Refugees, Office of the United Nations High Commissioner for Human Rights, International Organization for Migration, and Special Representative of the Secretary-General for Migration and Development. 2015. Search and Rescue at Sea, Disembarkation, and Protection of the Human Rights of Refugees and Migrants Now Imperative to Save Lives in the Bay of Bengal and Andaman Sea. Joint Statement issued in New York and Geneva, May 19, 2015. www.ohchr.org/en/NewsEvents/Pages/DisplayNews.aspx?NewsID=15976&LangID=E.

United Nations Office for the Coordination of Humanitarian Affairs. 2013. Humanitarian Bulletin: Myanmar, June 2013. Issue brief, June 2013. http://reliefweb.int/sites/reliefweb.int/files/resources/HB-AP-2013.FINAL_0.pdf.

Vit, Jonathan. 2016. Where Are the Rohingya Boat Survivors Now? IRIN, April 15, 2016. www.irinnews.org/news/2016/04/15/where-are-rohingya-boat-survivors-now.

Whiteman, Hilary. 2015. Indonesia Maid Ban Won't Work in Mideast, Migrant Groups Say. CNN, May 6, 2015. www.cnn.com/2015/05/06/asia/indonesia-migrant-worker-ban/.

CHAPTER FOUR

UNAUTHORIZED MARITIME MIGRATION IN THE GULF OF ADEN AND THE RED SEA

By Kate Hooper

Introduction

In recent years, growing numbers of migrants from the Horn of Africa have embarked on perilous boat journeys across the Red Sea and Gulf of Aden to Yemen. Their reasons for taking to the sea include fleeing political unrest and seeking out economic opportunities in the Gulf States or further afield. While some qualify for protection as refugees, others are economic migrants—a distinction that leads to different treatment under international and domestic law. Almost all of these migrants come from Ethiopia or Somalia.[1] Some depart from Obock, Djibouti, crossing the Red Sea to reach Yemen in a journey that takes about seven hours; others depart from Bossaso, on the Puntland (Somalia) coast, crossing the Gulf of Aden in one to three days (see Figure 1). These crossings take place in one of the most lawless maritime regions in the world. Many migrants die during the boat

---

1 For example, 99.9 percent of these migrants came from either Somalia or Ethiopia in 2010-14. United Nations High Commissioner for Refugees (UNHCR), "Yemen—New Arrivals at Coast from 2006 to October 2013," (UN dataset accessed August 11, 2016); Regional Mixed Migration Secretariat (RMMS), "Monthly Summaries," accessed August 18, 2016. While Somalia and Ethiopia are the primary points of departure, Djibouti mainly serves as a transit country for migrants. Similarly, the Eritrean coastline is well guarded by authorities, so most migrants leaving Eritrea do so by clandestinely crossing land borders with Sudan and Ethiopia. A growing number then travel onwards to Egypt or Libya to try and cross the Mediterranean to Europe. See RMMS, "Eritrea," updated June 2016.

journey,[2] and numerous reports document the horrific abuses migrants suffer at the hands of smugglers.[3]

Figure 1. Maritime Routes between the Horn of Africa and Yemen

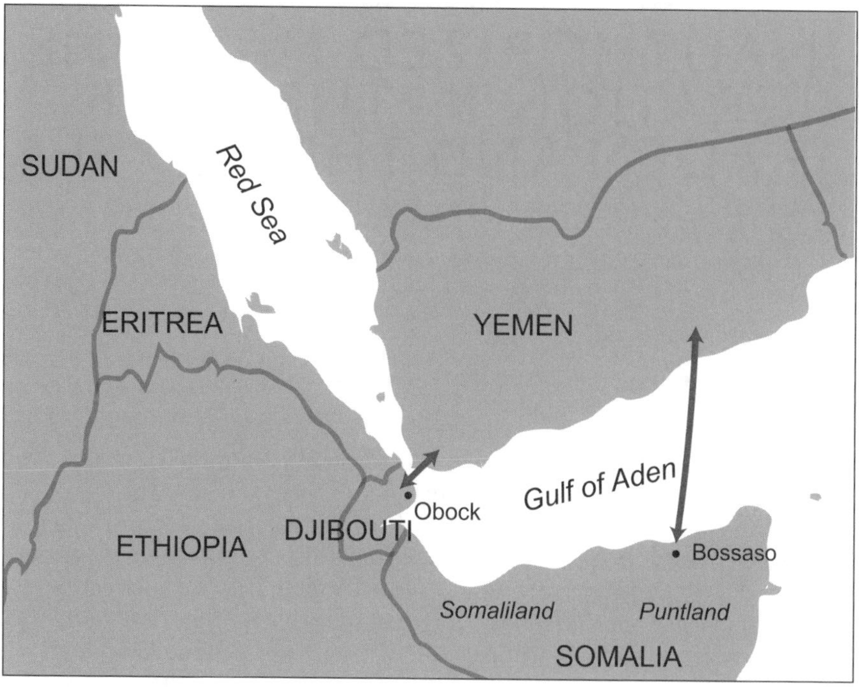

Source: Author's rendering. Original map from NuclearVacuum/Wikimedia, used under a Creative Commons BY-SA license.

Between 2006 and 2012, the number of migrants landing on the Yemeni coast each year (from both routes) more than quadrupled, growing from about 26,000 to 108,000 arrivals a year.[4] Although the number of

---

2 Ninety-five deaths were recorded for the Horn of Africa-Yemen crossing in 2015, and nearly 250 were reported in 2014—up from five in 2013 and four in 2012. See UNHCR, "New Arrivals in Yemen Comparison 2010-2013," updated October 2013; UNHCR, "New Arrivals in Yemen Comparison 2013-2016," updated February 29, 2016.

3 See, for example, RMMS, *Migrant Smuggling in the Horn of Africa & Yemen: The Political Economy and Protection Risks* (Nairobi: Danish Refugee Council, 2013); Human Rights Watch (HRW), *Hostile Shores: Abuse and Refoulement of Asylum Seekers and Refugees in Yemen* (New York: HRW, 2009); and United Nations Office on Drugs and Crime (UNODC), *Transnational Organized Crime in Eastern Africa: A Threat Assessment* (Vienna: UNODC, 2013).

4 UNHCR, "Yemen—New Arrivals at Coast from 2006 to October 2013."

arrivals fell to 62,000 in 2013, as Saudi Arabia cracked down on illegal immigration and deported tens of thousands of migrants, maritime arrivals in Yemen increased again in 2014, reaching almost 91,592.[5] However, the outbreak of civil war in Yemen in March 2015 disrupted this unidirectional flow, with many migrants fleeing Yemen for the Horn of Africa while others continued to arrive.[6] Between March 2015 and August 2016, the United Nations High Commissioner for Refugees (UNHCR) recorded the arrival of 180,000 migrants traveling from Yemen to Saudi Arabia, Oman, Djibouti, Somalia, and Ethiopia; one-third were Yemeni nationals, but two-thirds were migrants who had transited through Yemen after departing from Somalia or elsewhere.[7]

Beginning in the third quarter of 2015, crossings towards Yemen rebounded once more, despite continuing violence and instability. Surges in conflict have been a key driver of mixed migration flows in the region, not only providing many with the impetus to move in the first place, but also disrupting the law enforcement that might, in times of peace, inhibit unauthorized travel.[8] Widespread poverty and a lack of economic opportunities for these young populations is another crucial driver for the flows.[9] This chapter first sets out who is on the move and why, before examining the steps that national policymakers and international organizations are taking within the region to manage these mixed migration flows and to tackle the lucrative smuggling and trafficking industries that facilitate these journeys.

---

5 RMMS, "Regional Mixed Migration Summary for December 2014 Covering Mixed Migration Events, Trends and Data for Djibouti, Eritrea, South Sudan, Sudan, Ethiopia, Kenya, Puntland, Somalia, Somaliland and Yemen," (monthly summary, December 2014).

6 RMMS, "Regional Mixed Migration Summary for June 2015 Covering Mixed Migration Events, Trends and Data for Djibouti, Eritrea, South Sudan, Sudan, Ethiopia, Kenya, Puntland, Somalia, Somaliland and Yemen," (monthly summary, June 2015).

7 UNHCR, "Yemen: Regional Refugee and Migrant Response Plan," updated August 15, 2016.

8 See, for example, Olivia Akumu, "Shifting Tides: The Changing Nature of Mixed Migration Crossings to Yemen," RMMS, May 13, 2016.

9 According to World Bank calculations using UN Population Division data, 47 percent of Somalis and 41 percent of Ethiopians were between the ages of 0 and 14 in 2015. See World Bank, "Population Ages 0-14 (% of the Total)," accessed August 18, 2016.

I. Drivers of Maritime Migration in the Region

The Horn of Africa—encompassing Djibouti, Ethiopia, Eritrea, and Somalia—has been the origin of large-scale mixed migration flows[10] for many years, as people flee a combination of political instability, war, famine, and poverty. Migrants in the region may seek protection or opportunity in neighboring countries or may attempt to cross the Red Sea or Gulf of Aden to reach the oil-rich Gulf States. In the Gulf economies, which rely heavily on foreign labor of various skill levels, immigrants from the Horn join those from Asia, the Middle East, and North Africa to fill low- and unskilled jobs as domestic workers or laborers.[11] In 2015, international migrants made up 48 percent of the total population of Gulf Cooperation Council (GCC) countries.[12] That same year, 10 million migrants were living in Saudi Arabia—one of the primary destinations for migrants crossing into Yemen from the Horn of Africa—amounting to about one-third of its total population.[13] In Saudi Arabia, most migrants work as manual laborers or in the clerical and services sectors; up to 2 million were employed in domestic services as of 2013.[14]

Migration between the Horn of Africa and the Arabian Peninsula has a long history, with some scholars suggesting people first crossed from Africa to Eurasia via the Bab el-Mandeb strait (between present day Djibouti and Yemen) some 70,000 years ago. During the 19th and 20th centuries, migrants moved in both directions across the Gulf of Aden, as political and economic conditions shifted. Yemeni migrants traveled to the Horn of Africa in the mid-1930s, for example, to work on construction projects in Italian-occupied Ethiopia before political

---

10 Mixed migration flows include refugees and asylum seekers, unauthorized economic migrants, and victims of trafficking.

11 UNODC, *Transnational Organized Crime in Eastern Africa*, 3.

12 The Gulf Cooperation Council (GCC) countries are Bahrain, Kuwait, Oman, Qatar, Saudi Arabia, and the United Arab Emirates (UAE). See United Nations Department of Economic and Social Affairs (UN DESA), Population Division, "Trends in International Migrant Stock: The 2015 Revision" (UN database, POP/DB/MIG/Stock/Rev.2015); UN DESA, Population Division, "World Population Prospects: The 2015 Revision," Total Population—Both Sexes (UN database, 2015).

13 UN DESA, Population Division, "Trends in International Migrant Stock;" UN DESA, Population Division, "World Population Prospects."

14 RMMS, *The Letter of the Law: Regular and Irregular Migration in Saudi Arabia in a Context of Rapid Change* (Nairobi: Danish Refugee Council, 2014), 9.

turmoil during the 1960s led many to return home.[15] Employment opportunities in GCC countries have similarly attracted labor migration from both the Horn of Africa and Yemen since the economic boom of the 1970s.

More recently, maritime migration from the Horn of Africa across the Red Sea or Arabian Sea to Yemen is often linked to surges in conflict.[16] Between 1990 and 2010 the Horn of Africa experienced more than 200 armed conflicts, including a war that left Somalia without a functioning central government for 21 years.[17] Following the collapse of the Somali state in 1991, irregular maritime migration grew steadily into the early 2000s. The acceleration in maritime migration that began in 2006 (see Figure 2) coincided with rising political instability in Somalia, following battles for control of its capital, Mogadishu, and military intervention by Ethiopian, Kenyan, United Nations, and African Union troops against the Somali militant group al-Shabab.

---

15 Helen Lackner, ed., *Why Yemen Matters: A Society in Transition* (London: Saqi Books, 2014), 301.

16 Yemen Mixed Migration Task Force, "Mixed Migration from the Horn of Africa to Yemen," accessed July 23, 2015.

17 Uppsala Conflict Data Program data report 233 conflicts in this region between 1990 and 2010. These include 32 state-based armed conflicts (with a government as party to the conflict), 179 nonstate armed conflicts, and 22 campaigns of one-sided violence. Cited in Paul D. Williams, *Horn of Africa: Webs of Conflict & Pathways to Peace* (Washington, DC: The Wilson Center, 2011), 3.

Figure 2. Migrants Crossing into Yemen via the Red Sea and Arabian Sea, 2006-15, by Nationality

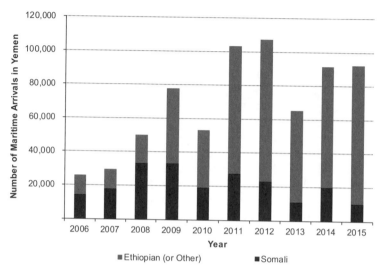

Notes: Data before 2010 is grouped into Somali and non-Somali arrivals, although the vast majority of non-Somali arrivals are Ethiopian. Between 2010 and 2015, Ethiopians accounted for 99.7-99.9 percent of this Ethiopia (or other) category annually.

Sources: United Nations High Commissioner for Refugees (UNHCR), "Yemen—New Arrivals at Coast from 2006 to October 2013," (UN dataset accessed August 11, 2016); UNHCR, "New Arrivals in Yemen Comparison 2010-2013," updated October 2013; and UNHCR, "New Arrivals in Yemen Comparison 2013-2016," updated February 29, 2016.

When UNHCR initiated the large-scale collection of data on maritime migration flows across the Gulf of Aden in 2006, most migrants were found to be Somali (55 percent in 2006, rising to 66 percent in 2008).[18] The circumstances driving Somali displacement since the late 1980s— conflict, state collapse, violence, and persecution—mean that most Somalis qualify for protection as refugees and have been granted prima facie refugee status in Yemen since 1988.[19] Other nationalities, such as Ethiopians, must undergo refugee status determinations conducted by

---

18 UNHCR, "Yemen—New Arrivals at Coast from 2006 to October 2013."

19 As defined by UNHCR, a prima facie approach recognizes the severity of conditions in a country or origin (or for stateless asylum seekers, a country of former habitual residence) and "acknowledges that those fleeing these circumstances are at risk of harm that brings them within the applicable refugee definition." As a result, individuals from such countries (in this case, Somalia) are granted refugee status without having to go through an individual status determination process. See UNHCR, *Guidelines on International Protection No.11: Prima Facie Recognition of Refugee Status* (Geneva: UNHCR, 2015).

UNHCR.[20] As the political situation in Somalia gradually improved—al-Shabab forces were pushed out of Mogadishu and other cities in 2010, and a government was formally installed in 2012—the numbers of Somalis journeying to Yemen fell. As Figure 2 illustrates, most migrants crossing into Yemen since 2008 are Ethiopian: their numbers rose significantly after 2010. In 2015 about 14,000 crossings via the Red Sea and 78,000 via the Gulf of Aden were recorded, of which 89 percent were made by Ethiopians.[21]

Rising instability, both in Ethiopia and in Yemen, is one of the factors driving Ethiopian migration to Yemen; it encourages people to leave Ethiopia and makes it easier to travel illicitly through an increasingly lawless Yemen to the Gulf States.[22] The resumption of journeys to Yemen in the second half of 2015 (see Figure 3), despite the ongoing civil war, illustrates this point.[23] Poverty and a lack of economic opportunity in Ethiopia, exacerbated by recurring drought and food insecurity, are other major drivers of migration when coupled with the knowledge that there is a huge market for migrant workers in GCC countries.[24] A 2012 survey found that economic considerations motivated most Ethiopian migration to Yemen; respondents cited low pay, poor job prospects, and high living costs at home, alongside pressure to provide for their families.[25] Research suggests that the majority of Ethiopians traveling in search of work do so as irregular migrants.[26] Unlike Somalis, therefore, most Ethiopians do not qualify for protection as refugees. Prior to March 2010, Yemen enforced a policy of arresting and deporting Ethiopians that arrived by boat and also did not recognize those designated as refugees by UNHCR in order to deter new arrivals from applying for asylum.[27] Although Yemen has since reformed this policy, allowing Ethiopians to apply for asylum, most do not apply and instead remain without legal status, working informally or paying smugglers to transport them onward to the Saudi Arabian border.[28]

---

20 RMMS, "Yemen," updated May 2016.
21 RMMS, "Regional Mixed Migration Summary for December 2015 Covering Mixed Migration Events, Trends, and Data for Djibouti, Eritrea, South Sudan, Sudan, Ethiopia, Kenya, Puntland, Somalia, Somaliland, and Yemen," (monthly summary, December 2015).
22 RMMS, *Migrant Smuggling in the Horn of Africa & Yemen*, 37–41.
23 See, for example, Akumu, "Shifting Tides."
24 UNODC, *Transnational Organized Crime in Eastern Africa*, 11.
25 RMMS, *Desperate Choices: Conditions, Risks and Protection Failures Affecting Ethiopian Migrants in Yemen* (Nairobi: Danish Refugee Council, 2012), 19–21.
26 RRMS, "Ethiopia," updated May 2016.
27 HRW, *Hostile Shores*, 11–40.
28 RMMS, *Desperate Choices*.

Figure 3. Migrants Arriving in Yemen by Sea Each Quarter, 2012-15

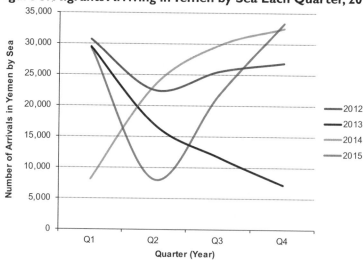

Sources: Regional Mixed Migration Secretariat (RMMS), "Monthly Summaries," accessed August 18, 2016; RMMS, "Trend Analysis," accessed August 18, 2016.

Geopolitical events can lead to a drop in arrivals, as seen in 2010 and 2013 (see Figure 2) and more recently, following the outbreak of civil war in Yemen in early 2015 (see Figure 3). Arrivals first fell in 2010, which UNHCR attributed to the declining number of Somalis crossing the Gulf of Aden following a crackdown on human trafficking by Puntland authorities and the rising insecurity of land routes to the northern regions of Somalia and through Ethiopia.[29] Saudi Arabia's Nitaqat ("Saudization") program, which encourages businesses to employ Saudi nationals and includes a crackdown on unauthorized migrant workers, led to another significant drop in crossings in 2013. Following an amnesty period during which unauthorized labor migrants could legalize their status or leave, Saudi authorities initiated mass deportations of unauthorized migrants in November 2013. In April of that year, the Saudi government also began constructing a 1,100-mile fence on the Saudi-Yemeni border to bolster national security and deter unwanted migration flows.[30] The Regional Mixed Migration Secretariat (RMMS) estimates that 170,000 Ethiopians were returned to Ethiopia between November 2013 and March 2014. Many returned destitute, having

---

29 Melissa Fleming, "Gulf of Aden: Somali Refugee Flow Slows Down Despite Ongoing Violence" (UNHCR news release, April 9, 2010).

30 BBC News, "Saudi Arabia Builds Giant Yemen Border Fence," BBC News, April 9, 2013.

spent significant sums to make the initial journey.[31] Even so, migrant arrivals into Yemen via the Red Sea and Gulf of Aden began to rise again in April 2014, eventually outpacing 2013 flows (see Figures 2 and 3). Many of those who were expelled undertook the journey once more in search of work.[32]

The outbreak of civil war in Yemen in March 2015 led to a significant drop in arrivals in the second quarter of the year (see Figure 3). By the end of 2015, there were 2.5 million people displaced within Yemen; and as of August 2016, 180,000 people (including many returning Ethiopian and Somali nationals) had fled Yemen for neighboring countries, including Somalia, Djibouti, and Ethiopia.[33] But even as people fled Yemen and the conflict continued, journeys eastward across the Red Sea and Gulf of Aden resumed in the third quarter of 2015 (see Figures 2 and 3). With monitoring operations disrupted by the conflict, the true number of arrivals could be even higher than the estimated 64,170 in the first half of 2016.[34]

II. Responses to Maritime Migration in the Region

Though maritime migration is not a new phenomenon in this region, its rapid escalation from 2006 onward and the rising death toll of migrants lost at sea have gained increased international attention.[35] Almost all migrants crossing from the Horn of Africa to Yemen pay smugglers to take them by boat from Obock, in Djibouti, or Bossaso, in

---

31 RMMS, "Ethiopia."

32 Christopher Horwood, "Deaths en Route from the Horn of Africa to Yemen and Along the Eastern Corridor from the Horn of Africa to South Africa," in *Fatal Journeys: Tracking Lives Lost during Migration*, eds. Tara Brian and Frank Laczko (Geneva: International Organization for Migration, 2014), 142.

33 UNHCR, "Yemen: Regional Refugee and Migrant Response Plan;" UNHCR, "Global Focus: Yemen," accessed July 21, 2016.

34 Akumu, "Shifting Tides;" RMMS, "Regional Mixed Migration in the Horn of Africa and Yemen in 2016: 1st Quarter Trend Summary and Analysis" (quarterly summary, 2016); RMMS, "Regional Mixed Migration in the Horn of Africa and Yemen in 2016: 2nd Quarter Trend Summary and Analysis" (quarterly summary, 2016).

35 See, for example, Reuters, "More than 60 Migrants Drown in Boat Sinking off Yemen: U.N.," Reuters, June 6, 2014; Kareem Fahim, "Shipwreck Kills Over a Dozen Ethiopian Migrants Trying to Reach Yemen," *The New York Times*, December 8, 2014; Saeed Al Batati, "African Migrants Face Death at Sea in Yemen," Al Jazeera, January 2, 2015.

Puntland (Somalia). In 2012 it was estimated that smugglers carrying migrants across the Red Sea and Gulf of Aden for about US $150 a head collectively made at least US $15 million—and this figure excludes additional bribes paid along the journey or after arrival in Yemen.[36]

The boats used by smugglers are usually in poor condition and very overcrowded—one report suggests that those with a 70- to 80-person capacity have carried as many as 250 migrants across the Gulf of Aden.[37] Some boats capsize en route. For example, in June 2014 a boat carrying 62 people sank in the Red Sea, killing all on board.[38] Numerous investigations describe incidents of suffocation amid overcrowding, as well as rape, physical assault, and murder at the hands of smugglers.[39] Migrants, many of whom cannot swim, have been reportedly forced overboard to avoid detection by authorities. In June 2013, the Danish Refugee Council warned of escalating brutality toward migrants upon their arrival in Yemen: it reported that smugglers and criminal gangs were kidnapping newly arrived migrants and extorting them and their families for ransom.[40] A 2014 RMMS study suggested women were particularly vulnerable to abuse, with reports of female migrants being abducted upon arrival and then subjected to sex trafficking or forced labor.[41] International organizations, including the Danish Refugee Council, now fund their own patrols and support Yemeni security forces in an effort to intercept new arrivals and protect them from predatory criminal elements.

In 2007, at least 1,400 migrants were reported to have died (or were missing and presumed dead), while crossing the Red Sea or Gulf of Aden. While these data likely underestimate fatalities, they hint at the magnitude of the true death toll at sea.[42] Since then, the number of dead or missing migrants has steadily fallen (see Table 1), although a spike in 2014 demonstrates the continuing dangers of these crossings. (For

---

36 UNODC, *Transnational Organized Crime in Eastern Africa*, 17–8.

37 HRW, *Hostile Shores*, 17.

38 Ariane Rummery, "Red Sea Tragedy Leaves 62 Dead in Deadliest Crossing of the Year" (UNHCR news release, June 6, 2014).

39 See, for example, HRW, *Hostile Shores*; UNODC, *Transnational Organized Crime in Eastern Africa*; Glen Johnson, "Sailing to Yemen with Human Traffickers," Al Jazeera, July 18, 2011.

40 Danish Refugee Council, "Protecting Migrants against Increased Violence," Reuters, June 5, 2013.

41 RMMS, *Abused & Abducted: The Plight of Female Migrants from the Horn of Africa to Yemen* (Nairobi: Danish Refugee Council, 2014).

42 For a detailed account of migrant deaths along these routes and how these data are collected (including the limitations), see Horwood, "Deaths en Route from the Horn of Africa," 139-76.

comparison, between January and September 2014, there were fewer deaths recorded in the Caribbean, but more fatalities recorded in the Bay of Bengal and the Mediterranean.[43])

Table 1. Number of Migrants Reported Dead or Missing in the Red Sea or Gulf of Aden, 2006-15

Year	Number of Migrants Reported Dead/Missing
2006	638
2007	1,400
2008	743
2009	376
2010	15
2011	131
2012	43
2013	5
2014	246
2015	95

Note: These data are compiled from NGO interviews with new arrivals in Yemen, who provide information about their journey, including the number of migrants on their boats and details of other boats they may have seen. It is likely these reports underestimate the total death toll along these routes.
Sources: UNHCR, "New Arrivals in Yemen Comparison 2010-2013;" UNHCR, "New Arrivals in Yemen Comparison 2013-2016;" Christopher Horwood, "Deaths en Route from the Horn of Africa to Yemen and Along the Eastern Corridor from the Horn of Africa to South Africa," in *Fatal Journeys: Tracking Lives Lost during Migration*, eds. Tara Brian and Frank Laczko (Geneva: International Organization for Migration, 2014), 153.

The declining recorded death rate since 2009 can be attributed in part to the routes recent migrants have chosen and to the attitudes of smugglers towards their human cargo. From 2009, more migrants began to use the shorter, safer route from Obock rather than the longer Bossaso route, infamous for extortion and abuses; however, this trend reversed in late 2014, with the majority of migrants once again opting to depart from Bossaso, reportedly to avoid the rising risks of abuse by smugglers along the Obock route, detection at sea, and detention by Yemeni military authorities upon arrival.[44] (Figure 4 sets out the shifting relative popularity of these two routes between 2008 and 2015.) Crucially, smugglers on both routes increasingly recognize the value of keeping migrants alive, if only to sell them to criminal networks in Yemen for further extortion.[45]

---

43 Tara Brian and Frank Laczko, "Counting Migrant Deaths: An International Overview," in *Fatal Journeys: Tracking Lives Lost during Migration.*, eds. Tara Brian and Frank Laczko (Geneva: International Organization for Migration, 2014), 18.
44 Akumu, "Shifting Tides;" RMMS, "Yemen."
45 RMMS, *Migrant Smuggling in the Horn of Africa & Yemen*, 22; HRW, *Hostile Shores*.

Figure 4. Migrants Arriving in Yemen, by Maritime Route, 2008-15

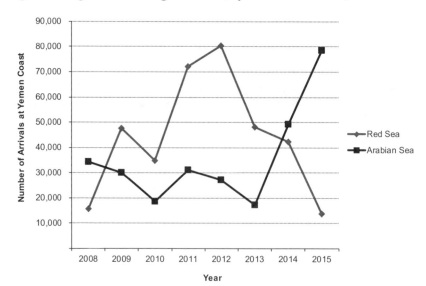

Sources: UNHCR, "Yemen—New Arrivals at Coast from 2006 to October 2013;" UNHCR, "New Arrivals in Yemen Comparison 2010-2013;" UNHCR, "New Arrivals in Yemen Comparison 2013-2016."

A. Policies to Protect Irregular Migrants Undertaking the Journey

Yemen is a signatory to the United Nations Convention on the Law of the Sea (1982), the International Convention for the Safety of Life at Sea (1974), and the International Convention on Maritime Search and Rescue (1979). Notably, Djibouti and Somalia are also signatories to the Convention on the Law of the Sea, and Djibouti, Eritrea, and Ethiopia are all signatories to the Convention for the Safety of Life at Sea. These instruments obligate state parties to assist and rescue any people found at sea—regardless of nationality, numbers, maritime zone, or mode of transport—and to deliver them to a place of safety.

In practice, the Gulf of Aden remains a very dangerous region and is renowned for piracy. By 2007, most incidents of piracy worldwide took place in the Gulf of Aden; piracy ransoms in Somalia were as high as US $160 million in 2011 (when the annual budget of the Puntland government stood at US $20 million).[46] In 2008, the U.S. Navy established a Maritime Security Patrol Area (MSPA), with air and naval patrols carried out by forces from the 16 Member States of the Combined Task Force 150 (CTF-150).[47] There is also now a lucrative business for private security firms, such as G4S, that provide armed guards for large ships traveling through the region.

Though international cooperation and private-sector contributions have improved the security of major shipping routes, few national or international patrols monitor smaller boats, including those that carry irregular migrants, particularly in open waters. The coasts of Yemen, where they meet the Red Sea and the Gulf of Aden, are patrolled by the Yemeni coast guard and security forces. These forces cooperate with teams from humanitarian organizations to intercept arrivals and transport them to UNHCR reception centers, where they are registered; provided with food, water, and medical care; and given the option to seek asylum if they wish. The Yemeni Red Crescent and the Danish Refugee Council also conduct joint patrols along the Red Sea coastline, while the Society for Humanitarian Solidarity (a Yemeni NGO) patrols the Gulf of Aden coastline.[48] Meanwhile, smugglers wary of detention by Yemeni security officials have been known to force their passengers to disembark several hundred meters off the Yemeni coast—often at night—and swim to shore.[49] Those migrants who cannot swim the distance are left to drown.

The scope of patrols is restricted by limited funding, insecurity, and corruption: one investigator traveling with migrants from Obock to Yemen documented the collusion of local Djiboutian police, who demanded bribes from each passenger.[50] A 2010 study suggests that the profits authorities accrue from this "migration economy" and its

---

46 Jatin Dua and Ken Menkhaus, "The Context of Contemporary Policy: The Case of Somalia," *Journal of International Criminal Justice* 10, no. 4 (2012): 754.

47 Combined Task Force 150 (CTF-150) operates in the Red Sea, Gulfs of Aden and Oman, and the Indian Ocean. Since its establishment in 2001, naval forces from Australia, Canada, Denmark, France, Germany, Italy, the Netherlands, New Zealand, Pakistan, Portugal, Singapore, South Korea, Spain, Turkey, the United Kingdom, and the United States have participated in it. See Combined Maritime Forces, "CTF-150: Maritime Security," accessed July 23, 2015.

48 UNHCR, *Yemen: Mixed Migration Update, January 2015* (Geneva: UNHCR, 2015).

49 HRW, *Hostile Shores*, 22.

50 Johnson, "Sailing to Yemen."

networks act as a "powerful disincentive to formally regulated border controls" in the region.[51]

B. National Initiatives to Address Mixed Migration Flows

Countries in the region have undertaken a number of national initiatives to address mixed migration flows, although implementation continues to be an issue. Several countries have passed antitrafficking and antismuggling legislation—including Law No. 133 in Djibouti on the *Fight against Trafficking in Persons and Illicit Smuggling of Migrants*, passed in March 2016. However, finding the financial and political capital to operationalize these laws remains a challenge.[52] Limited resources, corruption, and authorities' lack of familiarity with these legal protections have stymied the effective implementation and enforcement of these laws.[53] Another approach is to promote legal labor migration channels. In 2013, Ethiopia barred its citizens from leaving the country to work in the Middle East. It subsequently revised this overseas employment policy to include greater monitoring of recruitment agencies and punish illegal recruitment. Before lifting the ban in 2015, Ethiopian officials also held negotiations on legal migration channels with countries like Saudi Arabia and the United Arab Emirates.[54] Yet the continued emigration of Ethiopian nationals between 2013 and 2015, when the ban was in place, illustrates the limitations of state actions to control mixed migration flows in this region.

C. Regional Cooperation on Mixed Migration Flows

There have also been a number of efforts to bring together governments and civil society to gather information on and formulate common responses to irregular migration in the region. While progress has been made on information gathering, most notably in the form of

---

51 Sally Healy and Ginny Hill, "Yemen and Somalia: Terrorism, Shadow Networks and the Limitations of State-Building" (Chatham House Middle East and North Africa Programme Briefing Paper, Chatham House, London, October 2010), 9-10.

52 For more information on antitrafficking and antismuggling legislation in countries such as Djibouti, Ethiopia, Saudi Arabia, and Yemen, see U.S. Department of State, *Trafficking in Persons Report, June 2016* (Washington, DC: U.S. Department of State, 2016).

53 Bram Frouws and Christopher Horwood, "What If? Scenarios of Implemented and Enhanced Migration Legislation and Policies in the Horn of Africa and Yemen" (RMMS Discussion Paper, No. 1, RMMS, Nairobi, January 2015), 6.

54 U.S. Department of State, *Trafficking in Persons Report, June 2016*; RMMS, "Ethiopia."

the RMMS, cooperation on implementing responses has been much slower.

The first Mixed Migration Task Force (MMTF) in the region was set up in April 2007 in Nairobi, Kenya with IOM and UNHCR as co-chairs, and other UN agencies and international organizations as members. It was created with the aim of gathering information on and designing policies to address mixed migration from Somalia.[55] In May 2008, UNHCR convened a regional conference in Sana'a, Yemen on international migration and refugee protection in the Gulf of Aden. It was attended by government representatives from the Middle East and North Africa (MENA) region, regional and international organizations, and donor countries.[56] The resulting declaration called for more action to address the root causes of mixed migration flows in the region: specifically, the ongoing conflict in Somalia and the lack of economic opportunities across much of the Horn of Africa. It recommended establishing mixed migration task forces in affected countries (Yemen in particular), sharing information among government authorities on irregular migration, introducing legal migration channels, and promoting greater regional cooperation to protect migrants and combat smuggling and trafficking. Following this conference, an MMTF was established in Yemen in June 2008 to coordinate regional action on irregular maritime migration.[57] Similar task forces were subsequently established in both Somaliland and Puntland, as well as in Djibouti and Kenya. However, these task forces convene very infrequently, with consequently limited impact.

A number of regional conferences have also touched on mixed migration flows through the Horn of Africa and the Gulf of Aden in the last few years. One success story has been RMMS, which was established on the recommendation of these stakeholder meetings between 2008 and 2011 to collect, analyze, and disseminate data and in-depth research on mixed migration trends and policies in the Horn of Africa and Yemen

---

55 This Mixed Migration Task Force (MMTF) was set up under the Inter-Agency Standing Committee (IASC). See Mixed Migration Task Force Somalia, *Mixed Migration through Somalia and across the Gulf of Aden* (Geneva: UNHCR, 2008), 2.
56 The conference was funded by the European Commission and convened by UNHCR with the assistance of MMTF Somalia. See UNHCR, *Regional Conference on Refugee Protection and International Migration in the Gulf of Aden, Sana'a, Yemen, 19-20 May 2008, Summary Report* (Geneva: UNHCR, 2008).
57 MMTF Yemen is jointly chaired by UNHCR and International Organization for Migration, and administered by the Danish Refugee Council.

region (and beyond).[58] However, implementing many of the policy recommendations that arise from these meetings and from RMMS research has proved to be problematic.[59] Since 2011, the Regional Committee on Mixed Migration for the Horn of Africa and Yemen has convened government and NGO representatives annually to discuss mixed migration issues and formulate recommendations. And in November 2013, Yemen convened the Third Regional Conference on Asylum and Migration, which was held in Sana'a and produced a declaration calling for greater international coordination. Increased coordination, it stressed, would help build law enforcement capacity in the region and address the drivers of migration—including through expanded labor migration opportunities. But in both cases, the resources and political will to move forward on these nonbinding recommendations have proved elusive, especially in light of the ongoing civil war in Yemen.[60]

III. Conclusion

Yemen and the states that comprise the Horn of Africa are some of the poorest countries in the world and are beset by chronic insecurity and conflict.[61] Limited resources, coupled with weak state institutions, makes irregular maritime migration extremely difficult to bring under control. This challenge was acknowledged in the Sana'a Declaration, which highlighted the need to promote economic development in countries of origin and awareness of the dangers of maritime migration, while also improving reception conditions at destination.[62]

Recent decades have seen notable commitments—at least on paper—to the improvement of migration management, but implementation remains a challenge. Many countries in the region are signatories to the 1951 Refugee Convention and 1967 Protocol, as well as the Palermo

---

58 For more information on the activities and objectives of RMMS, see RMMS, "About RMMS," accessed August 23, 2016.

59 For a discussion of the outcomes of recent regional processes and instruments on migration flows through the Greater Horn of Africa, see Christopher Horwood with Kate Hooper, *Protection on the Move: Eritrean Refugee Flows through the Greater Horn of Africa* (Washington, DC: Migration Policy Institute, forthcoming).

60 Ibid.

61 In 2015, Yemen, Djibouti, and Ethiopia were ranked at 160, 168, and 174 (of 188) respectively on the United Nations Development Program (UNDP) Human Development Index; UNDP did not publish data for Somalia. See UNDP, *Human Development Report 2015: Work for Human Development* (New York: UNDP, 2015).

62 Regional Conference on Asylum and Migration, "Sana'a Declaration," November 13, 2013.

Protocols on trafficking and migrant smuggling, and have passed (or are passing) domestic antitrafficking legislation. In turn, regional conferences have produced numerous recommendations (such as the Sana'a Declaration) for managing mixed migration flows and tackling migrant-smuggling networks. But countries often lack the resources, capacity, or political will to fully implement and enforce these measures. Weak state institutions are a key issue: numerous studies describe the weak judiciary and law enforcement in these countries, illustrated by the reported collusion of local authorities in migrant-smuggling and trafficking operations.[63] Better management of migration thus often hinges on addressing broader governance issues such as improving the rule of law, strengthening government institutions, and tackling corruption as well as securing the financial resources to accomplish these goals. Donor governments in the region and beyond have both humanitarian and practical incentives to contribute to these efforts.

Without addressing the major drivers of migration in the region, such as chronic insecurity and poverty, people will continue to move in search of safety and opportunity. Besides placing a greater emphasis on border enforcement and measures to counter smuggling and trafficking, policymakers must promote safer alternatives to unauthorized maritime migration. One step is to educate people about the dangers of these illicit journeys across land and sea, including the risk of abduction and abuse, and the difficulties in reaching Saudi Arabia or other Gulf States. Another step is to better regulate existing labor migration channels by taking steps to monitor recruitment agencies and contracts, regulate costs, educate prospective migrants about their rights, and promote the welfare of their nationals in other countries.[64] And crucially, policymakers should consider expanding opportunities for legal migration. While negotiations to facilitate a greater degree of regional labor mobility remain nascent, more progress has been made toward reaching bilateral labor migration agreements, such as the talks taking place between Ethiopia and Saudi Arabia.[65] Such agreements have the potential to offer more people in the region safer, legal channels to pursue livelihoods abroad.

---

63 See, for example, Human Rights Watch, *Yemen's Torture Camps: Abuse of Migrants by Human Traffickers in a Climate of Impunity* (New York: HRW, 2014); Healy and Hill, *Yemen and Somalia*; RMMS, *Migrant Smuggling in the Horn of Africa & Yemen.*
64 Frouws and Horwood, "What If?"
65 Ethiopian News Agency, "Ethiopia to Sign Labor Exchange Deals with Saudi Arabia, UAE," Ethiopian News Agency, March 23, 2016; Nicolas Niarchos, "The Dangerous Route of Ethiopian Migrants," *The New Yorker*, July 20, 2016.

Works Cited

Akumu, Olivia. 2016. Shifting Tides: The Changing Nature of Mixed Migration Crossings to Yemen. Regional Mixed Migration Secretariat (RMMS), May 13, 2016. www.regionalmms.org/index.php/research-publications/feature-articles/item/1-shifting-tides-the-changing-nature-of-mixed-migration-c.

Al Batati, Saeed. 2015. African Migrants Face Death at Sea in Yemen. Al Jazeera, January 2, 2015. www.aljazeera.com/news/middleeast/2014/12/african-migrants-face-death-at-sea-yemen-20141230114436126121.html.

BBC News. 2013. Saudi Arabia Builds Giant Yemen Border Fence. BBC News, April 9, 2013. www.bbc.com/news/world-middle-east-22086231.

Brian, Tara and Frank Laczko. 2014. Counting Migrant Deaths: An International Overview. In *Fatal Journeys: Tracking Lives Lost during Migration*, eds. Tara Brian and Frank Laczko. Geneva: International Organization for Migration (IOM). http://publications.iom.int/system/files/pdf/fataljourneys_countingtheuncounted.pdf.

Combined Maritime Forces. N.d. CTF-150: Maritime Security. Accessed July 23, 2015. http://combinedmaritimeforces.com/ctf-150-maritime-security/.

Danish Refugee Council. 2013. Protecting Migrants against Increased Violence. Reuters, June 5, 2013. http://news.trust.org//item/20130605120630-apsif/.

Dua, Jatin and Ken Menkhaus. 2012. The Context of Contemporary Policy: The Case of Somalia. *Journal of International Criminal Justice* 10 (4): 749–66.

Ethiopian News Agency. 2016. Ethiopia to Sign Labor Exchange Deals with Saudi Arabia, UAE. Ethiopian News Agency, March 23, 2016. www.ena.gov.et/en/index.php/politics/item/1030-ethiopia-to-sign-labor-exchange-deals-with-saudi-arabia-uae.

Fahim, Kareem. 2014. Shipwreck Kills Over a Dozen Ethiopian Migrants Trying to Reach Yemen. *The New York Times*, December 8, 2014. www.nytimes.com/2014/12/09/world/middleeast/ethiopia-migrants-drown-trying-to-reach-yemen.html.

Fleming, Melissa. 2010. Gulf of Aden: Somali Refugee Flow Slows Down Despite Ongoing Violence. UNHCR news release, April 9, 2010. www.unhcr.org/4bbf07089.html.

Frouws, Bram and Christopher Horwood. 2015. What If? Scenarios of Implemented and Enhanced Migration Legislation and Policies in the Horn of Africa and Yemen. RMMS Discussion Paper, No. 1, RMMS, Nairobi, January 2015. www.regionalmms.org/images/DiscussionPapers/What_if.pdf.

Healy, Sally and Ginny Hill. 2010. Yemen and Somalia: Terrorism, Shadow Networks and the Limitations of State-Building. Chatham House Middle East and North Africa Programme Briefing Paper, Chatham House, London, October 2010. www.chathamhouse.org/sites/files/chathamhouse/public/Research/Africa/bp1010_yemensomalia.pdf.

Horwood, Christopher. 2014. Deaths en Route from the Horn of Africa to Yemen and Along the Eastern Corridor from the Horn of Africa to South Africa. In *Fatal Journeys: Tracking Lives Lost during Migration*, eds. Tara Brian and Frank Laczko. Geneva: IOM. http://publications.iom.int/system/files/pdf/fatal-journeys_countingtheuncounted.pdf.

Horwood, Christopher with Kate Hooper. Forthcoming. *Protection on the Move: Eritrean Refugee Flows through the Greater Horn of Africa*. Washington, DC: Migration Policy Institute.

Human Rights Watch (HRW). 2009. *Hostile Shores: Abuse and Refoulement of Asylum Seekers and Refugees in Yemen*. New York: HRW. www.hrw.org/sites/default/files/reports/yemen1209webwcover.pdf.

———. 2014. *Yemen's Torture Camps: Abuse of Migrants by Human Traffickers in a Climate of Impunity*. New York: HRW. www.hrw.org/report/2014/05/25/yemens-torture-camps/abuse-migrants-human-traffickers-climate-impunity.

Johnson, Glen. 2011. Sailing to Yemen with Human Traffickers. Al Jazeera, July 18, 2011. www.aljazeera.com/indepth/featur es/2011/07/2011715102915967252.html.

Lackner, Helen, ed. 2014. *Why Yemen Matters: A Society in Transition*. London: Saqi Books.

Mixed Migration Task Force Somalia. 2008. *Mixed Migration through Somalia and across the Gulf of Aden*. Geneva: United Nations High Commissioner for Refugees (UNHCR). www.unhcr.org/4877716c2.html.

Niarchos, Nicolas. 2016. The Dangerous Route of Ethiopian Migrants. *The New Yorker*, July 20, 2016. www.newyorker.com/news/news-desk/the-danger-ous-route-of-ethiopian-migrants.

Regional Conference on Asylum and Migration. 2013. Sana'a Declaration. November 13, 2013. www.unhcr.org/531dbb246.pdf.

Regional Mixed Migration Secretariat (RMMS). 2012. *Desperate Choices: Conditions, Risks and Protection Failures Affecting Ethiopian Migrants in Yemen*. Nairobi: Danish Refugee Council. www.regionalmms.org/images/ResearchInitia-tives/RMMSbooklet.pdf.

———. 2013. *Migrant Smuggling in the Horn of Africa & Yemen: The Political Economy and Protection Risks*. Nairobi: Danish Refugee Council. www.regionalmms. org/images/ResearchInitiatives/Migrant_Smuggling_in_the_Horn_of_Af-rica_and_Yemen._report.pdf.

———. 2014. *Abused & Abducted: The Plight of Female Migrants from the Horn of Africa to Yemen*. Nairobi: Danish Refugee Council. www.regionalmms.org/images/ResearchInitiatives/Abused__Abducted_RMMS.pdf.

———. 2014. *The Letter of the Law: Regular and Irregular Migration in Saudi Arabia in a Context of Rapid Change*. Nairobi: Danish Refugee Council. www.region-almms.org/images/ResearchInitiatives/RMMS_Letter_of_the_Law_-_Saudi_Arabia_report.pdf.

———. 2014. Regional Mixed Migration Summary for December 2014 Covering Mixed Migration Events, Trends and Data for Djibouti, Eritrea, South Sudan, Sudan, Ethiopia, Kenya, Puntland, Somalia, Somaliland and Yemen. Monthly summary, December 2014. www.regionalmms.org/monthlysummary/December_2014_RMMS_Summary.pdf.

———. 2015. Regional Mixed Migration Summary for December 2015 Covering Mixed Migration Events, Trends, and Data for Djibouti, Eritrea, South Sudan, Sudan, Ethiopia, Kenya, Puntland, Somalia, Somaliland, and Yemen. Monthly summary, December 2015. http://regionalmms.org/monthlysummary/RMMS_Monthly_Summary_December_2015.pdf.

———. 2015. Regional Mixed Migration Summary for June 2015 Covering Mixed Migration Events, Trends and Data for Djibouti, Eritrea, South Sudan, Sudan, Ethiopia, Kenya, Puntland, Somalia, Somaliland and Yemen. Monthly summary, June 2015. www.regionalmms.org/monthlysummary/June_2015_Summary.pdf.

———. 2016. Eritrea. Updated June 2016. www.regionalmms.org/index.php/country-profiles/eritrea.

———. 2016. Ethiopia. Updated May 2016. www.regionalmms.org/index.php/country-profiles/ethiopia.

———. 2016. Regional Mixed Migration in the Horn of Africa and Yemen in 2016: 1st Quarter Trend Summary and Analysis. Quarterly summary, 2016. http://regionalmms.org/trends/RMMSQ1Trends2016.pdf.

———. 2016. Regional Mixed Migration in the Horn of Africa and Yemen in 2016: 2nd Quarter Trend Summary and Analysis. Quarterly summary, 2016. http://regionalmms.org/trends/RMMS%20Mixed%20Migration%20Trends%20Q2%202016.pdf.

———. 2016. Yemen. Updated May 2016. www.regionalmms.org/index.php/country-profiles/yemen.

———. N.d. About RMMS. Accessed August 23, 2016. www.regionalmms.org/index.php/about-us/about-rmms1.

———. N.d. Monthly Summaries. Accessed August 18, 2016. www.regionalmms.org/index.php/data-trends/monthly-summaries.

———. N.d. Trend Analysis. Accessed August 18, 2016. http://regionalmms.org/index.php/data-trends/trend-analysis.

Reuters. 2014. More than 60 Migrants Drown in Boat Sinking off Yemen: U.N. Reuters, June 6, 2014. www.reuters.com/article/2014/06/06/us-yemen-migrants-idUSKBN0EH27D20140606.

Rummery, Ariane. 2014. Red Sea Tragedy Leaves 62 Dead in Deadliest Crossing of the Year. UNHCR news release, June 6, 2014. www.unhcr.org/5391c1e56.html.

United Nations Department of Economic and Social Affairs (UN DESA), Population Division. 2015. Trends in International Migrant Stock: The 2015 Revision. UN database, POP/DB/MIG/Stock/Rev.2015. www.un.org/en/development/desa/population/migration/data/estimates2/index.shtml.

———. 2015. World Population Prospects: The 2015 Revision. Total Population – Both Sexes. UN database. https://esa.un.org/unpd/wpp/Download/Standard/Population/.

United Nations Development Program (UNDP). 2015. *Human Development Report 2015: Work for Human Development.* New York: UNDP. http://hdr.undp.org/sites/default/files/2015_human_development_report.pdf.

United Nations High Commissioner for Refugees (UNHCR). 2008. *Regional Conference on Refugee Protection and International Migration in the Gulf of Aden, Sana'a, Yemen, 19-20 May 2008, Summary Report.* Geneva: UNHCR. www.unhcr.org/48808b1a2.html.

———. 2013. New Arrivals in Yemen Comparison 2010-2013. Updated October 2013. www.mmyemen.org/wp-content/uploads/2013/06/New-Arrivals-in-Yemen-Comparison-2010-October-2013.pdf.

———. 2015. *Guidelines on International Protection No.11: Prima Facie Recognition of Refugee Status.* Geneva: UNHCR. http://reliefweb.int/sites/reliefweb.int/files/resources/558a62299.pdf.

———. 2015. *Yemen: Mixed Migration Update, January 2015.* Geneva: UNHCR. www.unhcr.org/54e35b8f9.pdf.

———. 2016. New Arrivals in Yemen Comparison 2013-2016. Updated February 29, 2016. www.unhcr.org/en-us/protection/operations/4fd5a3de9/yemen-new-arrivals-2011-2016.html.

———. 2016. Yemen: Regional Refugee and Migrant Response Plan. Updated August 15, 2016. http://data.unhcr.org/yemen/regional.php.

———. N.d. Global Focus: Yemen. Accessed July 21, 2016. http://reporting.unhcr.org/node/2647#_ga=1.167181950.1730046848.1457990030.

———. N.d. Yemen—New Arrivals at Coast from 2006 to October 2013. UN dataset. Accessed August 11, 2016. www.mmyemen.org/wp-content/uploads/2013/06/Copy-of-UNHCRYemenNewArrivals_at_Coast-2006-October-2013-1.xls.

United Nations Office on Drugs and Crime (UNODC). 2013. *Transnational Organized Crime in Eastern Africa: A Threat Assessment.* Vienna: UNODC. www.unodc.org/documents/data-and-analysis/Studies/TOC_East_Africa_2013.pdf.

U.S. Department of State. 2016. *Trafficking in Persons Report, June 2016.* Washington, DC: U.S. Department of State. www.state.gov/documents/organization/258876.pdf.

Williams, Paul D. 2011. *Horn of Africa: Webs of Conflict & Pathways to Peace.* Washington, DC: The Wilson Center. www.wilsoncenter.org/sites/default/files/Horn%20of%20Africa%20Conflict%20Mapping%20Doc-%20FINAL.pdf.

World Bank. N.d. Population Ages 0-14 (% of the Total). Accessed August 18, 2016. http://data.worldbank.org/indicator/SP.POP.0014.TO.ZS.

Yemen Mixed Migration Task Force. 2015. Mixed Migration from the Horn of Africa to Yemen. Accessed July 23, 2015. www.mmyemen.org/?page_id=58.

CHAPTER FIVE

THE MARITIME APPROACHES TO AUSTRALIA

By Kathleen Newland

Introduction

Australia is a welcoming destination for international migrants, with the notable exception of those who seek to reach its territory by sea without prior authorization. In 2015, about 28 percent of the country's population of 24 million was made up of immigrants[1]— the second-highest proportion among the high-income members of the Organization for Economic Cooperation and Development (OECD). Only tiny Luxembourg has a higher ratio of migrants to native born among OECD members. Australian legal immigrant admissions levels are robust: 189,097 migrants were granted permission to settle permanently in financial year (FY) 2014-15.[2]

Australia also has a strong history of refugee admissions. It was an early signatory of the UN Convention Relating to the Status of Refugees; in fact, it was Australia's accession in 1954 that brought the treaty into force. In addition to immigrant admissions, 13,756 people were admitted to Australia or given leave to remain in 2014-15 under the humanitarian program, including 11,009 refugees and "special humanitarian"

---

1 United Nations Department of Economic and Social Affairs (UNDESA), *International Migration Report 2015: Highlights* (New York: UNDESA Population Division, 2016), 32; Australian Bureau of Statistics, *Australian Demographic Statistics: December Quarter 2015* (Canberra: Australian Bureau of Statistics, 2015).

2 Department of Immigration and Border Protection (DIBP), *2014-15 Migration Programme Report* (Canberra: DIBP, 2015). The Australian financial year, or fiscal year, is from July 1 to June 30.

cases resettled from overseas[3]—making Australia third only to the United States and Canada as the top global refugee resettlement destination.[4] Although the target for the humanitarian program remained the same—at 13,750 persons—for FY 2015-16 and FY 2016-17, in July 2015, the Australian government announced an additional 12,000 places would be made available for people displaced by the conflicts in Syria and Iraq. The first arrivals under this program arrived in November 2015.[5] The announcement also committed Australia to raising the humanitarian intake to 18,750 by FY 2018-19.[6]

To individuals designated by the government as "illegal maritime arrivals," however, Australia is remarkably unwelcoming. Australian government policy is to intercept boats carrying unauthorized migrants headed for Australia, "where safe to do so," and either to turn them back to their point of most recent embarkation or, if this is not feasible, to transfer them to another country for processing.[7] (Australia supports two overseas processing centers located in the Pacific island nation of Nauru and on Manus Island in Papua New Guinea.) Passengers on the intercepted boats are denied any chance of settling in Australia—even if their asylum claims are adjudicated favorably. In implementing this policy, Australia has taken harsher measures than any other developed country in its efforts to deflect, divert, and deter unauthorized maritime flows.[8]

As a country with no external land borders and a highly developed system of prescreening air arrivals, Australia's efforts to prevent illegal immigration focus overwhelmingly on maritime migration. (Unauthorized migrants who overstay their visas after having entered the

---

3 DIBP, "Fact Sheet—Australia's Refugee and Humanitarian Programme," accessed August 3, 2016.

4 United Nations High Commissioner for Refugees (UNHCR), *UNHCR Resettlement Handbook and Country Chapters* (Geneva: UNHCR, 2014).

5 DIBP, "Australia's Response to the Syrian and Iraqi Humanitarian Crisis," accessed August 3, 2016.

6 Prime Minister Malcom Turnbull and Minister for Immigration and Border Protection Peter Dutton, "Operation Sovereign Borders: No Successful People Smuggling Boats in Two Years" (press release, July 27, 2016).

7 Andrew and Renata Kaldor Centre on International Refugee Law, University of New South Wales, "Turning Back Boats" (fact sheet, University of New South Wales, February 26, 2015).

8 The United States comes closest, with its policy of not admitting refugees interdicted in the Caribbean (see Chapter 6), but it does not restrict resettlement opportunities for refugees in temporary protection at its base in Guantanamo, Cuba, nor does it resettle refugees to extremely poor countries.

country legally[9] seem to cause less concern, perhaps because they have undergone a screening process prior to arrival.) Success in preventing unauthorized maritime arrivals has been portrayed as a test of government competence by both government and opposition parties at various times, and consistently so by the populist media. While the harsh deterrence policies and practices have received strong criticism internationally and among human-rights advocates at home, they have drawn broad support from the Australian public. In the general election of 2013, the opposition candidate—and soon-to-be Prime Minister— Tony Abbott campaigned on a platform whose centerpiece was "Stop the Boats." His successor, Malcolm Turnbull, has maintained the policy.

The Abbott government (September 2013–September 2015) insisted that it had "established safe and lawful operational procedures, consistent with our [Australia's] international obligations and domestic laws and ensured a safe platform for return on each occasion."[10] Moreover, it pointed out that since its policies were fully implemented, with the turnbacks of boats to points of embarkation starting in December 2013 (including direct return to the country of origin[11]), no deaths at sea have been detected among unauthorized migrants trying to reach Australia. This defense has not mollified critics, including the UN High Commissioner for Human Rights, who asserted that Australia's policy "is leading to a chain of human-rights violations, including arbitrary detention and possible torture following return to home countries."[12]

Some fear that in its determination to "stop the boats," Australia is setting the pace for a race to the bottom in responsibility for refugee

---

9   Known as "unlawful noncitizens" in Australia.

10 Address by Scott E. Morrison, Minister of Immigration and Border Protection, "A New Force Protecting Australia's Borders," before the Lowy Institute for International Policy, Sydney, May 9, 2014. The "safe platforms for return" include the transfer of intercepted passengers to Australian lifeboats loaded with just enough fuel to reach the place of last embarkation (usually Indonesia).

11 According to the Andrew and Renata Kaldor Centre on International Refugee Law, "Over 1,100 Asylum Seekers Have Been Forcibly Returned to Sri Lanka since October 2012." See Andrew and Renata Kaldor Centre on International Refugee Law, "Sri Lanka and Australia after the War: A Forum on War Justice and the Indefinite Detention of Refugees," University of New South Wales, March 4, 2014; Andrew and Renata Kaldor Centre on International Refugee Law, "46 Vietnamese Were Returned Directly to Vietnam" (newsletter, Andrew and Renata Kaldor Centre for International Refugee Law, University of New South Wales, Sydney, May 11, 2015.

12 Opening Statement by Zeid Ra'ad Al Hussein, United Nations High Commissioner for Human Rights at the 27th Session of the Human Rights Council, Geneva, September 8, 2014.

protection in a context of maritime migration flows that include both humanitarian and economic migrants. The Abbott government was unresponsive to international or domestic criticism of its policies, and even recommended that other countries should follow its lead. Indeed, then Prime Minister Abbott told European governments in 2015 that "the only way you can stop the deaths [of maritime migrants in the Mediterranean] is to stop the boats," while his foreign minister said: "We have managed to stop the flow of people via the people smuggling trade but we have to be ever vigilant. So we are happy to share our experiences."[13]

Malcolm Turnbull, who became Prime Minister in September 2015, has stopped short of giving advice to European governments on how to handle immigration issues, citing geographical differences between Australia and Europe that fundamentally changed the circumstances of irregular maritime migration policy.[14] Nevertheless, expectations that unauthorized immigration and detention of migrants would play a lesser role in the July 2016 Australian election than it did in 2013 were quashed when Immigration Minister Peter Dutton made disparaging remarks about refugees who were "innumerate" as well as "illiterate in their own language." Turnbull backed his minister, claiming Dutton was an "outstanding Immigration Minister."[15] He then led the Liberal-National Coalition to a general election victory in July 2016 with its majority retained, albeit by only one seat. The major opposition party, Labor, did not advocate for substantial changes to the government's policy on maritime arrivals, likely because the policy seemed to have widespread public approval and because the party had been punished by the electorate in the 2013 election for adopting (and then reversing) a more liberal policy.

I. The Path to Zero Tolerance

Like most countries, Australia has long had a preference for planned and orderly migration—but it has not always rejected unauthorized

13 Jane Norman, "Tony Abbott Urges Europe to Adopt Stronger Border Protection Policies Following Migrant Boat Sinkings," Australian Broadcasting Corporation, April 21, 2015.

14 Katharine Murphy, "Turnbull Rebukes Abbott: I Won't Give Germany Advice about Refugees," The Guardian, November 13, 2015.

15 Francis Keany and Stephanie Anderson, "Election 2016: Malcolm Turnbull Backs 'Outstanding' Peter Dutton after Refugee Comments," Australian Broadcasting Corporation, May 18, 2016.

boat arrivals out of hand. The first "boat people" arrived in Australia in 1976 from Vietnam, and were accepted as refugees. Over the next several years, more than 2,000 refugees made their way from Indochina to Australia under their own power. Australia was an important partner in international cooperative arrangements to rescue, disembark, and resettle refugees in the aftermath of the Vietnam War, up to and including the Comprehensive Plan of Action in 1989.[16]

By the early 1990s, however, concern mounted that some boat people were not necessarily refugees, and in 1992 legislation was passed to permit the detention of unauthorized maritime arrivals. In 1994, detention was mandated. Arrivals by sea continued, however, and in 1999 Australia created separate asylum tracks for authorized and unauthorized entrants. Those who arrived legally (that is, with a visa) and then requested asylum could expect a permanent protection visa immediately upon acceptance of their asylum claim. For the unauthorized, a successful claim earned a three-year, temporary protection visa (TPV) that could be renewed only if the need for protection remained. Observers have pointed out that this practice is inconsistent with the Refugee Convention proviso that refugees must not be penalized for entering a country illegally to seek protection.[17]

The decision to discourage unauthorized maritime arrivals by denying them a permanent protection visa was accompanied by energetic efforts to stop maritime arrivals before they left their final point of transit, which for most was Indonesia. Under the terms of the Regional Cooperation Arrangement signed in 2000 by Australia, Indonesia, and the International Organization for Migration (IOM), Indonesia agreed to detain suspected unauthorized migrants (most of whom were assumed to be headed for Australia).[18] IOM agreed to screen the migrants and inform them of their options: (1) assisted voluntary return to their country of origin; (2) onward movement to a country they had permission to enter; or (3) assessment of their asylum claim, if they wished to make one, by the United Nations High Commissioner for Refugees (UNHCR) in Indonesia. Those who were found to be in need of protection were referred for resettlement; those who were not were referred back to IOM for repatriation. About 30 percent of those assessed by UNHCR were found to be refugees, and about one-quarter of these were

16 See Chapter 1.
17 IRIN, "Migration: Timeline of the Australian Asylum-Seeker Debate," IRIN, September 20, 2011.
18 Amy Nethery, Brynna Rafferty-Brown, and Savitri Taylor, "Exporting Detention: Australia-Funded Immigration Detention in Indonesia," *Journal of Refugee Studies* 26, no. 1 (2012): 88-109.

resettled in Australia.[19] Australia paid the largest share of the costs of all three partners in the Regional Cooperation Arrangement.

A major point of inflection in Australian policy toward maritime arrivals came in 2001, following the *M.V. Tampa* episode (see Chapter 1). The passengers rescued by the *Tampa*, most of them from Afghanistan and Iraq, were processed in the tiny Pacific island nation of Nauru. Offshore processing became the germ of Australia's "Pacific Strategy," later known as the "Pacific Solution." A suite of legislation, comprising the *Border Protection Act* (September 2001) and the *Migration Legislation Amendment* (June 2002), made major changes to the way the country dealt with unauthorized migrants attempting to reach Australia by sea. This legislation:

- Excised Christmas Island and several other offshore territories from Australia's asylum regime established by the *Migration Act of 1958*, which meant that people who landed there could not apply for asylum

- Established that unauthorized migrants intercepted at sea or on one of the excised territories would be ineligible for an Australian visa

- Instituted routine tracking and interception of "suspected illegal entry vessels" and their forcible return to (in most cases) Indonesia

- Authorized the transfer of persons intercepted at sea to a location outside Australia for the processing of their asylum claims, if any, and for repatriation if they were not found to be in need of protection.

Australia concluded agreements with Nauru and Papua New Guinea to host offshore processing centers. Here, intercepted migrants were detained in conditions condemned by human-rights groups as wholly inadequate to preserve the physical and mental health of the detainees (who, on Nauru, included substantial numbers of children). Processing times were slow, as was the wait for resettlement to a country other than Australia. Several detainees in the offshore centers died, by suicide, violence, or inadequate medical care.[20]

---

19 Erin Patrick and Betsy Cooper, "Appendix C: Australia and the Pacific Strategy," in *The New "Boat People": Ensuring Safety and Determining Status*, eds. Joanne van Selm and Betsy Cooper (Washington, DC: Migration Policy Institute, 2006), 83–4.
20 Monash University, Border Crossing Observatory, "Australian Border Deaths Database," accessed July 22, 2016.

The Pacific Solution ushered in a dramatic decline in boat arrivals, but it sparked other problems. Protests and condemnations of conditions in the offshore detention centers mounted (this was true of the mainland centers as well). Australia's image abroad as a defender of humane values suffered, especially after two migrant ships sank within a year of the strategy's introduction in 2001, resulting in the loss of 579 lives. People at home and abroad wondered if the results of the Pacific Solution were worth its human, financial, and reputational costs. In the first few years (up to 2005), 58 percent of those assessed to be refugees in the offshore processing centers were resettled to Australia.[21]

Finding other countries to take refugees intercepted by Australian forces was difficult. The United States, facing similar problems with refugees interdicted in the Caribbean, signed a mutual assistance agreement with Australia in 2007, under which each country would resettle up to 200 refugees intercepted by the other. The goal was to meet their protection obligations while denying unauthorized migrants their preferred "migration outcome."[22] In fact, very few people were transferred under this arrangement.

After the 2007 elections in Australia brought a Labor government to power, the Labor leadership denounced the Pacific Solution and formally brought an end to most of its features in 2008, closing the offshore processing centers and pulling back on the pursuit of migrant ships. Domestically, it abolished the TPV for refugees who had arrived illegally in favor of permanent residence, and reduced the use of mandatory detention. Perhaps predictably, the number of unauthorized boat arrivals began to climb steadily. By 2010, it had reached about 6,000 and had again become a domestic political issue. The Labor Party changed its leadership, and the new Prime Minister declared the intention to build—or rebuild—a regional strategy that would again feature offshore processing.

Some new approaches were also proposed: for example, in 2011 the government negotiated an arrangement with Malaysia to swap 800 asylum seekers who arrived in Australia by boat for 4,000 refugees from Myanmar in Malaysia. The arrangement was invalidated by the Australian High Court before it could be implemented, however. Among other reasons, the High Court cited the nonbinding nature of the agreement and the fact that Malaysia is not a signatory to the Refugee Convention. If refugees sent to Malaysia by Australia were forced to

21 Patrick and Cooper, 85–7.
22 Nick Squires, "US and Australia to Swap Asylum Seekers," *The Telegraph*, April 18, 2007.

return to a country where their lives or freedom would be in danger, this would violate Australia's obligations under the Refugee Convention. In the meantime, the government signed an agreement with Papua New Guinea to reestablish an offshore processing center on Manus Island. While the number of arrivals dipped in 2011, they resumed a strong upward trend in 2012. The year 2013 saw a new record set, exceeding 20,700 arrivals,[23] setting in motion a full-scale political and operational crisis. As has been noted, unauthorized maritime migration was a major issue in the election campaign of 2013.[24]

II. The Policy Framework of 2015-16

Liberal Party leader Tony Abbott became Prime Minister in a Liberal-National Coalition (LNC) government in September 2013 and created Operation Sovereign Borders on his first day in office.[25] It was the centerpiece of an effort to stop unauthorized maritime arrivals from reaching Australia. From a high of 48 boats in July 2013, only five arrived in October 2013 and another five in November. Just one boat reached Australia in 2014, in the month of July (its passengers were transferred to Nauru).[26] None arrived in the following two years. As of June 22, 2016, a total of 28 boats carrying migrants had been turned away by actions under Operation Sovereign Borders since the coalition government assumed power in September 2013. Most of the features of the Pacific Solution have been reinstated and reinforced, and new

---

23 Marie McAuliffe and Victoria Mence, "Global Irregular Maritime Migration: Current and Future Challenges" (Occasional Paper Series 07/2014, DIBP, Irregular Migration Research Programme, April 2014).

24 Although in 2016 both parties supported the governments' hardline stance on irregular maritime arrivals, Labor leader Bill Shorten suggested that his party, if elected, would abandon the process of Temporary Protection Visas (TPVs) and grant permanent residency to around 30,000 asylum seekers who had arrived under the previous Labor government. See Joe Kelly and Rosie Lewis, "Federal Election 2016: Rudd-Gillard Asylum Seekers to Get Visas," *The Australian*, June 16, 2016.

25 Operation Sovereign Borders is "a military-led, whole-of-government effort to counter maritime people smuggling," involving 15 government departments and agencies, according to its commander, Lieutenant General Angus Campbell. See Remarks by Angus Campbell, Lieutenant General of the Australian Army, "Operation Sovereign Borders: Initial Reflections and Future Outlook," to the Australian Strategic Policy Institute, Barton, Australia, May 15, 2014.

26 DIBP, "Operation Sovereign Borders," accessed August 5, 2016.

measures have been introduced—many of them extremely controversial. Several have spurred legal and diplomatic action.[27]

Figure 1. Number of Boats and Maritime Migrant Arrivals in Australia, by Calendar Year, 1989 to 2014

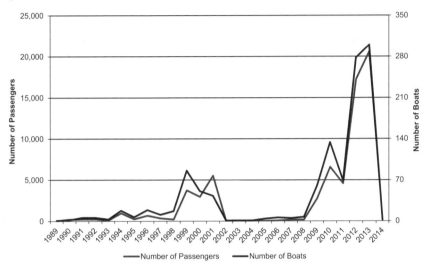

Source: Janet Phillips, "Boat Arrivals and Boat 'Turnbacks' in Australia since 1976: A Quick Guide to the Statistics," Parliament of Australia, September 11, 2015.

The interception of boats and embarkation of their passengers by Australian ships, along with the refusal of the Australian government to accept the obligation to protect refugees among those passengers, contradicts the position of the UNHCR Executive Committee: a state that voluntarily takes control of a seaworthy vessel has the same responsibilities for any refugees onboard as it would have if those refugees were inside its territory. A minimalist interpretation of the obligation of nonrefoulement[28] leaves other states, less capable than Australia, with the responsibility of protection.

---

27 See, for example, Gabrielle Appleby, "Australia's Rigid Immigration Barrier," *The New York Times*, May 7, 2015; Kaitlyn Pennington-Hill, "Australia Makes a U-Turn with the Revival of the Pacific Solution: Should Asylum Seekers Find a New Destination?" *Washington University Global Studies Law Review* 13, no. 3 (2015): 585–603.

28 "Refoulement" is legal term for forcible return; as used in the context of the 1951 Refugee Convention, "nonrefoulement" expresses the obligation of states not to return refugees to a place where their lives or liberty would be in danger.

Turnbacks and towbacks into Indonesian territorial waters strained Australia's relations with that country[29] and may be seen as a violation of the *Law of the Sea*. The Australian government acknowledged that of 12 towbacks toward Indonesia, six involved inadvertent breaches of Indonesian territorial waters, for which Australia was compelled to apologize. Relations between the two countries deteriorated further in June 2015, when allegations surfaced that the smugglers piloting a boat carrying 65 asylum seekers (most from Bangladesh, Myanmar, and Sri Lanka) were paid AU $40,000 to return to Indonesia with the asylum seekers after being intercepted in international waters by Australian boats. The Australian government neither confirmed nor denied the charge, consistent with its policy of not commenting on "on-water" operations, even as the government of Indonesia asked for an explanation and said that if the incident occurred it represented a "new low" in Australian policy. The Indonesian government launched an investigation and asked the Australian ambassador for an explanation.[30] Legal scholars have concluded that if the alleged payment to the smugglers was made, it may be a violation of the Protocol against the Smuggling of Migrants by Land, Air, and Sea of the International Convention against Transnational Organized Crime.[31]

Most of the asylum seekers intercepted at sea under Operation Sovereign Borders have been subjected to indefinite, mandatory detention in harsh conditions in the overseas processing centers in Nauru and Manus Island, along with very slow processing. A collection of more than 2,000 confidential reports to the Australian government from personnel employed at the center in Nauru were leaked to *The Guardian* newspaper in 2016;[32] the incidents of abuse, self-harm, and trauma they detailed appeared to confirm the charges that the conditions amount to a violation of fundamental rights, with the detention of children a particular concern (see Box 1).

In addition, the legality of the detention centers has been called into question. In April 2016, the Supreme Court of Papua New Guinea ruled that the center on Manus Island breached the fundamental right of the

29 Australian Associated Press, "Tony Abbott Asylum Boat Plan Puts Cooperation at Risk, Indonesia Warns," *The Guardian*, September 26, 2013.

30 *The Guardian*, "Indonesia Seeks Answers on Claims Australia Paid People Smugglers," *The Guardian*, June 13, 2015.

31 Andrew and Renata Kaldor Centre on International Refugee Law, "In Focus: Paying People Smugglers," University of New South Wales, July 1, 2015.

32 Paul Farrell, Nick Evershed, and Helen Davidson, "The Nauru Files: Cache of 2,000 Leaked Reports Reveal Scale of Abuse of Children in Australian Offshore Detention," *The Guardian*, August 10, 2016.

detainees to liberty.[33] In May 2016, the United Nations Human Rights Council concluded, during the 25th session of its Universal Periodic Review, that the Manus Island center was illegal. The government of Papua New Guinea accepted the ruling, and the prime minister announced that the center would be closed.[34] Although in February 2016 the Australian High Court had ruled that the government was acting lawfully in its maintenance of offshore detention centers (provided that the government does not support detention beyond what is reasonably necessary for processing),[35] the two governments announced in August 2016 that the Manus Island center would be closed. No information was provided at the time of the announcement about what would happen to the 854 asylum seekers held in the center. The Australian immigration minister pledged that none of them would be allowed to settle in Australia, and stated that their only options would be to repatriate (although 98 percent of those whose refugee claims had been assessed were found to be refugees and therefore could not legally be sent back to their home countries) or to settle in Papua New Guinea—one of the least developed nations in the world.[36]

Further, the physical and mental health care these asylum seekers receive has been called into question, particularly in light of the self-immolation of an Iranian detainee[37] and stories of medical emergencies in which necessary steps to prevent the deaths of detainees (such as evacuating patients to Australian hospitals) were not taken.[38] A trauma expert and psychologist deployed to the offshore processing centers in Nauru and Manus Island criticized the current policies for inflicting some of the worst trauma he had ever seen.[39] Finally, limited media access to the Nauru detention facility—and the AU $8,000 visa fee required for press entry (as of 2014)—has led to criticisms that Nauru

---

33 Ben Doherty, "Papua New Guinea Tells UN it Accepts Court Decision on Manus Island Illegality," *The Guardian*, May 6, 2016.

34 Stephanie Anderson, "Manus Island Detention Centre to be Shut, Papua New Guinea President Peter O'Neill Says," Australian Broadcasting Corporation, April 27, 2016.

35 Madeline Gleeson, "Glimmers of Hope for Detained Asylum Seekers in the High Court's Nauru Decision," The Conversation, February 3, 2016.

36 Brett Cole, "Australia Will Close Detention Center on Manus Island but Still Won't Accept Asylum Seekers," *The New York Times*, August 17, 2016; Paul Farrell and Paul Karp, "Peter Dutton Attacks Guardian and ABC over Reporting of Nauru Files," *The Guardian*, August 18, 2016.

37 Sky News, "Asylum-Seeker Dies after Self-Immolation," Sky News, April 29, 2016.

38 Henry Belot, "PNG Demands Answers from Manus Island Contractors ISOS after Hamid Khazei's Death," *Sydney Morning Herald*, June 6, 2016.

39 Ben Doherty and David Marr, "The Worst I've Ever Seen—Trauma Expert Lifts Lid on 'Atrocity' of Australia's Detention Regime," *The Guardian*, June 19, 2016.

and Australia were collaborating in trying to enforce a media blackout (allegations Nauru's government has denied).[40]

The reinstatement of TPVs as the standard form of protection for recognized refugees who entered Australia illegally makes it difficult for refugees to focus on the long-term goals and investments necessary to integrate and build a new life. As has been noted, TPVs are issued for a duration of three years, after which refugees have to prove their need for continuing protection. This is contrary to the terms of the Refugee Convention, under which it is the responsibility of the protecting state to show that cessation of refugee status is based on deep and lasting change in the country of origin.

Box 1. Children in Detention

In November 2014, the Australian Human Rights Commission reported on the findings of an inquiry into the results of prolonged immigration detention on the physical and mental health of approximately 800 children who had been detained with no pathway to protection or settlement in Australia. (This number, it should be noted, represents a significant drop from the 1,992 children who were in detention as of July 2013.) Some 186 of these children were detained on Nauru, and the rest in mainland Australia or on Christmas Island. The commission concluded that "the evidence documented in this report demonstrates unequivocally that prolonged detention of children leads to serious negative impacts on their mental and emotional health and development ... It is also clear that the laws, policies, and practices of Labor and Coalition Governments are in serious breach of the rights guaranteed by the Convention on the Rights of the Child and the International Covenant on Civil and Political Rights."

In the face of such criticism, but without softening its position that offshore detention is necessary to deter boat arrivals, the government reduced the detention of child asylum seekers both on Australian territory and in the offshore detention centers. As of June 30, 2016, 49 children were still detained in Nauru and none in Australia.

Sources: Australian Human Rights Commission, *The Forgotten Children: National Inquiry into Children in Immigration Detention* (Sydney: Australian Human Rights Commission, 2014); Department of Immigration and Border Protection (DIBP), *Immigration Detention and Community Statistics Summary* (Canberra: DIBP, 2016).

---

40 Amanda Meade, "Only 'Respectful and Objective Media' Outlets Welcome, Says Nauru," *The Guardian*, June 21, 2016.

Some of the measures instituted after the LNC government took office in September 2013 were equally controversial. In June 2014, a boat carrying[41] Sri Lankans was intercepted by an Australian ship. After screening the passengers on the ship—in a process that many observers regarded as inadequate—the asylum seekers were transferred to a Sri Lankan naval vessel and returned to Sri Lanka. Irregular departure from Sri Lanka is in itself a crime, and none of the passengers were given the opportunity for a full hearing of their asylum claims, even offshore. At about the same time, a boat carrying 157 Sri Lankan asylum seekers was intercepted, having departed from India. They were held *incommunicado* on an Australian customs vessel for more than one month, and no information on their whereabouts or their state of heath was made available to their relatives or anyone else outside of the Australian government. The High Court of Australia issued an injunction against their direct return to Sri Lanka (although later, in January 2015, the High Court ruled that their detention was lawful), and after being briefly held in a detention center on the Australian mainland, they were eventually moved to Nauru for adjudication of their claims.

The lack of transparency in Operation Sovereign Borders, as illustrated by the incident above, is another point of controversy. In the first year of its implementation, no information about the methods or outcomes of the operation was released to the public—making it impossible for critics to hold the government accountable for violations of migrants' rights or Australian law. The operation's commander argued that it is necessary to "carefully manage the release of information" in order to protect the Australian personnel carrying out sensitive operations and to deny smugglers any data that would help them plan their routes, exploit gaps in surveillance, and evade detection.[41] On the first anniversary of Operation Sovereign Borders, however, the then Minister of Immigration and Border Protection revealed some operational details and results of the previous year's work in order to bolster the government's case that its policies have been successful.

Finally, Australia has made agreements with extremely poor countries in its region to settle refugees from its offshore processing centers. These include agreements with Nauru and Papua New Guinea (the sites of those centers) and, as of September 2014, with Cambodia (see Box 2). There is great concern about the capacity of those countries to absorb refugees and offer them meaningful protection.[42]

---

41 Remarks of Lieutenant General Angus Campbell, "Operation Sovereign Borders."
42 See, for example, Human Rights Watch, "Australia: Reconsider Nauru Refugee Transfers to Cambodia" (press release, November 20, 2014).

Box 2. The Australia-Cambodia Agreement of September 2014

Under the terms of Australia's agreement with Cambodia, refugees picked up at sea by Australian forces and transferred to Nauru for status determination may be offered resettlement in Cambodia. Cambodia is a signatory to the 1951 Refugee Convention. Cambodia began conferring refugee status in 2009, and in 2014 hosted 63 refugees, none of whom has received the residence permit necessary to work in the formal economy. Cambodia is among the poorest countries in the world and suffers from weak human-rights protections, corruption, poor services, and inadequate infrastructure. Moreover, it has been accused of refouling Uighur asylum seekers to China and Montagnards to Vietnam.

According to the agreement, Australia will bear the costs of processing and transferring refugees, and will provide settlement assistance for their first 12 months in Cambodia (with medical assistance continuing longer). Australia has also pledged an additional AU $40 million in development assistance to Cambodia. The International Organization for Migration agreed (at the request of Australia, Cambodia, and Nauru) to assist in the refugees' transfer and integration.

While the government of Cambodia has agreed that any refugees who go from Nauru to Cambodia will have the rights guaranteed in the Refugee Convention (including the right to work and to family reunification, health insurance and language training, travel documents, and access to citizenship), many observers have expressed grave doubts that Cambodia is capable of delivering on this intention—particularly since, after a period of adjustment in Phnom Penh, refugees will be required to settle outside the capital, where it will likely be extremely difficult for them to establish a livelihood and integrate socially.

In June 2015, the first four refugees moved from the offshore processing center in Nauru to Cambodia. One more moved in November. It is unprecedented for a wealthy, capable country to transfer refugees to an extremely poor, underdeveloped one. Refugees are normally resettled from, not to, such countries. So poor were conditions in Cambodia that by late May 2016, all four of the first refugees resettled as part of the 2014 deal had "voluntarily" returned to the countries they initially fled; one returned to Myanmar and three to Iran. One refugee advocate claims that this was the original intention of the Australian government. Only one refugee resettled from Nauru remained in Cambodia as of August 2016, although the Australian government insisted that the option to move to Cambodia remained open.

Sources: Andrew and Renata Kaldor Centre for International Refugee Law, "Fact Sheet: The Cambodia Agreement," University of New South Wales, April 11, 2016; Madeline Gleeson, "In Focus: Resettlement of Refugees from Nauru to Cambodia," Andrew and Renata Kaldor Centre on International Refugee Law, University of New South Wales, August 9, 2016; International Organization for Migration, "Cambodia Receives First Group of Refugees from Nauru" (press release, June 4, 2015); Lauren Crothers, "Last Refugee Among Group Australia Sent to Cambodia Returns to Home Country," *The Guardian,* June 8, 2016.

The hardline approach taken by the LNC government has not gone unchallenged. Criticism from the opposition Labor Party, however, has been muted, presumably because the party's 2010 policy shift while in office (described above) had moved in the same direction. But minority parties, human-rights advocates, and legal experts have charged that the policies violate both Australian and international law. UNHCR has repeatedly made demarches, and, unusually, public statements urging the reconsideration of Australian practices. In answer, the government passed legislation in 2014 that altered domestic law and made it difficult to challenge the state's violation of its obligations under international law.

The *Migration and Maritime Powers Legislation Amendment (Resolving the Asylum Legacy Caseload) Act 2014*, signed on December 15, 2014, represents a sweeping reformulation of Australia's obligations toward refugees, and its relation to the body of international law designed to protect them. Schedule 5 of the act is titled "Clarifying Australia's international law obligations." It amends the *Migration Act of 1958* by adding a new section that deals with removals of unlawful aliens. This addition (Section 197c) has two clauses. The first says: "For the purposes of Section 198, it is irrelevant whether Australia has nonrefoulement obligations in respect of an unlawful non-citizen." The second says: "An officer's duty to remove as soon as reasonably practicable an unlawful non-citizen under Section 198 arises irrespective of whether there has been an assessment, according to law, of Australia's nonrefoulement obligations in respect of the non-citizen."[43] Simply stated, the new section removes the core protection of the Refugee Convention for unauthorized arrivals by obligating authorities to remove them as quickly as possible from Australia even if their need for protection has

---

43 *Migration and Maritime Powers Legislation Amendment (Resolving the Asylum Legacy Caseload) Act 2014* (Cth), schedule 5, part 1, division 1 (December 15, 2014), *Federal Register* C2014A00135 (April 24, 2015); *Migration Act 1958* (Cth) (July 1, 2016), *Federal Register* C2016C00712 (July 4, 2016).

not yet been ascertained. For asylum seekers who travel unauthorized by sea, the denial of protection begins even before they reach Australia.

Interestingly, on the day before the bill was passed, the Secretary of the Department of Immigration and Border Protection gave a speech, "Sovereignty in an Age of Global Interdependency," in which he described one of two elements necessary for the global order, in these terms: "The second element involves all states working within an international system, which has clear rules of procedure and engagement, and agreed mechanisms to facilitate cooperation. The global order relies upon adherence to rules-based behavior—from the resolution of trade disputes and territorial boundaries, to the aversion of war, and the making of peace."[44]

The new law gives the Minister of Immigration and Border Protection sweeping, largely unchecked, powers to interdict people on the high seas, detain them indefinitely, and send them to any country, whether a signatory to the Refugee Convention or not (it may be worth recalling that the High Court had earlier rejected an Australian agreement with Malaysia because that nation is not a signatory to the Convention).

One aim of the law, as its title indicates, is to reduce the caseload of some 30,000 asylum seekers who remained in detention in mainland Australia at the time of the bill's passage, a legacy of the period before the policy of offshore processing was applied to all maritime arrivals. TPVs, for people found to be refugees, were reintroduced by the law's amendments.

The law also creates a new visa category, which was the price of support from a minority party whose support was essential for passage of the bill into law.[45] The Safe Haven Enterprise Visa (SHEV) gives refugees in Australia on three-year TPVs the option to transfer to a SHEV, which would allow them to work or study in a designated region of the country for five years and would render them eligible for permanent residence under one of several nonrefugee visa categories (i.e., skilled workers, employer sponsored, family reunification) if they can satisfy the conditions.[46] Both TPVs and SHEVs are available for maritime arrivals who entered Australia before January 2014. Asylum seekers

44 Remarks by Michael Pezullo, Secretary, DIBP, "Sovereignty in an Age of Global Interdependency: The Role of Borders," before the Australian Strategic Policy Institute, Barton, Australia, December 4, 2014.
45 Lenore Taylor, "Scott Morrison Concessions Seem Unlikely to Save Asylum Bill from Senate Defeat," *The Guardian*, December 2, 2014.
46 DIBP, "Safe Haven Enterprise Visas" (fact sheet, DIBP, July 2015).

who were interdicted at sea subsequently were taken to the offshore processing centers in Manus Island or Nauru.

Another controversial provision of the new law is its removal or restriction of merit reviews for many asylum seekers. The importance of review can be seen in the Department of Immigration and Border Protection's own data, which show that its asylum decisions have been overturned, on average, between 20 percent and 37 percent of the time by the Refugee Review Tribunal. For maritime arrivals, this rate has been much higher—about 70 to 80 percent, and as high as 100 percent for some national groups.[47]

Additional legislation in 2015, known as the *Migration Amendment (Maintaining the Good Order of Immigration Detention Facilities) Bill 2015* generated additional concern by giving officers in Australia's offshore detention centers broad, discretionary authority to use force to maintain order.[48] Moreover, the *Australian Border Force Act* (which merged the enforcement functions of the Department of Immigration and the Department of Trade as of July 1, 2015) made it a crime for staff at the detention centers to disclose information about events in the centers without authorization; thus, any unauthorized reporting about abuses of authority or other dangerous conditions could be punishable by up to two years' imprisonment.[49] Although disclosure of such information is permitted when the employee believes it necessary to prevent threats to the life or health of an individual, it is the whistleblower who bears the burden of proof that an exception applies. Testimony to a parliamentary inquiry, which conveys immunity, is the only way employees can confidently bring forth information about abuses of detainees in the offshore processing centers without fear of prosecution.[50] While no one has been prosecuted as of July 2016 under

---

47 Andrew and Renata Kaldor Centre on International Refugee Law, "Submission to the Senate Legal and Constitutional Affairs Legislation Committee: Migration and Maritime Powers Legislation Amendment (Resolving the Legacy Caseload) Bill 2014 (Cth)," University of New South Wales, October 31, 2014.

48 Andrew and Renata Kaldor Centre on International Refugee Law, "Legislative Brief: Migration Amendment (Maintaining the Good Order of Immigration Detention Facilities) Bill 2015," University of New South Wales, May 28, 2015.

49 *Australian Border Force Act 2015* (Cth) (July 1, 2015), *Federal Register* C2015A00040 (July 10 2015); Paul Farrell, "Detention Doctors and Nurses Rally in Opposition to Asylum Seeker Disclosure Laws," *The Guardian*, June 29, 2015; Khanh Hoang, "Border Force Act Entrenches Secrecy Around Australia's Asylum Seeker Regime," The Conversation, July 1, 2015.

50 Ben Doherty, Paul Farrell, and Agencies, "New Inquiry into Detention Centres Will Allow Whistleblowers to Give Evidence," *The Guardian*, October 12, 2015.

the terms of the law, members of the medical community have been investigated by the federal police and others have had their contract of employment terminated. Some doctors are challenging the act's restriction on freedom of speech in court.[51]

Soon after assuming the office of Prime Minister, Malcolm Turnbull confirmed that his government would maintain his predecessor's hardline stance on asylum seekers, avowing that it was his government's policy that none of the current detainees on Manus Island and Nauru would ever resettle in Australia. Instead, he claimed that Australia would do all it could in order to encourage the asylum seekers to return to their countries of origin.[52] Further to this, the Immigration and Border Protection Minister, the Foreign Minister, and Turnbull have rejected offers from developed countries to resettle the asylum seekers held in offshore detention centers. After New Zealand offered to resettle 150 refugees per year, Dutton rejected this offer on the basis that it would only encourage human traffickers to continue smuggling people and that it would enable the asylum seekers to enter Australia through the backdoor, since New Zealand citizens are permitted to settle in Australia.[53] Instead, Australian policy on resettlement has been to approach poorer countries to handle the matter. In October 2015, the government approached the Philippines in a potential AU $150 million deal to resettle some of its detained asylum seekers.[54] The President of the Philippines rejected this offer, claiming that, as an impoverished and overcrowded country, the Philippines could not take any refugees.[55] But in 2016, Australia recommenced talks with six countries, including Indonesia, Malaysia, and the Philippines, to resettle some of the asylum seekers detained on Manus Island and Nauru.[56]

51 Ben Doherty, "Immigration Detention Doctors Challenge Border Force Act's Secrecy Clause in Court," *The Guardian*, July 26, 2016.

52 Jeremy Story Carter, "'They Will Never Come to Australia': Turnbull Maintains Tough Stance on Asylum Seekers," Australian Broadcasting Corporation, September 23, 2015.

53 Helen Davidson, "Turnbull Rejects New Zealand Offer to Take 150 Refugees from Detention," *The Guardian*, April 28, 2016.

54 Austin Ramzy, "Australia Negotiating to Send Refugees to Philippines," *The New York Times*, October 9, 2015.

55 *The Straits Times*, "Philippines' Aquino Rejects Permanent Refugees from Australia," *The Straits Times,* October 27, 2015.

56 Reuters, "Australia Resumes Talks with Six Countries to Resettle Asylum Seekers," Reuters, February 19, 2016.

III. Conclusion

Even as Australia continues to welcome refugees through its resettlement program, it has essentially withdrawn from the global asylum regime, shielded by the seas that surround it. Protecting its maritime borders from migrants and refugees has come at a cost to its reputation, diplomatic relations, and public purse. But successive governments have come to see it as a political and practical imperative.

The controversies surrounding Australia's policies toward unauthorized maritime arrivals illustrate the great difficulty of balancing the need for capable states to protect refugees and treat all migrants humanely against their responsibility to bring order to immigration and asylum processes, instill public confidence in the state's ability to safeguard national borders, and combat the crimes associated with human smuggling. While current Australian policy addresses the symptoms of the problem of unauthorized migration, it does not address the broader, long-term dynamics of movement in the Asia-Pacific region, and it has raised obstacles to regional cooperation on migration issues. Controlling movement to one place, in one timeframe, is not solving a problem but only shifting it to other states, in this case less capable ones.

Perhaps the growth of public confidence in the ability of Australian policymakers to "stop the boats" will allow these policymakers to address a more ambitious agenda, including participating in, or indeed leading, the resolution of region-wide problems (such as, for example, the displacement and statelessness of the Rohingya population in Myanmar).[57] Lessons from Australia's experience as a highly successful country of immigration and a leader on humanitarian issues are sorely needed in its region and the world.

---

57 When asked if Australia would use its resettlement program to help in providing durable solutions for several thousand Rohingya refugees rescued in the Bay of Bengal/Andaman Sea region in the spring of 2015, Prime Minister Tony Abbott answered: "Nope, nope, nope." See Shalailah Medhora, "'Nope, Nope, Nope': Tony Abbott Says Australia Will Take No Rohingya Refugees," *The Guardian*, May 20, 2015.

Works Cited

Al Hussein, Zeid Ra'ad. 2014. Opening Statement by United Nations High Commissioner for Human Rights at the 27th Session of the Human Rights Council, Geneva, September 8, 2014. www.ohchr.org/EN/NewsEvents/Pages/DisplayNews.aspx?NewsID=14998&LangID=E.

Anderson, Stephanie. 2016. Manus Island Detention Centre to be Shut, Papua New Guinea President Peter O'Neill Says. Australian Broadcasting Corporation, April 27, 2016. www.abc.net.au/news/2016-04-27/png-pm-oneill-to-shut-manus-island-detention-centre/7364414.

Andrew and Renata Kaldor Centre on International Refugee Law, University of New South Wales. 2014. Sri Lanka and Australia after the War: A Forum on War Justice and the Indefinite Detention of Refugees. University of New South Wales, March 4, 2014. www.kaldorcentre.unsw.edu.au/event/sri-lanka-and-australia-after-war-forum-post-war-justice-and-indefinite-detention-refugees.

———. 2014. Submission to the Senate Legal and Constitutional Affairs Legislation Committee: Migration and Maritime Powers Legislation Amendment (Resolving the Legacy Caseload) Bill 2014 (Cth). University of New South Wales, October 31, 2014. www.kaldorcentre.unsw.edu.au/publication/submission-senate-legal-and-constitutional-affairs-legislation-committee-migration-and.

———. 2015. 46 Vietnamese Were Returned Directly to Vietnam. Newsletter, Andrew and Renata Kaldor Centre for International Refugee Law, University of New South Wales, Sydney, May 11, 2015. http://us3.campaign-archive2.com/?u=90dc25d76301c1f5080ba74ba&id=c339145f92.

———. 2015. In Focus: Paying People Smugglers. University of New South Wales, July 1, 2015. www.kaldorcentre.unsw.edu.au/news/focus-paying-people-smugglers-did-australian-government-breach-international-law.

———. 2015. Legislative Brief: Migration Amendment (Maintaining the Good Order of Immigration Detention Facilities) Bill 2015. University of New South Wales, May 28, 2015. www.kaldorcentre.unsw.edu.au/publication/legislative-brief-migration-amendment-maintaining-good-order-immigration-detention.

———. 2015. Turning Back Boats. Fact sheet, University of New South Wales, February 26, 2015. www.kaldorcentre.unsw.edu.au/publication/%E2%80%98turning-back-boats%E2%80%99.

———. 2016. Fact Sheet: The Cambodia Agreement. University of New South Wales, April 11, 2016. www.kaldorcentre.unsw.edu.au/publication/cambodia-agreement.

Appleby, Gabrielle. 2015. Australia's Rigid Immigration Barrier. *The New York Times*, May 7, 2015. www.nytimes.com/2015/05/08/opinion/australias-rigid-immigration-barrier.html.

Australian Associated Press. 2013. Tony Abbott Asylum Boat Plan Puts Cooperation at Risk, Indonesia Warns. *The Guardian*, September 26, 2013. www.theguardian.com/world/2013/sep/26/indonesian-navy-abbott-asylum-policy-risks.

Australian Border Force Act 2015 (Cth). July 1, 2015. *Federal Register* C2015A00040
(July 10 2015). www.legislation.gov.au/Details/C2015C00319.

Australian Bureau of Statistics. 2015. *Australian Demographic Statistics: December
Quarter 2015.* Canberra: Australian Bureau of Statistics. www.ausstats.abs.
gov.au/ausstats/subscriber.nsf/0/7645CB8797196A85CA257FDA001D5E8
7/$File/31010_dec%202015.pdf.

Australian Human Rights Commission. 2014. *The Forgotten Children: National Inquiry
into Children in Immigration Detention.* Sydney: Australian Human Rights
Commission. www.humanrights.gov.au/our-work/asylum-seekers-and-
refugees/publications/forgotten-children-national-inquiry-children.

Belot, Henry. 2016. PNG Demands Answers from Manus Island Contractors ISOS
after Hamid Khazei's Death. *Sydney Morning Herald*, June 6, 2016. www.smh.
com.au/national/png-demands-answers-from-manus-island-contractors-
isos-after-hamid-khazaeis-death-20160606-gpcbcy.html.

Campbell, Angus. 2014. Operation Sovereign Borders: Initial Reflections and Future
Outlook. Remarks by the Lieutenant General of the Australian Army to the
Australian Strategic Policy Institute, Barton, Australia, May 15, 2014. www.
aspi.org.au/_data/assets/pdf_file/0016/21634/SovereignBorders_Reflec-
tions.pdf.

Cole, Brett. 2016. Australia Will Close Detention Center on Manus Island but Still
Won't Accept Asylum Seekers. *The New York Times*, August 17, 2016. www.
nytimes.com/2016/08/18/world/australia/manus-detention-center-pap-
ua-new-guinea.html?_r=0.

Crothers, Lauren. 2016. Last Refugee Among Group Australia Sent to Cambodia Returns to Home Country. *The Guardian*, June 8, 2016. www.theguardian.com/
australia-news/2016/may/28/last-refugee-among-group-australia-sent-to-
cambodia-returns-to-home-country.

Davidson, Helen. 2016. Turnbull Rejects New Zealand Offer to Take 150 Refugees
from Detention. *The Guardian*, April 28, 2016. www.theguardian.com/
australia-news/2016/apr/29/turnbull-rejects-new-zealand-offer-to-take-
150-refugees-from-detention.

Department of Immigration and Border Protection (DIBP). 2015. *2014-15 Migration
Programme Report.* Canberra: DIBP. www.border.gov.au/ReportsandPublica-
tions/Documents/statistics/2014-15-Migration-Programme-Report.pdf.

———. 2015. Safe Haven Enterprise Visas. Fact sheet, DIBP, July 2015. www.refu-
geecouncil.org.au/wp-content/uploads/2015/08/Fact-Sheet-Safe-Haven-
Enterprise-visas.pdf.

———. 2016. *Immigration Detention and Community Statistics Summary.* Canberra:
DIBP. www.border.gov.au/ReportsandPublications/Documents/statistics/
immigration-detention-statistics-30-June-2016.pdf.

———. N.d. Australia's Response to the Syrian and Iraqi Humanitarian Crisis. Accessed August 3, 2016. www.border.gov.au/Trav/Refu/response-syrian-
humanitarian-crisis.

———. N.d. Fact Sheet—Australia's Refugee and Humanitarian Programme. Accessed August 3, 2016. www.border.gov.au/about/corporate/information/
fact-sheets/60refugee.

———. N.d. Operation Sovereign Borders. Accessed August 5, 2016. www.border. gov.au/about/operation-sovereign-borders/counter-people-smuggling-communication/english/in-australia/fact-sheet.

Doherty, Ben. 2016. Immigration Detention Doctors Challenge Border Force Act's Secrecy Clause in Court. *The Guardian*, July 26, 2016. www.theguardian.com/australia-news/2016/jul/27/immigration-detention-doctors-challenge-border-force-acts-secrecy-clause-in-court.

———. 2016. Papua New Guinea Tells UN it Accepts Court Decision on Manus Island Illegality. *The Guardian*, May 6, 2016. www.theguardian.com/australia-news/2016/may/07/papua-new-guinea-tells-un-it-accepts-court-decision-on-manus-island-illegality.

Doherty, Ben, Paul Farrell, and Agencies. 2015. New Inquiry into Detention Centres Will Allow Whistleblowers to Give Evidence. *The Guardian*, October 12, 2015. www.theguardian.com/australia-news/2015/oct/13/detention-inquiry-aims-circumvent-border-force-act-whistleblowers-report.

Doherty, Ben and David Marr. 2016. The Worst I've Ever Seen—Trauma Expert Lifts Lid on "Atrocity" of Australia's Detention Regime. *The Guardian*, June 19, 2016. www.theguardian.com/australia-news/2016/jun/20/the-worst-ive-seen-trauma-expert-lifts-lid-on-atrocity-of-australias-detention-regime.

Farrell, Paul. 2015. Detention Doctors and Nurses Rally in Opposition to Asylum Seeker Disclosure Laws. *The Guardian*, June 29, 2015. www.theguardian. com/australia-news/2015/jun/30/detention-doctors-rally-in-opposition-to-asylum-seeker-disclosure-laws.

Farrell, Paul, Nick Evershed, and Helen Davidson. 2016. The Nauru Files: Cache of 2,000 Leaked Reports Reveal Scale of Abuse of Children in Australian Offshore Detention. *The Guardian*, August 10, 2016. www.theguardian.com/australia-news/2016/aug/10/the-nauru-files-2000-leaked-reports-reveal-scale-of-abuse-of-children-in-australian-offshore-detention.

Farrell, Paul and Paul Karp. 2016. Peter Dutton Attacks Guardian and ABC over Reporting of Nauru Files. *The Guardian*, August 18, 2016. www.theguardian.com/australia-news/2016/aug/18/peter-dutton-says-he-wont-be-defamed-by-guardian-and-abc-over-nauru-files.

Gleeson, Madeline. 2016. Glimmers of Hope for Detained Asylum Seekers in the High Court's Nauru Decision. The Conversation, February 3, 2016. https://theconversation.com/glimmers-of-hope-for-detained-asylum-seekers-in-the-high-courts-nauru-decision-54036.

———. 2016. In Focus: Resettlement of Refugees from Nauru to Cambodia. Andrew and Renata Kaldor Centre on International Refugee Law, University of New South Wales, August 9, 2016. www.kaldorcentre.unsw.edu.au/news/focus-resettlement-refugees-nauru-cambodia.

Guardian, The. 2015. Indonesia Seeks Answers on Claims Australia Paid People Smugglers. *The Guardian*, June 13, 2015. www.theguardian.com/australia-news/2015/jun/13/indonesia-seeks-answers-on-claims-australia-paid-traffickers-to-turn-back.

Hoang, Khanh. 2015. Border Force Act Entrenches Secrecy Around Australia's Asylum Seeker Regime. The Conversation, July 1, 2015. https://theconversation.com/border-force-act-entrenches-secrecy-around-australias-asylum-seeker-regime-44136.

Human Rights Watch. 2014. Australia: Reconsider Nauru Refugee Tranfers to Cambodia. Press release, November 20, 2014. www.hrw.org/news/2014/11/20/australia-reconsider-nauru-refugee-transfers-cambodia.

International Organization for Migration. 2015. Cambodia Receives First Group of Refugees from Nauru. Press release, June 4, 2015. www.iom.int/news/cambodia-receives-first-group-refugees-nauru.

IRIN. 2011. Migration: Timeline of the Australian Asylum-Seeker Debate. IRIN, September 20, 2011. www.irinnews.org/printreport.aspx?reportid=93760.

Keany, Francis and Stephanie Anderson. 2016. Election 2016: Malcolm Turnbull Backs "Outstanding" Peter Dutton after Refugee Comments. Australian Broadcasting Corporation, May 18, 2016. www.abc.net.au/news/2016-05-18/dutton-warns-illiterate-refugees-will-take-aussie-jobs/7424198.

Kelly, Joe and Rosie Lewis. 2016. Federal Election 2016: Rudd-Gillard Asylum Seekers to Get Visas. The Australian, June 16, 2016. www.theaustralian.com.au/federal-election-2016/federal-election-2016-ruddgillard-asylumseekers-to-get-visas/news-story/e6105eb5fe345d872cbb28a9b9e5e42f.

McAuliffe, Marie and Victoria Mence. 2014. Global Irregular Maritime Migration: Current and Future Challenges. Occasional paper series 07/2014, DIBP, Irregular Migration Research Programme, April 2014. www.border.gov.au/ReportsandPublications/Documents/research/global-irregular-maritime-migration.pdf.

Meade, Amanda. 2016. Only "Respectful and Objective Media" Outlets Welcome, Says Nauru. The Guardian, June 21, 2016. www.theguardian.com/world/2016/jun/22/only-respectful-and-objective-media-outlets-are-welcome-says-nauru.

Medhora, Shalailah. 2015. "Nope, Nope, Nope": Tony Abbott Says Australia Will Take No Rohingya Refugees. The Guardian, May 20, 2015. www.theguardian.com/world/2015/may/21/nope-nope-nope-tony-abbott-says-australia-will-take-no-rohingya-refugees.

Migration Act 1958 (Cth). July 1, 2016. Federal Register C2016C00712 (July 4, 2016). www.legislation.gov.au/Details/C2016C00712.

Migration and Maritime Powers Legislation Amendment (Resolving the Asylum Legacy Caseload) Act 2014 (Cth). December 15, 2014. Federal Register C2014A00135 (April 24, 2015). www.legislation.gov.au/Details/C2014A00135.

Monash University, Border Crossing Observatory. N.d. Australian Border Deaths Database. Accessed July 22, 2016. http://artsonline.monash.edu.au/thebordercrossingobservatory/publications/australian-border-deaths-database/.

Morrison, Scott E. 2014. A New Force Protecting Australia's Borders. Address by the Minister of Immigration and Border Protection before the Lowy Institute for International Policy, Sydney, May 9, 2014. www.lowyinstitute.org/news-and-media/audio/podcast-future-border-protection-scott-morrison-mp.

Murphy, Katharine. 2015. Turnbull Rebukes Abbott: I Won't Give Germany Advice about Refugees. The Guardian, November 13, 2015. www.theguardian.com/australia-news/2015/nov/13/turnbull-wont-offer-germany-advise-on-syrian-refugee-crisis.

Nethery, Amy, Brynna Rafferty-Brown, and Savitri Taylor. 2012. Exporting Detention: Australia-Funded Immigration Detention in Indonesia. *Journal of Refugee Studies* 26 (1): 88-109. http://jrs.oxfordjournals.org/content/26/1/88.full.

Norman, Jane. 2015. Tony Abbott Urges Europe to Adopt Stronger Border Protection Policies Following Migrant Boat Sinkings. Australian Broadcasting Corporation, April 21, 2015. www.abc.net.au/news/2015-04-21/asylum-seekers-abbott-urges-europeeee-stronger-border-protection/6408552.

Patrick, Erin and Betsy Cooper. 2006. Appendix C: Australia and the Pacific Strategy. In *The New "Boat People": Ensuring Safety and Determining Status*, eds. Joanne van Selm and Betsy Cooper. Washington, DC: Migration Policy Institute. www.migrationpolicy.org/research/new-boat-people-ensuring-safety-and-determining-status.

Pennington-Hill, Kaitlyn. 2015. Australia Makes a U-Turn with the Revival of the Pacific Solution: Should Asylum Seekers Find a New Destination? *Washington University Global Studies Law Review* 13 (3): 585–603.

Pezullo, Michael. 2014. Sovereignty in an Age of Global Interdependency: The Role of Borders. Remarks by the Secretary of DIBP before the Australian Strategic Policy Institute, Barton, Australia, December 4, 2014. www.border.gov.au/newsandmedia/Documents/sovereignty-age-interdependency-04122014.pdf.

Ramzy, Austin. 2015. Australia Negotiating to Send Refugees to Philippines. *The New York Times*, October 9, 2015. www.nytimes.com/2015/10/10/world/australia/australia-migrants-refugees-resettlement-philippines.html?_r=0.

Reuters. 2016. Australia Resumes Talks with Six Countries to Resettle Asylum Seekers. Reuters, February 19, 2016. www.reuters.com/article/us-australia-asylum-idUSKCN0VT054.

Sky News. 2016. Asylum-Seeker Dies after Self-Immolation. Sky News, April 29, 2016. www.skynews.com.au/news/top-stories/2016/04/29/asylum-seeker-dies-after-self-immolation.html.

Squires, Nick. 2007. US and Australia to Swap Asylum Seekers. *The Telegraph*, April 18, 2007. www.telegraph.co.uk/news/worldnews/1549000/US-and-Australia-to-swap-asylum-seekers.html.

Story Carter, Jeremy. 2015. "They Will Never Come to Australia": Turnbull Maintains Tough Stance on Asylum Seekers. Australian Broadcasting Corporation, September 23, 2015. www.abc.net.au/radionational/programs/drive/prime-minister-malcolm-turnbull-tough-stance-on-asylum-seekers/6799610.

Straits Times, The. 2015. Philippines' Aquino Rejects Permanent Refugees from Australia. *The Straits Times*, October 27, 2015. www.straitstimes.com/asia/se-asia/philippines-aquino-rejects-permanent-refugees-from-australia.

Taylor, Lenore. 2014. Scott Morrison Concessions Seem Unlikely to Save Asylum Bill from Senate Defeat. *The Guardian*, December 2, 2014. www.theguardian.com/australia-news/2014/dec/03/asylum-bill-temporary-protection-visas.

Turnbull, Malcom and Peter Dutton. 2016. Operation Sovereign Borders: No Successful People Smuggling Boats in Two Years. Press release, July 27, 2016. www.minister.border.gov.au/peterdutton/2016/Pages/Operation_Sovereign_Borders_no_successful_people_smuggling_boats_in_two_years.aspx.

United Nations Department of Economic and Social Affairs (UNDESA). 2016. *International Migration Report 2015: Highlights*. New York: UNDESA Population Division. www.un.org/en/development/desa/population/migration/publications/migrationreport/docs/MigrationReport2015_Highlights.pdf.

United Nations High Commissioner for Refugees (UNHCR). 2014. *UNHCR Resettlement Handbook and Country Chapters*. Geneva: UNHCR. www.unhcr.org/4a2ccf4c6.html.

CHAPTER SIX

MARITIME MIGRATION IN THE UNITED STATES AND THE CARIBBEAN

By Kathleen Newland and Sarah Flamm

Introduction

Patterns of unauthorized maritime migration across the Caribbean Sea have long been dominated by the attempts of migrants and asylum seekers to reach the United States, and the efforts of U.S. government authorities to stop them. Since 1981, the government has instructed the U.S. Coast Guard to intercept unauthorized persons approaching U.S. shores by sea.[1] A policy that started as a response to discrete episodes of mass irregular immigration from the Caribbean has evolved into a standing method of border enforcement. It was originally adopted in order to foil defiance of U.S. immigration laws and prevent a perceived threat to the welfare and safety of U.S. communities receiving large numbers of unauthorized immigrants. Now, interception is also presented by U.S. officials as a national security measure. By this logic, if unauthorized migrants and migrant smugglers can easily penetrate U.S. sea borders, so can terrorists, criminals, and others who intend harm to the United States and its people. In fiscal year[2] (FY) 2015, 3,828 people were intercepted at sea by the U.S. Coast Guard, more than three-quarters from Cuba.[3] They were either returned directly to their countries of origin or, if they express a fear of persecution on being returned, taken to the U.S. naval station at

---

1 This case study expands and updates an earlier Migration Policy Institute (MPI) analysis of maritime migration in the Caribbean; see Kathleen Newland, "Appendix B: The U.S. and the Caribbean," in *The New "Boat People": Ensuring Safety and Determining Status*, eds. Joanne van Selm and Betsy Cooper (Washington, DC: MPI, 2006).
2 The U.S. fiscal year runs from October 1 to September 30.
3 U.S. Coast Guard, "Alien Migrant Interdiction: U.S. Coast Guard Maritime Migrant Interdictions," updated January 19, 2016.

Guantánamo, Cuba for refugee status determination.[4] Some continue to make it through the Coast Guard shield: for example, 60 Cubans arrived by boat to the Florida Keys over a two-day period in July 2016.[5]

As the maritime border of the United States has become more difficult to approach, increasing numbers of people are traveling by air or sea to Mexico, Ecuador, or other countries in Central and South America, and then traveling north to approach the U.S. southern border by land.[6] Efforts to prevent migrant arrivals by sea have also drastically reduced opportunities for refugees from island states in the Caribbean to present their claims for international protection to U.S. authorities.

Following the September 11, 2001 terrorist attacks, the U.S. government deployed increasingly advanced surveillance technology and omnipresent security[7] at U.S. borders and beyond, including at sea. There has been a shift in policy as well: since 9/11 interception has been, for the first time, explicitly linked to the deterrence of refugee as well as migrant flows. In the 1980s and 1990s, interception was presented as a necessary measure that could include safeguards to ensure that refugees fleeing by boat were not prevented from seeking and finding protection—and indeed, as a measure that might rescue them in the course of mortally dangerous journeys. Although deeply flawed in practice, the safeguards put in place at that time acknowledged the need, although not a legal obligation, to open a humanitarian channel through the Coast Guard barrier. Since 9/11, however, this stance has been abandoned on the grounds that the effort of intercepting boats and screening passengers for refugee status creates an unacceptable diversion of law enforcement resources from antiterrorism priorities.

---

4   The facility that houses refugees and asylum seekers in Guantánamo is completely separate from the military prison holding terrorism suspects.
5   David Goodhue, "40 Cubans Arrive Monday Night to Florida Keys," *Miami Herald,* July 18, 2016.
6   Jens Manuel Krogstad, "Surge in Cuban Immigration to U.S. Continues into 2016," Pew Research Center, August 5, 2016; Abel Fernández, "Cuban Migrants Force their Way across the Panama-Costa Rica Border," *Miami Herald,* April 14, 2016; Luis Chaparro, "Texas Shelters, Churches Fear Sudden Influx of Cuban Migrants Will Overwhelm Them," Fox News Latino, May 18, 2016.
7   The U.S. Coast Guard collaborates with U.S. Customs and Border Protection (CBP) and U.S. Immigration and Customs Enforcement (ICE) to operate a 24/7 maritime screening operations facility at the National Targeting Center (NTC) in Virginia. The Indications and Warning Center at NTC screens 100 percent of the crew and passengers of vessels required to submit an advanced notice of arrival.

The deterrence of refugee flows is now embraced by authorities as a goal, rather than as an unfortunate byproduct of border protection.

The policy of interception and direct return of travelers to their countries of origin has led many observers to conclude that the U.S. government is in violation of its obligations under the 1951 Convention Relating to the Status of Refugees. Meanwhile, the position of the U.S. government, as confirmed by the Supreme Court,[8] is that these obligations do not apply outside U.S. territorial waters. The government nonetheless maintains that any intercepted person who expresses a need for protection will have that need evaluated according to international standards and acted upon appropriately. There is widespread concern, however, that both the evaluation and the response are inadequate from a protection standpoint, and that, as practiced, relevant procedures discriminate on the basis of nationality. The most important example of discrimination is the contrast between the treatment of Cuban nationals, who in the 50 years since 1966 have been granted legal status if they reach the United States without authorization, and unauthorized migrants of other nationalities, who are subject to detention and can be placed in removal proceedings as soon as they enter U.S. territory.

U.S. policies of interception at sea, particularly as they affect Caribbean nationals, thus raise significant concerns about deterrence, discrimination, and forcible return of refugees to situations where they may face danger to their lives or liberty.[9] This chapter reviews the evolution of U.S. policy toward unauthorized maritime migration and shows how the legacy of the 1980s and 1990s shapes current migration patterns—and responses to them. It also describes briefly the policies of other Caribbean countries that receive unauthorized migrants by sea.

I. A Brief History of U.S. Interception of Migrants and Refugees at Sea

According to the U.S. Coast Guard Historian's Office, "From 1794 through 1980 the Coast Guard conduct[ed] migrant interdiction only as an adjunct to a primary mission such as Search and Rescue or ... the

---

8 *Sale v. Haitian Centers Council, Inc.* 509 U.S. Reports 155 (1993).
9 The legal term for this is "refoulement" and is described in the 1951 UN Convention Relating to the Status of Refugees.

boarding of a suspicious vessel."[10] The earliest interdictions occurred after the banning and criminalization of the slave trade in the late 18th and early 19th centuries, when the Coast Guard acted to prevent slave ships from landing in the United States or from transporting U.S.-based slaves to places where the trade was still permitted, such as Cuba.

More recent U.S. interception policies have been heavily influenced by domestic political and foreign policy interests, particularly in relation to Cuba. Coast Guard vessels intercepted migrants from Cuba in the mid-1960s, but primarily in a rescue mode and to impose some order on an outflow that was seen, in the Cold War context of the time, as composed of prima facie refugees.[11] Apart from some concern about the infiltration of spies, Cubans were generally welcomed. The dangers and chaos of sea voyages were replaced by a negotiated series of charter flights in 1965 (characterized by the U.S. government as "freedom flights") to bring Cubans directly to the United States. (The government of Fidel Castro acquiesced in the departure of political opponents.) More than 260,000 Cubans arrived in the United States in this way between 1965 and 1971, and quickly became legal permanent residents.[12]

A challenge to the United States' open-door policy toward Cuban refugees was mounted by the Cuban government in 1980. After a series of political confrontations with the United States, Fidel Castro announced in 1980 that Cuban police and military forces would not prevent boat departures from the port of the small town of Mariel. Thousands of Cubans scrambled to find places aboard Miami-bound boats, and members of the Cuban community in the United States mounted a flotilla of private vessels that set out from Florida to pick up people from Cuba, in violation of U.S. immigration law. Castro also took the opportunity to deport inmates of some Cuban prisons and mental institutions, sending them off with the maritime flows. The ensuing chaos, in which 27 migrants died at sea, overwhelmed U.S. reception and processing capabilities. The U.S. Coast Guard was deployed to prevent U.S. residents from sailing to Cuba to participate in what became known as the Mariel boatlift. Coast Guard vessels also intercepted Cuban boats and

---

10 U.S. Coast Guard, "Alien Migrant Interdiction: History of the U.S. Coast Guard in Illegal Immigration (1794–1971)," updated January 12, 2016.

11 A prima facie refugee is an individual who, due to official recognition of the severity of conditions in their country of origin (or, in the case of stateless persons, their country of residence), is considered to be entitled to refugee status without completing a more individualized refugee status determination process.

12 U.S. Coast Guard, "Alien Migrant Interdiction: History of the U.S. Coast Guard in Illegal Immigration."

transported their passengers to reception points from which they were dispersed to processing centers around the United States.

The Coast Guard intercepted about 1,700 vessels during the Mariel operation, and a total of 124,776 Cuban migrants arrived in the United States between April 1 and September 25, 1980. All were permitted to stay, although some of the criminals (those convicted of serious, non-political crimes) were jailed.[13] About 25,000 Haitian nationals, and smaller numbers from other Caribbean countries, also sailed to the United States in this period.[14] Most were able to disappear into ethnic communities (particularly in Florida) or claim asylum under the newly passed *U.S. Refugee Law of 1980.*

Migrant interdiction, in the contemporary sense (preventing spontaneous arrivals), can be traced back to the response to the Mariel boatlift. To prevent any repetition of the uncontrolled flows, President Reagan issued Presidential Proclamation 4865 on "High Seas Interdiction of Illegal Aliens" on September 28, 1981. It declared, in part, "The entry of undocumented aliens from the high seas is hereby suspended and shall be prevented by the interdiction of certain vessels carrying such aliens."[15]

Of course, saying it did not make it so, but with the proclamation the policy and practice of interception were firmly established. In FY 1982, 171 migrants were intercepted by the Coast Guard, all of them from Haiti. The number of interceptions fluctuated in an upward trend over the next eight years, reaching a peak of 5,863 in 1989. Almost all were in the Caribbean, and in most years Haitians dominated. Interdictions of people from many countries apart from Cuba and Haiti took place along the Atlantic and Pacific coasts as well, particularly Chinese nationals, but in much smaller numbers (see Table 1).

---

13 Andrew Glass, "Castro Launches Mariel Boatlift, April 20, 1980," Politico, April 20, 2009; Global Security, "Mariel Boatlift," accessed August 8, 2016.

14 Ruth Ellen Wasem, *Cuban Migration to the United States: Policies and Trends* (Washington, DC: Congressional Research Service, 2009).

15 Ronald Reagan, "Proclamation 4865 of September 29, 1981—High Seas Interdiction of Illegal Aliens," *Federal Register* 46, no. 190 (October 1, 1981): 48107.

Table 1. Total Migrant Interdictions at Sea by U.S. Coast Guard, by Nationality, FY 1982–2014

Year	Haiti	DR	PRC	Cuba	MX	EC	Other	Total
1982	171	0	0	0	0	0	0	171
1983	511	6	0	44	0	0	5	566
1984	1,581	181	0	7	2	0	37	1,808
1985	3,721	113	12	51	0	0	177	4,074
1986	3,422	189	11	28	1	0	74	3,725
1987	2,866	40	0	46	1	0	38	2,991
1988	4,262	254	0	60	11	0	13	4,600
1989	4,902	664	5	257	30	0	5	5,863
1990	871	1,426	0	443	1	0	95	2,836
1991	2,065	1,007	138	1,722	0	0	58	4,990
1992	37,618	588	181	2,066	0	0	174	40,627
1993	4,270	873	2,511	2,882	0	0	48	10,584
1994	25,302	232	291	38,560	0	0	58	64,443
1995	909	3,388	509	525	0	0	36	5,367
1996	2,295	6,273	61	411	0	2	38	9,080
1997	288	1,200	240	421	0	0	45	2,194
1998	1,369	1,097	212	903	30	0	37	3,648
1999	1,039	583	1,092	1,619	171	298	24	4,826
2000	1,113	499	261	1,000	49	1,244	44	4,210
2001	1,391	659	53	777	17	1,020	31	3,948
2002	1,486	177	80	666	32	1,608	55	4,104
2003	2,013	1,748	15	1,555	0	703	34	6,068
2004	3,229	5,014	68	1,225	86	1,189	88	10,899
2005	1,850	3,612	32	2,712	55	1,149	45	9,455
2006	1,198	3,011	31	2,810	52	693	91	7,886
2007	1,610	1,469	73	2,868	26	125	167	6,338
2008	1,583	688	1	2,216	47	220	70	4,825
2009	1,782	727	35	799	77	6	41	3,467
2010	1,377	140	0	422	61	0	88	2,088
2011	1,137	222	11	985	68	1	50	2,474
2012	977	456	23	1,275	79	7	138	2,955
2013	508	110	5	1,357	31	1	82	2,094
2014	1,103	293	0	2,111	48	0	32	3,587
2015	561	257	10	2,927	27	3	43	3,828
Total	120,380	37,196	5,956	75,750	1,002	8,269	2,061	248,525

Notes: The U.S. fiscal year (FY) runs from October 1 to September 30. DR = Dominican Republic; PRC = People's Republic of China, MX = Mexico, EC = Ecuador.
Source: U.S. Coast Guard, "Alien Migrant Interdiction: U.S. Coast Guard Maritime Migrant Interdictions," updated January 19, 2016.

Following the installation of the popularly elected President Aristide in Haiti in 1989, boat departures and interceptions dropped dramatically between 1989 and 1990. A military coup in late 1991, however, prompted departures from Haiti to soar again in 1992. Almost 38,000 Haitians were intercepted by the U.S. Coast Guard in FY 1992. President George H. W. Bush issued Executive Order 12807 on May 24, 1992, calling for "instructions to the Coast Guard in order to enforce the suspension of the entry of undocumented aliens at sea and the interdiction of any defined vessel carrying such aliens." The instructions included: (1) stopping and boarding vessels; (2) questioning those on board, examining their documents, and taking such actions as necessary to prevent unauthorized noncitizens from entering the United States; and (3) returning the vessel and its passengers to the country from which it came, although with the stipulation that the Attorney General could exercise discretion to decide that a refugee will not be returned involuntarily.[16] The measures outlined in the order were to be carried out only beyond the territorial waters of the United States.

To enforce the directive, the Coast Guard placed 17 cutters, five Navy ships, and nine aircraft in the Windward Passage between Haiti and Cuba under Operation Able Manner to intercept Haitian boats from January 15, 1993 through November 1994.

In the meantime, boat departures from Cuba were increasing, as were tensions on the island after several ferryboats were hijacked in July and August 1994 by would-be migrants. At least 37 migrants and two Cuban government employees were killed or drowned between July 13 and August 8.[17] In echoes of 1980, the Cuban government blamed the United States for encouraging the disorder and, on August 11, ordered security forces not to obstruct boat departures. The Coast Guard was deployed to prevent private U.S. vessels from carrying out another Cuban boatlift, and a few days later, on August 19, the U.S. government initiated a Cuban Mass Emergency Plan to prevent the illegal entry of unauthorized Cubans into the United States. Reversing the policy in place since 1966, Cubans interdicted at sea would not be taken to the United States; rather, they would be delivered to the U.S. naval facility at Guantánamo Bay, or to another "safe haven" facility in Panama.[18] Thirty-five cutters were stationed in the Straits of Florida for interception duty as part of Operation Able Vigil. In the week of August 22,

---

16 George H. W. Bush, "Executive Order 12807 of May 24, 1992—Interdiction of Illegal Aliens," *Federal Register* 57, no. 105 (June 1, 1992): 23133.

17 U.S. General Accounting Office (GAO), *Cuba: U.S. Response to the 1994 Cuban Migration Crisis* (Washington, DC: GAO, 1995).

18 Ibid.

1994 alone, more Cubans (10,190) were intercepted than in the decade between 1983 and 1993.

In both operations, intercepted migrants had no opportunity to proceed directly to the United States, even if they were able to demonstrate a credible fear of persecution. After President Clinton assumed office in 1993, the policy of summary return of all Haitians intercepted at sea was modified. At that point, U.S. authorities attempted to determine refugee status on board Coast Guard vessels outfitted for the purpose—a practice that raised questions of safety and fairness[19]—but the available spaces were quickly overwhelmed by the sheer number of people whose cases needed to be reviewed. Adjudications were suspended, and Haitians intercepted at sea were held at Guantánamo. When the restoration of the Aristide government in late 1994 brought a measure of calm, at least temporarily, to their homeland, most of the intercepted Haitians were repatriated. Even if there were refugees among them, the country was deemed safe enough for return.

II. The Legacy of the 1980s and 1990s

Operation Able Vigil ended in September 1994 after the conclusion of a bilateral migration agreement between Cuba and the United States. (This, and a companion agreement in 1995, remained the only formal U.S.-Cuba bilateral agreements until President Obama reopened diplomatic relations with Cuba in December 2014.) The agreement provided for the admission of 20,000 Cubans per year, both refugees and immigrants, to be processed in Havana and admitted directly to the United States.[20] The Cuban government agreed to crack down on boat departures, but not to penalize people who had left and returned in order to participate in the direct departure program. The goal of the agreement was to provide a legal pathway to the United States so that Cubans would not risk their lives on the high seas. The Cuban exceptionalism of U.S. immigration policy was thus maintained. Most of the Cubans who had left by boat and been held in Guantánamo or Panama were

---

19 See Azadeh Dastyari, *United States Migrant Interdiction and the Detention of Refugees in Guantánamo Bay* (Cambridge: Cambridge University Press, 2015).
20 U.S. Department of State, "Cuba: Implementation of Migration Agreement" (statement, October 12, 1994).

eventually paroled into the United States,[21] but henceforth Cubans picked up by the Coast Guard would be returned to Cuba and instructed on how to apply for direct departure. Outside the framework of the U.S.-Cuba migration agreements, however, a vestige of earlier practice lives on: Cubans who manage to evade the Coast Guard patrols and land on U.S. soil are allowed to remain in the United States and adjust their status to legal permanent residence after one year—the so-called "wet-foot/dry-foot" policy. This policy gives Cubans an incentive to continue to attempt unauthorized entry by sea even though alternative, legal channels are available, if imperfect.

The main alternative is to apply for direct departure through the processing center at the U.S. Interests Section of the Embassy of Switzerland in Havana and, since July 2015, at the newly opened U.S. Embassy in Havana.[22] U.S. officers conduct screening interviews to determine if individuals qualify for refugee status—i.e., by demonstrating, among other things, "persecution or a well-founded fear of persecution on account of race, religion, nationality, membership in a particular social group, or political opinion."[23] Cubans can also apply for immigrant visas if they qualify by, for example, having family members in the United States.

In addition to Cubans and Haitians, the third-largest national group among the migrants intercepted at sea by the U.S. Coast Guard is those from the Dominican Republic. A peak in arrivals from the Dominican Republic in 1995–96 prompted the deployment of another Coast Guard operation, Able Response, in which 9,500 people were interdicted or forced to turn back to the Dominican Republic (see Table 1). In 2004, Dominicans accounted for more than half of the nearly 10,000 interceptions in the Caribbean; by 2014 their share had dropped to just 8

---

21 A person who is not otherwise eligible for a visa may be allowed to enter the United States in case of a compelling emergency through the use of humanitarian parole. Parole does not confer any immigration benefits, but persons who is granted parole may apply for another status for which they are eligible. In the case of Cubans, once they reach the United States they may apply for permanent residency under the *Cuban Adjustment Act*. See U.S. Citizenship and Immigration Services (USCIS), "Humanitarian Parole," updated August 18, 2016.

22 The United States and Cuba long lacked formal diplomatic relations, and hence no official embassies operated. Instead, the U.S. Interests Section in Havana and the equivalent Cuba Interest Section in Washington, DC served to represent national interests. In July 2015, the embassies were reopened. See Karen DeYoung, "In Historic Cuba Visit, Kerry Presides over Raising of U.S. Flag over Embassy in Havana," *The Washington Post*, August 15, 2015.

23 *Immigration and Nationality Act of 1965*, Public Law 89–236 (1965), § 101(a)(42) (A).

percent of total interceptions.[24] Overall, Dominicans receive the same treatment as Haitians in terms of screening and return.

U.S. operations to counter unauthorized immigration in the Caribbean–North American region have necessitated an increase in international cooperation, information sharing, and joint security operations. For instance, a partnership approach is utilized in the Bahamas and Turks and Caicos, whereby the U.S. Coast Guard is given permission to patrol their large expanse of territorial waters to prevent illegal immigration as well as the drug trade.[25] International cooperation is also important when resettling refugees and providing for their well-being while awaiting settlement. The United Nations High Commissioner for Refugees (UNHCR) and the International Organization for Migration (IOM) have a strong presence, including offices, in most Caribbean countries. Along with humanitarian organizations, they provide technical support to governments in matters relating to refugees, including interim care.

The simultaneous Haitian and Cuban migration crises of the mid-1990s, although the numbers involved were small in relation to the U.S. population, opened a new era in U.S. interception policy and practice in the Caribbean, marked by a determination to prevent unauthorized arrivals by boat and to deal harshly with those who defy the ban. When in 2004 political chaos and violence again reached a peak in Haiti, forcing President Aristide to flee the country for a second time and spurring the U.S. government to mount another interdiction operation, President George W. Bush emphasized, "I have made it abundantly clear to the Coast Guard that we will turn back any refugee that attempts to reach our shore."[26] Attorney General John Ashcroft characterized Haitian boat arrivals as a threat to national security because of the diversion of Coast Guard resources. Such statements indicated that U.S. interception policy in the Caribbean had moved beyond rescue and prevention, with safeguards for refugees, to a policy of pure deterrence.

---

24 U.S. Coast Guard, "Alien Migrant Interdiction: U.S. Coast Guard Maritime Migrant Interdictions."

25 Operation Bahamas Turks and Caicos (OPBAT) is a tripartite agreement established in 1983 primarily focused on drug interdiction, but is also used for disaster response, search and rescue, and, increasingly, to counter illegal immigration. See Cleola Hamilton, "Rescue at Sea Operations, Interception and Disembarkation: Screening Identification and Referral Mechanisms for Mixed Arrivals in the Bahamas" (presentation by the Parliamentary Secretary, Ministry of Foreign Affairs and Immigration, the Bahamas, at the Caribbean Regional Conference on the Protection of Vulnerable Persons in Mixed Migration Flows – Promoting Cooperation and Identification of Good Practices, Nassau, the Bahamas, May 23, 2013).

26 George W. Bush, "President Bush Welcomes Georgian President Saakashvili to the White House" (remarks at a photo opportunity, February 25, 2004).

The persistence of this deterrence-based policy was demonstrated in 2010, after an earthquake measuring 7.0 on the Richter scale struck southwestern Haiti on January 12, causing widespread devastation around the Haitian capital of Port-au-Prince. The death and casualty toll as a result of the disaster numbered in the hundreds of thousands. The American response was twofold. On the one hand, the U.S. government pledged $100 million as part of a disaster-relief program just days after the event[27] and announced that Haitian migrants in the United States illegally would be granted Temporary Protected Status (TPS).[28] TPS grants Haitian nationals already present in the United States at the time of the earthquake legal residence and the right to work for 18 months. Since 2010 the TPS of Haitian nationals has been extended multiple times and is currently valid until July 22, 2017.[29] On the other hand, the Homeland Security Secretary, Janet Napolitano, announced that potential migrants from Haiti must not seek to enter the United States without authorization and that those caught at sea attempting to make the crossing would be repatriated. Napolitano argued that a migrant crisis would divert U.S. attention from relief efforts.[30] One week after the earthquake struck, on January 19, 2010, military officials announced an operation dubbed Vigilant Sentry, in which a U.S. Navy and Coast Guard task force was deployed in Haiti's territorial waters to prevent a migrant exodus as well as to deliver supplies to the beleaguered population.[31]

III. Recent Developments in Migration Flows and Policy

For migrants who are intercepted at sea, the door to the United States is quite firmly shut, even if they have valid refugee claims. Those of any nationality who pass a credible-fear screening are taken to Guantána-

---

27 James Sturcke, "Haiti Quake: Obama Announces $100m US Aid Package," *The Guardian*, January 14, 2010.

28 U.S. Department of Homeland Security (DHS), "Statement from Homeland Security Secretary Janet Napolitano on Temporary Protected Status (TPS) for Haitian Nationals" (press release, January 15, 2010).

29 USCIS, "Temporary Protected Status Extended for Haiti" (press release, August 25, 2015).

30 Spencer S. Hsu, "Officials Try to Prevent Haitian Earthquake Refugees from Coming to U.S." *The Washington Post*, January 18, 2010.

31 Bruno Waterfield, "Haiti Earthquake: U.S. Ships Blockade Coast to Thwart Exodus to America," *The Telegraph*, January 19, 2010.

mo. If, during adjudication procedures in Guantánamo, they are found to have valid refugee claims, the U.S. government seeks a third country to accept them for resettlement. Australia, Nicaragua, Spain, and Venezuela are among the countries that have accepted Cuban refugees for resettlement from Guantánamo.[32] They are not considered for resettlement in the United States, even if they have close family ties there—a policy that is meant to deter maritime migration. However, the actions of the executive branch vis-à-vis Cuban migrants are constrained by the *Cuban Adjustment Act*,[33] which gives access to legal status to Cubans who reach dry land in the United States.

Non-Cubans who arrive by boat in the United States without authorization are subject to summary return if they do not meet the credible-fear test and to mandatory detention during their adjudication period if they do. By contrast, several thousand refugees come directly from Cuba to the United States every year under the terms of the U.S.–Cuba Migration Agreement. The number of arrivals was about 6,360 in FY 2005 and 4,205 in FY 2013. Only four Haitians were granted refugee status between 2010 and 2014.[34] U.S. Department of Homeland Security (DHS) records dating back to 1995 indicate that no nationals from other Caribbean countries have been granted refugee status in the United States.[35] In 2012, there were 155 Cubans, 217 Dominicans, 827 Haitians, and 232 Jamaicans who sought asylum after reaching the United States by land, sea, or air.[36]

The logic behind current U.S. policy in the Caribbean is that even refugees will not approach U.S. shores without authorization if they are convinced that the journey across the Caribbean will not lead to legal stay and protection in the United States. Some have tried instead to reach other countries: Haitians have arrived by boat in Cuba, the Bahamas, Jamaica, and the Dominican Republic.[37] Meanwhile, many Cubans now travel by land to the U.S. southwestern border via Mexico, which allows them to take advantage of the "dry-foot" policy. There were 43,159 such land arrivals in FY 2015—an increase of more than

---

32 Wasem, *Cuban Migration to the United States.*

33 *Cuban Adjustment Act*, Public Law 89-732, *U.S. Statutes at Large* 80 (1966): 1161.

34 DHS Office of Immigration Statistics, *2014 Yearbook of Immigration Statistics* (Washington, DC: DHS, 2016).

35 DHS Office of Immigration Statistics, *2004 Yearbook of Immigration Statistics* (Washington, DC: DHS, 2006).

36 U.S. Department of Justice (DOJ), Executive Office for Immigration Review, *Asylum Statistics: FY 2011–2015* (Washington, DC: DOJ, 2016).

37 Wasem, *Cuban Migration to the United States.* Note that most Haitian travel to the Dominican Republic by land.

78 percent over 2014—and this figure had already been exceeded in the first ten months of FY 2016.[38]

Even with the dramatic increase in Cuban arrivals at the land borders of the United States (and small numbers from other countries), some migrants continue to attempt maritime journeys. Immediately after the December 17, 2014 announcement of a thaw in U.S.-Cuban relations,[39] Cuban boat departures accelerated—presumably because Cubans anticipated the repeal of the *Cuban Adjustment Act* and the end of the wet-foot/dry-foot policy. The numbers of Cubans intercepted in the second half of December 2014, after the announcement, rose 164 percent over the first half. The number of irregular Cuban boat departures more than doubled between FY 2013 and FY 2015, reaching a volume not seen since the crisis of 1994. Of these departures, 2,927 were intercepted at sea in FY 2015, the largest number of interceptions since 1994.[40] (Haitian interceptions, meanwhile, nearly doubled from FY 2013 to FY 2014, but then sank back again to about the FY 2013 level in FY 2015.[41]) Most disturbingly, a reported 87 percent of those intercepted were traveling in homemade, unseaworthy craft described by the Coast Guard as "really unsafe."[42] Few Cubans can afford smugglers' fees, which may be as much as US $10,000 per person, and mounting frustration with economic stagnation in post-Fidel Cuba is prompting migrants to use methods that have already resulted in "a trail of deaths."[43]

These and other developments in Caribbean and Central American migration patterns highlight the grave concerns that arise from a policy of deterrence that makes no allowance for the fact that unauthorized journeys by sea are often the only means of escape open to refugees. If such individuals are systematically prevented from making such an escape, the system of international protection is seriously weakened. At best, the responsibility of protecting these refugees is unilaterally deflected to other states; at worst, they are forced to

---

38 Krogstad, "Surge in Cuban Immigration."

39 Speech by Barack Obama, President of the United States, *Statement by the President on Cuba Policy Changes*, Washington, DC, December 17, 2014.

40 U.S. Coast Guard, "Alien Migrant Interdiction: U.S. Coast Guard Maritime Migrant Interdictions."

41 Ibid.

42 Remarks by a U.S. Coast Guard representative at a private meeting arranged by the Bureau of Population, Refugees, and Migration (PRM) at the U.S. Department of State, Washington, DC, October 29, 2015.

43 Frances Robles, "In Rickety Boats, Cuban Migrants Again Flee to U.S.," *The New York Times*, October 9, 2014.

remain in a situation where they are vulnerable to persecution. Harsh treatment of unauthorized asylum seekers challenges Article 31 of the Refugee Convention, which says that states party to the Convention should not impose penalties on refugees because they have arrived illegally.

The procedures for assessing a credible fear of persecution among Haitians intercepted at sea appear, since February 2004, to be so exacting as to fail to meet even the barest of minimum standards of international refugee law. Haitians are given no information on how to request asylum; they must spontaneously and unmistakably make themselves heard by officials on board Coast Guard vessels to get even the credible-fear interview, a procedure known as the "shout test." When implementation of this practice began, refugee experts found Haiti "too dangerous to permit the return of Haitians to their country,"[44] UNHCR pleaded with governments to respect the right of Haitians to seek asylum, and the U.S. State Department advised Americans to leave the country.[45] In the first few days after President Bush's 2004 announcement, 905 Haitians were intercepted by the Coast Guard. Only three passed the shout test, and not one was found to have a credible fear of persecution. All were forcibly returned to Haiti[46]—an "inexplicably low" recognition rate, according to UNHCR.[47] In 2005, 1,850 Haitians were intercepted at sea; only one was granted refugee status.[48] The deterrent effect of interdiction coupled with the low rate of recognition was evident as the number of Haitians to attempt the sea voyage declined in the years that followed. The number of Haitians prescreened on Coast Guard vessels decreased from 2,493 in 2005 to a low of 440 in 2010.[49] Since that time, nearly every Haitian intercepted at sea has been returned directly to Haiti.

44 Human Rights Watch (HRW), "Haiti: U.S. Return of Asylum Seekers Is Illegal" (news release, February 29, 2004).

45 UN High Commissioner for Refugees (UNHCR), "UNHCR Urges International Support for Haitians and Right of Asylum" (news release, February 26, 2004); Letter from Mark Franken, Chair of Refugee Council USA, to President George W. Bush, March 3, 2004.

46 HRW, *Submission to the Committee on the Elimination of Racial Discrimination during its Consideration of the Fourth, Fifth and Sixth Periodic Reports of the United States of America, CERD 72nd Session* (New York: HRW, 2008).

47 Remarks by Kolude Doherty, UNHCR Regional Representative for the United States and the Caribbean, at a roundtable on "Haiti in Turmoil: Assistance, Protection, and Flight" at MPI, Washington, DC, March 18, 2004.

48 Wasem, *Cuban Migration to the United States.*

49 Author email correspondence with Michael Valverde, Refugee, Asylum, and International Operations Directorate, Office of International Operations, USCIS, June 13, 2014.

Intercepted Cubans, on the other hand, are asked if they have concerns about returning to Cuba, and are automatically given a credible-fear interview if they answer in the affirmative. If they arrive by boat under their own power in the United States, they are not subject to expedited removal procedures and are usually released from detention shortly after filing an asylum claim. Cubans who arrive in this manner are eligible to adjust to lawful permanent residence within one year.

The differential treatment accorded to Cubans as compared with other maritime migrants from the Caribbean raises issues of discrimination on the grounds of nationality. Cubans continue to take the risks of traveling by sea because they know that if they reach the United States, they will be allowed to stay; as a result, in 2015 Cubans made up 76 percent of all Coast Guard interdictions (see Table 2). The comparatively lower numbers of Haitians and other nationalities indicate that, for them, the cost-benefit calculation has shifted against unauthorized maritime migration. (Although few Chinese migrants are intercepted in the Caribbean, those who do are asked, via a written form, why they left China. Some special protection programs apply to those who left for reasons of coercive family-planning measures.)

Table 2. U.S. Maritime Migrant Interdictions by Nationality, 1982–2015

Country	2015		1982–2015	
	Number of Interdictions	Share of all Interdictions	Number of Interdictions	Share of All Interdictions
Cuban	2,927	76%	75,698	30%
Haitian	561	15%	120,226	48%
Dominican	257	7%	37,196	15%
Mexican	27	1%	1,002	0%
Chinese	10	0%	5,956	2%
Ecuadorian	3	0%	8,269	3%
Other	43	1%	2,058	1%
Total	3,828	100%	248,316	100%

Source: U.S. Coast Guard, "Alien Migrant Interdiction: Total Interdictions – Fiscal Year 1982 to Present," updated January 19, 2016.

The *Refugee Protection Act of 2013*, introduced by Senator Patrick Leahy (D-VT) during a prior session of Congress, contained provisions regarding individuals interdicted at sea that could have helped address inequities between migrants of different nationalities.[50] The legislation would have required an asylum interview for any migrant intercepted at sea who expressed a fear of return. It would also have required DHS to establish a uniform asylum-screening procedure that provided the interdicted individual a "meaningful opportunity to express a fear of return through a translator and ... information about their ability to inform U.S. officers about a fear of return." The *Refugee Protection Act* would have also required that successful asylum seekers be given the opportunity "to seek protection in a country where he or she has family or other ties or, absent such ties, to be resettled in the United States."[51] However, after being introduced by Senator Leahy it was referred to the Senate Judiciary Committee, where it died. No further legislative efforts of such scope have attempted to redress the uneven treatment of different nationalities under U.S. law.

IV. Refugee Policy in Caribbean Countries

Although Caribbean countries are more often sources of refugees, several countries such as the Dominican Republic, the Bahamas, and Trinidad and Tobago also host refugees.

The Dominican Republic is the only country in the Caribbean that has enacted asylum legislation.[52] At the end of 2015, it was host to 615 recognized refugees and had 758 asylum claims pending.[53] Dwarfing these numbers, however, were the 133,770 people, almost all Haitians, who were present in the country and covered by the UNHCR mandate to assist stateless people.[54] This group consists almost entirely of people of Haitian descent, who were stripped of their Dominican citizenship in 2013 and have had very limited ability to reclaim it despite the opening

---

50 *Refugee Protection Act of 2013*, S 645, 113th Cong., 1st sess., *Congressional Record* 159, no. 42, daily ed. (March 21, 2013): S2149.

51 Ibid., Section 24.

52 The Dominican Republic enacted asylum legislation in 1983 and created institutions to oversee its implementation in 1984. See Salvador Jorge Blanco, "Decreto presidencial No. 2330 de 10 de septiembre de 1984, reglamento de la Comisión Nacional para los Refugiados" (decree by the president of the Dominican Republic, September 10, 1984); Women's Refugee Commission, *Refugee Policy Adrift: The United States and Dominican Republic Deny Haitians Protection* (New York: Women's Refugee Commission, 2003).

53 UNHCR, *Global Trends: Forced Displacement in 2015* (Geneva: UNHCR, 2016), Annex Table I.

54 Ibid.

of a formal channel to do so in 2014.[55] Many Haitians and Dominicans of Haitian descent have reportedly been forced to return to Haiti without consideration of their citizenship claims or their potential refugee status. Although Haitians travel to the Dominican Republic by land rather than by sea, the Dominican Republic's policies influence maritime departures, as some of those expelled may take to the sea to avoid violence, persecution, or severe deprivation in Haiti.

In the period following the January 12, 2010 earthquake in Haiti, the Dominican Republic was one of several countries that temporarily admitted Haitian refugees to receive disaster relief and medical attention, leading to a reported influx of 500,000 or more Haitians.[56] However, several months after the quake, the Dominican Republic (as well as Jamaica and the Bahamas, which had also accepted disaster victims), began deporting Haitian refugees en masse, amid concerns that they were causing disease outbreaks and exacerbating already high unemployment levels in struggling host-country economies.[57]

Critics, including the U.S. State Department and UNHCR, claim that the Dominican asylum system, run by the National Commission for Refugees (CONARE), is dysfunctional in practice.[58] UNHCR has estimated that more than 200 asylum cases, corresponding to 820 individual claimants and their families—most of them Haitian nationals fleeing political turmoil in the 1990s and 2000s—have remained unresolved for more than a decade.[59] Other asylum seekers on the waiting list were from Sri Lanka, Cuba, Colombia, and Iran. While they wait, these individuals lack documentation and employment authorization. The process of clearing the asylum backlog has been excruciatingly slow.

In the Bahamas there was no consistent system for processing and protecting refugees and asylum seekers until 2013, despite it being a signatory to the 1951 Convention and the 1967 Protocol. However, since

55 HRW, *We Are Dominican: Arbitrary Deprivation of Nationality in the Dominican Republic* (New York: HRW, 2015).

56 Randal C. Archibold, "As Refugees from Haiti Linger, Dominicans' Good Will Fades," *The New York Times,* August 30, 2011.

57 These countries have experienced high unemployment rates in the past several years. In 2014, the rate was an estimated 14.2 percent in Jamaica, 14.5 percent in the Dominican Republic, and 15 percent in the Bahamas. See Central Intelligence Agency (CIA), "World Factbook—Unemployment Rate," accessed August 30, 2016.

58 U.S. Department of State, *Dominican Republic 2013 Human Rights Report* (Washington, DC: U.S. Department of State, 2014).

59 U.S. Conference of Catholic Bishops (USCCB), Migration and Refugee Services, *MRS/USCCB Mission to the Dominican Republic* (Washington, DC: USCCB, 2012).

2014 the Bahamian government has improved its practices and now individuals trained by UNHCR provide screenings for asylum applicants and then refer them to the Ministry of Foreign Affairs and Immigration (MFA) for refugee adjudication if they are found to have a credible fear of persecution. Following MFA approval, the candidates are forwarded to the cabinet for a final decision.[60] However, the Bahamas follows the U.S. lead in interdictions. Cubans intercepted in Bahamian waters, whether by the U.S. or Bahamian Coast Guard, have their asylum claims processed in the Bahamas. Intercepted Haitians are summarily returned to Haiti. At the end of 2015, UNHCR reported that the Bahamas was hosting eight refugees and had 21 asylum cases pending; another 86 people were receiving some other form of assistance or protection from UNHCR.[61]

Trinidad and Tobago is also a signatory to the UN Refugee Convention and Protocol, but the government has not yet passed legislation to implement its obligations under these conventions.[62] So, in effect, refugees have no enforceable rights in the country, including no right to work. The government delegates care of asylum seekers to the Living Water Community (LWC), a local Roman Catholic social services agency that both provides for their immediate needs and looks for settlement opportunities for them in other Caribbean countries as well as in Trinidad and Tobago. LWC reports that many persons who file asylum claims in Trinidad and Tobago eventually abandon their applications, and either leave the country or walk away from the LWC because the agency cannot guarantee protection. Trinidad and Tobago hosted 114 refugees and 25 asylum seekers at the end of 2015.[63] In addition to Cubans, they included nationals from Ghana, Nigeria, and Senegal.[64]

The Cuban government has no formal mechanism to process the asylum claims of foreign nationals, and has not signed the 1951 Convention or the 1967 Protocol. However, the Cuban Constitution does provide for asylum to be granted to individuals who are persecuted for their beliefs or their actions in pursuit of specified political ideals. For the small number of asylum cases, the government works with UNHCR (although the agency does not have an office in the country) and other humanitar-

---

60 U.S. Department of State, *Bahamas 2014 Human Rights Report* (Washington, DC: U.S. Department of State, 2015).

61 UNHCR, *Global Trends*, Annex Table I.

62 U.S. Department of State, *Trinidad and Tobago 2013 Human Rights Report* (Washington, DC: U.S. Department of State, 2014).

63 UNHCR, *Global Trends*, Annex Table I.

64 Carol Matroo, "100 Refugees Seek TT Asylum," *Trinidad and Tobago Newsday*, January 12, 2014.

ian organizations to provide protection and assistance, pending third-country settlement.[65] According to UNHCR, Cuba hosted 303 refugees at the end of 2015, and had 25 asylum cases pending.[66]

The scarcity of opportunities to seek asylum within the Caribbean region stems in large part from a tendency of authorities in Caribbean countries to regard unauthorized migrants, especially those traveling by sea, as strictly economic migrants, regardless of the turmoil that may envelop their countries of origin. Migration among the Caribbean countries accounts for only about 10 percent of overall migration, as North America remains the favored destination. Among intra-Caribbean migration flows people typically travel from poorer to more prosperous countries in the region; Haiti, the Dominican Republic, Guyana, and Jamaica are the main countries of origin, and the Bahamas, the British and U.S. Virgin Islands, and Turks and Caicos are the main destinations.[67]

V. Looking Ahead

The U.S. Coast Guard, as an instrument of U.S. migrant interception policy, has interdicted maritime travelers from 63 countries. The epicenter of its efforts lies in the Caribbean region, in particular the waters that separate Cuba and Haiti from the United States. Relevant policy development has been crisis driven, shaped by the Mariel boatlift from Cuba in 1980, large exoduses from Haiti and Cuba in the wake of political turmoil in the mid-1990s, and national-security concerns following the terrorist attacks of September 11, 2001. But migration in the region is also heavily influenced by the U.S. government's continuing ambivalence about Cuban migration, embodied in the wet-foot/dry-foot policy.

Interception and return of maritime migrants and acceptance of Cuban migrants who reach dry land, in combination with the fear that thawing relations between the United States and Cuba may result in the end of this privileged position has created a classic "squeezing the balloon" effect, with most Cuban abandoning the sea routes and attempting to reach the United States by land. The ongoing surge of

---

65 U.S. Department of State, *Cuba 2013 Human Rights Report* (Washington, DC: U.S. Department of State, 2014).
66 UNHCR, *Global Trends*, Annex Table I.
67 International Organization for Migration, "Responding to Migration Challenges in the Caribbean" (press release, December 3, 2009).

Cuban migration from December 2014 through 2016, through South and Central America north to the U.S.–Mexico border,[68] is a serious irritant in relations between the United States and the South and Central American countries affected by the influx. It has also roiled the relations among countries on the route. The affected countries are united only in blaming the United States for causing the problems.

Three issues have been central to the disputes: 1) the growth of smuggling networks that facilitate migrant journeys across multiple borders and the threats they pose to migrants and to the rule of law; 2) the stranding of migrants in transit countries as they run out of money or face administrative barriers as they move northward; and 3) the discrimination against other groups of migrants compared to the Cubans, which rankles the governments of those nationals who do not enjoy privileged access to the United States.

In actions reminiscent of the closing of the Balkan route from Greece to northern Europe (see Chapter 2), starting in the winter of 2015, Central and South American countries have tried to close their borders to Cubans. Both Ecuador and Costa Rica have revoked visa-free travel for Cubans and said that new Cuban migrants without authorization would be deported.[69] Violence has ensued along the Costa Rican border with both Panama and Nicaragua as frustrated migrants forced their way across. Panama struck a deal with Mexico to fly almost 4,000 Cubans to Ciudad Juarez on the U.S.-Mexico border, and then closed its border with Colombia in May 2016.[70] Colombia said it would no longer issue transit visas to Cubans and has equated official facilitation of onward travel to human trafficking.[71] Nicaragua, one of Cuba's closest allies, closed its border with Costa Rica to prevent Cubans (and other migrants) from traveling north.[72] As a result, an estimated 9,500 Cuban migrants were stranded in Costa Rica.[73] Since Nicaragua is the only land route from Costa Rica through Central America to Mexico and the

68 Krogstad, "Surge in Cuban Immigration."

69 Zach Dyer, "Cuban Migrants Continue Arriving as Costa Rica Declares 'Mission Accomplished,'" *The Tico Times*, March 17, 2016; TeleSUR, "Undocumented Cubans in Ecuador Face Deportation," TeleSUR, July 7, 2016.

70 BBC News, "Nicaragua Turns Back Cuban Migrants to Costa Rica," BBC News, November 16, 2015; Sofia Menchu, "Deal Reached to Allow Stranded Cuban Migrants out of Costa Rica," Reuters, December 29, 2015.

71 Jim Wyss, "Colombia Denies Airlift for Cuban Migrants, to Begin Deportations," *Miami Herald,* August 2, 2016.

72 BBC News, "Nicaragua Turns Back Cuban Migrants."

73 José Meléndez, "Costa Rica Says its Doors are Closed to Cubans," *Miami Herald,* April 11, 2016.

U.S. border, the closing of its border prompted Costa Rica, Guatemala, El Salvador, and Mexico to cooperate on a land-and-air bridge to transport the stranded Cubans to the U.S. border.[74]

Even as El Salvador participated in the bridge arrangement, its foreign minister complained of the inherent unfairness of the wet-foot/dry-foot policy.[75] The president of Costa Rica also blamed the United States for the continuing migrant crisis in Central America.[76] Finally, in August 2016, nine Latin American foreign ministers sent a letter to U.S. Secretary of State John Kerry calling for revision of the *Cuban Adjustment Act* and the wet-foot/dry-foot policy, writing that they have "encouraged a disorderly, irregular, and unsafe flow of Cubans who, risking their lives, pass through our countries in order to reach the U.S. ....this situation has generated a migratory crisis that is affecting our countries."[77]

It remained unclear, as of late 2016, what impact, if any, the thaw in U.S.-Cuban relations would have on U.S. immigration policy over the long term. In the immediate aftermath of the announcement by President Obama of a détente with the Castro government, U.S. government officials announced that the wet-foot/dry-foot policy would remain in place. Repeal of the *Cuban Adjustment Act,* or changes to it, would require congressional action.

Policies forged during crises do not always age well, as they often contradict more enduring concerns and principles. But U.S. interception policy in the Caribbean has endured for more than 35 years, and there is little indication that it will eventually return to its origins as a means of bringing order and greater safety to maritime travel, while leaving open the possibility for refugees to get the protection they need. In the meantime, profound concerns that U.S. policies are abetting refoulement, deterrence, and discrimination in the Caribbean require close examination and countries in the region seek more normal, lawful migration patterns through calmer seas.

---

74 *The Economist,* "The Last Wave: The Urge to Leave in Strong, but the Opportunity is Diminishing," *The Economist,* January 16, 2016.

75 Associated Press, "Cuban Migrants Stranded in Costa Rica Finally Begin Journey to US," *The Guardian,* January 13, 2016.

76 Zach Dyer, "Cuban Migrants Continue Arriving."

77 Government of Ecuador, Ministry of Foreign Relations and Human Mobility, "Nine Latin American Countries Sign Letter Urging the United States to Review its Policy on Cuban Immigration" (press release, August 29, 2016).

Works Cited

Archibold, Randal C. 2011. As Refugees from Haiti Linger, Dominicans' Good Will Fades. *The New York Times,* August 30, 2011. www.nytimes. com/2011/08/31/world/americas/31haitians.html.

Associated Press. 2016. Cuban Migrants Stranded in Costa Rica Finally Begin Journey to US. *The Guardian,* January 13, 2016. www.theguardian.com/world/2016/jan/13/cuba-migrants-stranded-costa-rica-us-nicaragua.

BBC News. 2015. Nicaragua Turns Back Cuban Migrants to Costa Rica. BBC News, November 16, 2015. www.bbc.com/news/world-latin-america-34832184.

Blanco, Salvador Jorge. 1984. Decreto presidencial No. 2330 de 10 de septiembre de 1984, reglamento de la Comisión Nacional para los Refugiados. Decree by the president of the Dominican Republic, September 10, 1984. www. refworld.org/docid/3dbe9dfb6.html.

Bush, George H. W. 1992. Executive Order 12807 of May 24, 1992—Interdiction of Illegal Aliens. *Federal Register* 57, no. 105 (June 1, 1992): 23133. www.uscg. mil/hq/cg5/cg531/AMIO/eo12807.pdf.

Bush, George W. 2004. President Bush Welcomes Georgian President Saakashvili to the White House. Remarks at a photo opportunity, February 25, 2004. https://georgewbush-whitehouse.archives.gov/news/releases/2004/02/text/20040225-1.html.

Central Intelligence Agency (CIA). N.d. World Factbook—Unemployment Rate. Accessed August 30, 2016. www.cia.gov/library/publications/resources/the-world-factbook/fields/2129.html#jm.

Chaparro, Luis. 2016. Texas Shelters, Churches Fear Sudden Influx of Cuban Migrants Will Overwhelm Them. Fox News Latino, May 18, 2016. http://latino.foxnews.com/latino/news/2016/05/18/texas-shelters-churches-fear-sudden-influx-cuban-migrants-will-overwhelm-them.

Cuban Adjustment Act. Public Law 89-732. *U.S. Statutes at Large* 80. November 2, 1966. http://uscode.house.gov/statutes/pl/89/732.pdf.

Dastyari, Azadeh. 2015. *United States Migrant Interdiction and the Detention of Refugees in Guantánamo Bay.* Cambridge: Cambridge University Press.

DeYoung, Karen. 2015. In Historic Cuba Visit, Kerry Presides over Raising of U.S. Flag over Embassy in Havana. *The Washington Post,* August 15, 2015. www. washingtonpost.com/world/national-security/us-flag-to-fly-again-over-newly-reopened-embassy-in-cuba/2015/08/14/a6797036-41cf-11e5-8e7d-9c033e6745d8_story.html.

Doherty, Kolude. 2004. Remarks by the UNHCR Regional Representative for the United States and the Caribbean at a roundtable on Haiti in Turmoil: Assistance, Protection, and Flight. Migration Policy Institute, Washington, DC, March 18, 2004.

Dyer, Zach. 2016. Cuban Migrants Continue Arriving as Costa Rica Declares "Mission Accomplished." *The Tico Times,* March 17, 2016. www.ticotimes.net/2016/03/17/cuban-migrants-continue-arriving-costa-rica-declares-mission-accomplished.

Economist, The. 2016. The Last Wave: The Urge to Leave in Strong, but the Opportunity is Diminishing. *The Economist*, January 16, 2016. www.economist.com/news/americas/21688425-urge-leave-strong-opportunity-diminishing-last-wave.

Fernández, Abel. 2016. Cuban Migrants Force their Way across the Panama-Costa Rica Border. *Miami Herald*, April 14, 2016. www.miamiherald.com/news/nation-world/world/americas/cuba/article71802002.html.

Franken, Mark. 2004. Letter from the Chair of Refugee Council USA to President George W. Bush, March 3, 2004.

Glass, Andrew. 2009. Castro Launches Mariel Boatlift. Politico, April 20, 2009. www.politico.com/story/2009/04/castro-launches-mariel-boatlift-april-20-1980-021421.

Global Security. N.d. Mariel Boatlift. Accessed August 8, 2016. www.globalsecurity.org/military/ops/mariel-boatlift.htm.

Goodhue, David. 2016. 40 Cubans Arrive Monday Night to Florida Keys. *Miami Herald*, July 18, 2016. www.miamiherald.com/news/local/community/florida-keys/article90437807.html.

Government of Ecuador, Ministry of Foreign Relations and Human Mobility. 2016. Nine Latin American Countries Sign Letter Urging the United States to Review its Policy on Cuban Immigration. Press release, August 29, 2016. www.cancilleria.gob.ec/en/nine-latin-american-countries-sign-letter-urging-the-united-states-to-review-its-policy-on-cuban-immigration/.

Hamilton, Cleola. 2013. Rescue at Sea Operations, Interception and Disembarkation: Screening Identification and Referral Mechanisms for Mixed Arrivals in the Bahamas. Presentation by the Parliamentary Secretary, Ministry of Foreign Affairs and Immigration, the Bahamas, at the Caribbean Regional Conference on the Protection of Vulnerable Persons in Mixed Migration Flows – Promoting Cooperation and Identification of Good Practices, Nassau, the Bahamas, May 23, 2013. www.unhcr.org/51dc011f21.html.

Hsu, Spencer S. 2010. Officials Try to Prevent Haitian Earthquake Refugees from Coming to U.S. *The Washington Post*, January 18, 2010. www.washingtonpost.com/wp-dyn/content/article/2010/01/17/AR2010011701893.html?sid=ST2010011703508.

Human Rights Watch (HRW). 2004. Haiti: U.S. Return of Asylum Seekers is Illegal. News release, February 29, 2004. www.hrw.org/news/2004/02/29/haiti-us-return-asylum-seekers-illegal.

———. 2008. *Submission to the Committee on the Elimination of Racial Discrimination during its Consideration of the Fourth, Fifth and Sixth Periodic Reports of the United States of America, CERD 72nd Session*. New York: HRW. www.hrw.org/reports/2008/us0208/us0208webwcover.pdf.

———. 2015. *We Are Dominican: Arbitrary Deprivation of Nationality in the Dominican Republic*. New York: HRW. www.hrw.org/report/2015/07/01/we-are-dominican/arbitrary-deprivation-nationality-dominican-republic.

Immigration and Nationality Act of 1965. Public Law 89–236, 1965. www.uscis.gov/ilink/docView/SLB/HTML/SLB/0-0-0-1/0-0-0-29/0-0-0-101/0-0-0-195.html.

International Organization for Migration. 2009. Responding to Migration Challenges in the Caribbean. Press release, December 3, 2009. www.iom.int/news/responding-migration-challenges-caribbean.

Krogstad, Jens Manuel. 2016. Surge in Cuban Immigration to U.S. Continues into 2016. Pew Research Center, August 5, 2016. www.pewresearch.org/fact-tank/2016/08/05/cuban-immigration-to-u-s-surges-as-relations-warm.

Matroo, Carol. 2014. 100 Refugees Seek TT Asylum. *Trinidad and Tobago Newsday*, January 12, 2014. www.newsday.co.tt/news/0,189071.html.

Meléndez, José. 2016. Costa Rica Says its Doors are Closed to Cubans. *Miami Herald*, April 11, 2016. www.miamiherald.com/news/nation-world/world/americas/cuba/article71239892.html.

Menchu, Sofia. 2015. Deal Reached to Allow Stranded Cuban Migrants out of Costa Rica. Reuters, December 29, 2015. www.reuters.com/article/us-cuba-migrants-idUSKBN0UC01L20151229.

Newland, Kathleen. 2006. Appendix B: The U.S. and the Caribbean. In *The New "Boat People": Ensuring Safety and Determining Status*, eds. Joanne van Selm and Betsy Cooper. Washington, DC: Migration Policy Institute. www.migrationpolicy.org/research/new-boat-people-ensuring-safety-and-determining-status.

Obama, Barack. 2014. Speech by the President of the United States on Cuba Policy Changes. Washington, DC, December 17, 2014. www.whitehouse.gov/the-press-office/2014/12/17/statement-president-cuba-policy-changes.

Reagan, Ronald. 1981. Proclamation 4865 of September 29, 1981—High Seas Interdiction of Illegal Aliens. *Federal Register* 46, no. 190 (October 1, 1981): 48107. www.archives.gov/federal-register/codification/proclamations/04865.html.

Robles, Frances. 2014. In Rickety Boats, Cuban Migrants Again Flee to U.S. *The New York Times*, October 9, 2014. www.nytimes.com/2014/10/10/us/sharp-rise-in-cuban-migration-stirs-worries-of-a-mass-exodus.html.

Sale v. Haitian Centers Council, Inc. 509 U.S. Reports 155, 1993. https://supreme.justia.com/cases/federal/us/509/155/.

Sturcke, James. 2010. Haiti Quake: Obama Announces $100m US Aid Package. *The Guardian*, January 14, 2010. www.theguardian.com/world/2010/jan/14/haiti-quake-obama-us-aid.

TeleSUR. 2016. Undocumented Cubans in Ecuador Face Deportation. TeleSUR, July 7, 2016. www.telesurtv.net/english/news/Undocumented-Cubans-in-Ecuador-Face-Deportation-20160707-0027.html.

United Nations High Commission for Refugees (UNHCR). 2004. UNHCR Urges International Support for Haitians and Right of Asylum. News release, February 26, 2004.

———. 2016. *Global Trends: Forced Displacement in 2015.* Geneva: UNHCR. www.unhcr.org/en-us/statistics/unhcrstats/576408cd7/unhcr-global-trends-2015.html.

U.S. Citizenship and Immigration Services (USCIS). 2015. Temporary Protected Status Extended for Haiti. Press release, August 25, 2015. www.uscis.gov/ news/news-releases/temporary-protected-status-extended-haiti.

———. 2016. Humanitarian Parole. Updated August 18, 2016. www.uscis.gov/humanitarian/humanitarian-parole.

U.S. Coast Guard. 2015. Remarks of by a U.S. Coast Guard representative at a private meeting arranged by the Bureau of Population, Refugees, and Migration at the U.S. Department of State, Washington, DC, October 29, 2015.

———. 2016. Alien Migrant Interdiction: History of the U.S. Coast Guard in Illegal Immigration (1794–1971). Updated January 12, 2016. www.uscg.mil/hq/ cg5/cg531/AMIO/amiohist.asp.

———. 2016. Alien Migrant Interdiction: Total Interdictions – Fiscal Year 1982 to Present. Updated January 19, 2016. www.uscg.mil/hq/cg5/cg531/AMIO/ FlowStats/FY.asp.

———. 2016. Alien Migrant Interdiction: U.S. Coast Guard Maritime Migrant Interdictions. Updated January 19, 2016. www.uscg.mil/hq/cg5/cg531/AMIO/ FlowStats/currentstats.asp.

U.S. Conference of Catholic Bishops (USCCB), Migration and Refugee Services. 2012. *MRS/USCCB Mission to the Dominican Republic.* Washington, DC: USCCB. www.usccb.org/about/migration-policy/fact-finding-mission-reports/upload/DR-Haiti-Report-Final.pdf.

U.S. Congress, Senate. *Refugee Protection Act of 2013.* S 645. 113th Cong., 1st sess. *Congressional Record* 159, no. 42, daily ed. (March 21, 2013): S2139. www. congress.gov/113/bills/s645/BILLS-113s645is.pdf.

U.S. Department of Homeland Security (DHS). 2010. Statement from Homeland Security Secretary Janet Napolitano on Temporary Protected Status (TPS) for Haitian Nationals. Press release, January 15, 2010. www.dhs.gov/ news/2010/01/15/secretary-napolitano-temporary-protected-status-tps-haitian-nationals.

U.S. Department of Homeland Security, Office of Immigration Statistics. 2006. *2004 Yearbook of Immigration Statistics.* Washington, DC: DHS. www.dhs.gov/ sites/default/files/publications/Yearbook2004.pdf.

———. 2016. *2014 Yearbook of Immigration Statistics.* Washington, DC: DHS. www. dhs.gov/sites/default/files/publications/ois_yb_2014.pdf.

U.S. Department of Justice (DOJ), Executive Office for Immigration Review. 2016. *Asylum Statistics: FY 2011–2015.* Washington, DC: DOJ. www.justice.gov/eoir/ file/asylum-statistics/download.

U.S. Department of State. 1994. Cuba: Implementation of Migration Agreement. Statement, October 12, 1994. http://dosfan.lib.uic.edu/ERC/bureaus/ lat/1994/941010ShellyCuba.html.

———. 2014. *Cuba 2013 Human Rights Report.* Washington, DC: U.S. Department of State. www.state.gov/j/drl/rls/hrrpt/2013/wha/220434.htm.

———. 2014. *Dominican Republic 2013 Human Rights Report.* Washington, DC: U.S. Department of State. www.state.gov/j/drl/rls/hrrpt/2013/wha/220439. htm.

———. 2014. *Trinidad and Tobago Republic 2013 Human Rights Report*. Washington, DC: U.S. Department of State. www.state.gov/documents/organization/220685.pdf.

———. 2015. *Bahamas 2014 Human Rights Report*. Washington, DC: U.S. Department of State. www.state.gov/documents/organization/236874.pdf.

U.S. General Accounting Office (GAO). 1995. *Cuba: U.S. Response to the 1994 Cuban Migration Crisis*. Washington, DC: GAO. www.gao.gov/archive/1995/ns95211. pdf.

Valverde, Michael. 2014. Author email correspondence with official from the Refugee, Asylum, and International Operations Directorate, Office of International Operations, USCIS, June 13, 2014.

Wasem, Ruth Ellen. 2009. *Cuban Migration to the United States: Policies and Trends*. Washington, DC: Congressional Research Service. www.fas.org/sgp/crs/ row/R40566.pdf.

Waterfield, Bruno. 2010. Haiti Earthquake: U.S. Ships Blockade Coast to Thwart Exodus to America. *The Telegraph,* January 19, 2010. www.telegraph.co.uk/ news/worldnews/centralamericaandthecaribbean/haiti/7030237/Haiti-earthquake-US-ships-blockade-coast-to-thwart-exodus-to-America.html.

Women's Refugee Commission. 2003. *Refugee Policy Adrift: The United States and Dominican Republic Deny Haitians Protection*. New York: Women's Refugee Commission. www.womensrefugeecommission.org/resources/ document/216-refugee-policy-adrift-the-united-states-and-dominican-republic-deny-haitians-protection.

Wyss, Jim. 2016. Colombia Denies Airlift for Cuban Migrants, to Begin Deportations. *Miami Herald,* August 2, 2016. www.miamiherald.com/news/nation-world/ world/americas/colombia/article93381367.html.

ACKNOWLEDGMENTS

I would like to thank the Irregular Migration Research Programme (now the Irregular Migration and Border Research Programme) at the Australian Department of Immigration and Border Protection for commissioning the Migration Policy Institute (MPI) to produce a paper on unauthorized maritime migration. That paper grew beyond the dimensions, scope, and timeframe originally envisioned, but the Programme provided the impetus that became this book. I am particularly grateful to Marie McAuliffe, who was a stimulating interlocutor, and opened doors to interviews in Australia as well as providing valuable source material—not least her own work. Her colleagues Victoria Mence and Chris Ritchie also provided great support. The then-Deputy Secretary of the Department of Immigration and Border Protection, Wendy Southern, gave encouragement and was a warm host during two trips to Australia.

The Regional Office for Asia and the Pacific of the International Organization for Migration (IOM) provided the opportunity to extend our research on the Bay of Bengal/Andaman Sea/Straits of Malacca region. An earlier draft of our case study on that region was jointly published with IOM and benefited from the comments of Andrew Bruce, Rabab Fatima, and their colleagues at IOM Bangkok.

The former UN High Commissioner for Refugees, António Guterres, gave impetus to my thinking about rescue at sea by inviting me to speak at the High Commissioner's Dialogue in 2014, and by applying his unique combination of intellectual rigor and political passion to the issue.

The completion of the book was made possible by the support MPI's International Program receives from the Open Society Foundations. We are extremely grateful for their support, and for the always useful feedback provided by Maria Teresa Rojas.

Most of all, I am grateful to my MPI colleagues: Elizabeth Collett, who took on the most daunting case study of the Mediterranean, Kate Hooper who wrote the chapter on the Red Sea/Gulf of Aden routes, and Sarah Flamm, who expanded the Caribbean study beyond U.S. policy to include the issues facing other Caribbean countries. Thanks also to Louis Metcalfe, who assisted us with research in the final round of updates. Finally, MPI's outstanding Communications team, led by

Michelle Mittelstadt, worked magic on the final draft to turn it into a publishable manuscript. Special thanks to Michelle, to Lauren Shaw for her meticulous and graceful editing, and to Liz Heimann for layout of the book.

I join millions of migrants and refugees everywhere in a debt of gratitude to Peter Sutherland, the Special Representative for International Migration of the UN Secretary-General. He has refused to let the world turn away from the responsibility owed to migrants and refugees as fellow human beings with inherent rights and dignity—and tremendous ability to contribute to the societies that welcome them. He and his senior advisor, Gregory Maniatis, have been supporters and contributors to this project from its earliest stage.

Finally, I would like to thank Jurek Martin for his patient encouragement and steadfast belief through an unreasonable number of late evenings at work, anxious mornings, spoiled weekends and vacations, and so on. I could not do it without him.

Kathleen Newland
Co-Founder and Senior Fellow, Migration Policy Institute

ABOUT THE AUTHORS

 Kathleen Newland is Co-Founder of the Migration Policy Institute (MPI). She is also the Founding Director of the International diaspora Engagement Alliance (IdEA) during its incubation phase at MPI from 2011–13; IdEA was established as a partnership among MPI, the U.S. Department of State, and U.S. Agency for International Development. She is a Member of the MPI Board of Trustees.

Previously, at the Carnegie Endowment for International Peace, she was a Senior Associate and then Co-Director of the International Migration Policy Program (1994–2001). She sits on the board of overseers of the International Rescue Committee and the boards of directors of USA for UNHCR, the Stimson Center, Kids in Need of Defense (KIND), and the Foundation for The Hague Process on Migrants and Refugees. She is a Chair Emerita of the Women's Commission for Refugee Women and Children.

Prior to joining the Migration Program at the Carnegie Endowment, Ms. Newland worked as an independent consultant for such clients as the UN High Commissioner for Refugees (UNHCR), the World Bank, and the office of the Secretary-General of the United Nations. From 1988–1992, Ms. Newland was on the faculty of the London School of Economics. During that time, she also co-founded (with Lord David Owen) and directed Humanitas, an educational trust dedicated to increasing awareness of international humanitarian issues. From 1982 to 1988, she worked at the United Nations University in Tokyo as Special Assistant to the Rector. She began her career as a researcher at Worldwatch Institute in 1974.

Ms. Newland is author or editor of eight books, including *Developing a Road Map for Engaging Diasporas in Development: A Handbook for Policymakers and Practitioners in Home and Host Countries* (MPI and International Organization for Migration, 2012); *Diasporas: New Partners in Global Development Policy* (MPI, 2010); *No Refuge: The Challenge of Internal Displacement* (United Nations, 2003); and *The State of the World's Refugees* (UNHCR, 1993). She has also written 17 shorter monographs as well as numerous policy papers, articles, and book chapters.

Ms. Newland is a graduate of Harvard University and the Woodrow Wilson School at Princeton University. She did additional graduate work at the London School of Economics.

Elizabeth Collett is the Founding Director of MPI Europe and Senior Advisor to MPI's Transatlantic Council on Migration. She is based in Brussels, and her work focuses in particular on European migration and immigrant integration policy. Ms. Collett convenes MPI Europe's working group on the future of the Common European Asylum System (EU Asylum: Towards 2020), bringing together senior policymakers from more than a dozen European countries to discuss future asylum policy reform.

Prior to joining MPI, Ms. Collett was a Senior Policy Analyst at the European Policy Centre, a Brussels-based think tank, and was responsible for its migration program, which covered all aspects of European migration and integration policy. She has also worked in the Migration Research and Policy Department of the International Organization for Migration in Geneva and for the Institute for the Study of International Migration in Washington, DC. She also served as a Research Associate at the Centre for Migration Policy and Society, Oxford University (2011–13), and consulted for numerous governmental ministries and nongovernmental organizations, including foundations, nonprofits, and UN agencies.

Ms. Collett holds a master's degree in foreign service (with distinction) from Georgetown University, where she specialized in foreign policy and earned a certificate in refugee and humanitarian studies, and a bachelor's degree in law from the University of Oxford.

Kate Hooper is an Associate Policy Analyst with International Program at MPI, where her research areas include labor migration, diaspora engagement, and immigrant integration.

Previously, Ms. Hooper interned with the Centre for Social Justice, where she provided research support on UK social policy and deprivation issues, and a political communications firm in Westminster, United Kingdom.

She holds a master's degree with honors from the University of Chicago's Committee on International Relations, and a bachelor's degree in history from the University of Oxford. She also holds a certificate in international political economy from the London School of Economics.

Sarah Flamm is a former Research Assistant at MPI, where she worked on the International Program and the Labor Markets Initiative.

Previously, Ms. Flamm worked as a Stanford in Government Fellow at the International Labor Organization (ILO) in Geneva, where she focused on child labor and trafficking issues. She studied day laborers' access to health care in San Francisco as a Community-Based Research Fellow, working with the city health department and a local nonprofit. Ms. Flamm has also worked in the Voting Section at the U.S. Department of Justice.

Ms. Flamm holds a bachelor's degree in public policy with a concentration in immigration policy and a Spanish minor as well as a master's degree in public policy, both from Stanford University.

ABOUT THE MIGRATION POLICY INSTITUTE

The Migration Policy Institute (MPI) is an independent, nonpartisan, nonprofit think tank in Washington, DC dedicated to analysis of the movement of people worldwide.

MPI provides analysis, development, and evaluation of migration and refugee policies at local, national, and international levels. It aims to meet the rising demand for pragmatic and thoughtful responses to the challenges and opportunities that large-scale migration, whether voluntary or forced, presents to communities and institutions.

Founded in 2001 by Demetrios G. Papademetriou and Kathleen Newland, MPI grew out of the International Migration Policy Program at the Carnegie Endowment for International Peace.

MPI is guided by the philosophy that international migration needs active, intelligent management. When such policies exist and are responsibly administered, they bring benefits to immigrants, communities of origin and destination, and sending and receiving countries.

MPI's work proceeds from four central propositions:

- Fair, smart, transparent, and rights-based immigration and refugee policies can promote social cohesion, economic vitality, and national security.

- Given the opportunity, immigrants become net contributors and create new social and economic assets.

- Sound immigration and integration policies result from balanced analysis, solid data, and the engagement of a spectrum of stakeholders—from community leaders and immigrant organizations to the policy elite—interested in immigration policy and its human consequences.

- National policymaking benefits from international comparative research, as more and more countries accumulate data, analysis, and policy experience related to global migration.

For more on MPI, visit: www.migrationpolicy.org.